*International and Comparative Law
of the Commonwealth*

International and Comparative Law
of the Commonwealth

Ralph Braibanti, R. Y. Jennings, David R. Deener,
J. N. D. Anderson, L. C. Green, Alona E. Evans,
Ivan R. Feltham, Rita F. Taubenfeld and
Howard J. Taubenfeld, Robert R. Wilson

Edited by Robert R. Wilson

Number 33 in a series published for the
Duke University Commonwealth Studies Center
Duke University Press, Durham, N.C.
1968

Printed in the United States of America
by Kingsport Press, Inc., Kingsport, Tenn.

Preface

The rapidity of development in the Commonwealth has been a striking feature of the mid-twentieth century. Legal questions as well as policy issues attending this development have taken various forms. Some of the matters involved relate to public international law, others to comparative law. The continuing and relative importance of some of the issues raised would seem to justify academic discussion of them and private conference opportunity for comparison of views. Realization of this provided occasion for the Conference on International and Comparative Law of the Commonwealth which took place at Duke University on October 27 and 28, 1966. Names of participants in the Conference appear on page vi of the present volume.

Papers presented at the conference have been included in the volume, but not the discussion which followed presentation of each paper. Those contributing papers included, in the order in which their contributions appear, Professor Ralph Braibanti of Duke University, Professor R. Y. Jennings of Cambridge University (who was unable to be present in person for the presentation of his paper), Professor David R. Deener of Tulane University, Professor J. N. D. Anderson of the Institute of Advanced Legal Studies and of the School of Oriental and African Law at the University of London, Professor Leslie C. Green of the University of Alberta, Professor Alona E. Evans of Wellesley College, Mr. Ivan R. Feltham of the firm of Baker and McKenzie, Chicago, and Professor Howard Taubenfeld of the Southern Methodist University Law School (of whose paper Mrs. Rita F. Taubenfeld is co-author, although Mrs. Taubenfeld was not in attendance at the conference).

The convenor of the conference is indebted to many persons for their respective parts in connection with it. President Douglas Knight of Duke University presided at the dinner held on the first evening of the conference. Speakers at this dinner meeting were Dr. Arthur Larson, Director of the Rule of Law Research Center at Duke University, Mr. G. W. Haight, Chairman of the American Bar Association's Committee on Comparative Law, and Mr. H. C. L. Merillat, then Executive Director of the American Society of International Law. Professor R. Taylor Cole, Provost of Duke University, welcomed the visiting members to Duke University. Participants who served as chairmen or discussion leaders for the various sessions were (in alphabetical order): Hans Baade, Duke University Law School; M. Margaret Ball, Duke University; Alfred Canon, Southwestern at Memphis; Robert E. Clute, University of Georgia; Robert I. Crane, Duke University; David Deener, Tulane University; Salo Engel, University of Tennessee; Peter Fliess, Louisiana State University; Craufurd Goodwin, Duke University; Kazimierz Grzybowski, Duke University; John Halderman, Duke University; David Henry, Department of Justice, Government of Canada; John M. Howell, Dean of East Carolina University; Ralph G. Jones, Texas Technological College; W. W. Kulski, Duke University; Hodge O'Neal, Duke University Law School; Don C. Piper, University of Maryland; Oscar Svarlien, University of Florida; Herman Walker, State University College, New Paltz, New York; Seymour W. Wurfel, Law School, University of North Carolina at Chapel Hill.

The editor of the present volume acknowledges with high appreciation the assistance of many persons whose co-operation made the conference possible. Professor Ralph Braibanti in his capacity as Chairman of the Committee on Commonwealth Studies at Duke University has encouraged the inclusion of the papers as a volume in the Commonwealth-Studies Series. Dean David R. Deener's counsel on the choice of topics was extremely helpful. Mrs. C. W. Ralston and Professor William H. Simpson of Duke University rendered assistance of great value in the administrative arrangements for the conference, and in the preparation of materials for publication Mrs. Ralston's assistance has been invaluable. The Duke University Press has with characteristic courtesy facilitated publication.

The holding of the conference and the publication of the symposium were made possible through a grant from the Ford Foundation. For opinions expressed in the present volume, however, the respective authors alone are responsible.

Robert R. Wilson

Durham, North Carolina
June 30, 1967

Contents

Contents

International and Comparative Law
of the Commonwealth

The Role of Law in Political Development

Ralph Braibanti*

> Men should not think it slavery to live according
> to the rule of the constitution; for it is their salvation.
>
> Aristotle's *Politics*

The principal contention of this brief essay is that the study of
legal institutions and the legal community has been neglected in
analyses of the political development of new states. Yet not only
is the strengthening of legal institutions crucial to the viability of
new political systems, it is equally true that law also has a role as
an agent of social change, as a source for the diffusion of attitudes, ideas, and norms which may have a modernizing and
innovative impact on the social order.

I

A suggestive point of departure are two references separated in
time by some two centuries and in space by some ten thousand
miles—two kinds of separation which have some bearing on what
I propose to discuss. My purpose in using these two references is
a simple one, namely to suggest that conditions and attitudes
regarding legal institutions in the new states and in analyses of
political development are somewhat different from those which

---

* James B. Duke Professor of Political Science and Chairman, Center for Commonwealth Studies, Duke University.

prevailed in the early days of American nationhood. We shall start with Edmund Burke's comment on the American colonies that "in no country, perhaps in the world, is the law so general a study. The profession itself is numerous and powerful, and in most provinces it takes the lead. . . . I hear that they have sold nearly as many of Blackstone's *Commentaries* in America as in England."[1] Burke's description is enriched by figures which are well known in American history, namely, that twenty-five of the fifty-two signers of the Declaration of Independence were lawyers, as were thirty-one of the fifty-five members of the Continental Congress.[2] Lawyers were indeed the high priests of early American political development, a development dominated by what to Tocqueville appeared to be an aristocracy of the robe.[3] To be sure, a century later the priests may have become deacons or even acolytes to party politicians as Bryce writes in 1888 of lawyers' waning influence, but even in that observation he contrasts this with the "first and second generations of the Republic"[4] when legal influences dominated the evolution of our political system. When we turn to the corpus of analytics relating to our own emerging nationhood we find hundreds of studies like A. Lawrence Lowell's *Essays on Government* replete with references to the dominance of lawyers and, more important for our purposes now, to the significant confluence of legal and political norms in the evolution of a viable state system.

Our second reference is taken from the contemporary political thought of one of many states newly sovereign after World War II. Again, we shall use this reference as an indicator suggestive of a larger complex of dispositions. President Mohammad Ayub Khan of Pakistan, addressing lawyers in 1960, suggested that they

1. See "Speech on Conciliation with America" (1775), Burke's *Works* (Boston, 1865), II, 124–125.

2. Heinz Eulau and John D. Sprague, *Lawyers in Politics: A Study in Professional Convergence* (New York, 1964), p. 11.

3. Alexis de Tocqueville, *Democracy in America*, Henry Reeve text, ed. Phillips Bradley (New York, 1945). Tocqueville's classic analysis of the legal aristocracy can be found in Vol. I, pp. 272–280 of this edition. See also a critique of the views of Tocqueville and Bryce on this matter in Eulau and Sprague, *Lawyers in Politics*, esp. pp. 32–39.

4. James Bryce, *The American Commonwealth* (New York, 1908), II, 570.

often fabricated evidence in the support of their clients, that the legal profession was overstaffed and that this, "apart from locking useful manpower unnecessarily, created cut-throat competition in the profession, ushering in all sorts of abuses."[5] This, of course, was not a new view of lawyers on the Indo-Pakistani subcontinent; on the contrary, it was consistent with the views of many British officers during imperial rule, including Sir Malcolm Darling, F. L. Brayne, and Philip (Mason) Woodruff.[6] President Ayub's view of the situation in Pakistan is similar to the attitude of at least one of the Indian law commission's analyses of the same condition in contemporary India. Thus the Setalvad Commission could say in its fourteenth report that law schools were "attracting by and large students of mediocre ability and indifferent merit," and that "the lawyer has lost his leadership in public life."[7] It quoted with approval the statement of an Indian lawyer that the time has arrived when "we must make up our minds whether we think that democracy means that anybody should become a lawyer and engage in any cut-throat competition or whether it means that anyone who has a talent can join in any honourable profession."[8] The Law Reform Commission in Pakistan expressed similar apprehension of legal training though it was much more moderate in tone.[9] This attitude toward not only lawyers but toward legal institutions as well is common with respect to the newly developing states. Thus Guyot, writing on Burma, characterizes "law as a 'contentious' profession and medicine as a 'con-

5. Full text accessible in Government of Pakistan, *Speeches and Statements of Field Marshal Mohammad Ayub Khan* (Karachi, 1961), III, 27. This point of view is reiterated somewhat more strongly in Ayub's autobiography, *Friends Not Masters* (Karachi, 1967), pp. 102–107.

6. See, for example, Darling's striking description and analysis of what he regards as the evil economic consequences of excessive litigation in the Punjab in his *The Punjab Peasant in Prosperity and Debt* (4th ed.; London, 1947), pp. 67–69. Brayne's Socratic dialogue attacking the "curse and the futility" of litigation is both amusing and uncommonly perceptive: F. L. Brayne, *Socrates in an Indian Village* (8th ed.; London, 1946), pp. 108–113. A delightful fictional account of the same phenomenon is Philip Woodruff's *Call the Next Witness* (London, 1945).

7. Government of India, Ministry of Law, Law Commission of India, *Fourteenth Report: Reform of Judicial Administration* (New Delhi, 1960), I, 556.

8. *Ibid.*, pp. 556–557.

9. Government of Pakistan, Ministry of Law, *Report of the Law Reform Commission, 1958–59* (Karachi, 1959), pp. 115–116.

structive' one, which seems roughly to have been their roles in
Burma."[10] The "overbalance" of lawyers, assuming the validity of
this judgment of law and medicine, represents, this political
scientist concludes, "a misallocation of educational resources."
Such views are very commonly held. They may be summarized in
this way: in developing states, too many lawyers and a consequent disproportionate emphasis on legal modes of thought (or
legalistic formalism) are antithetical to the needs of political and
economic development. Presumably legal modes of thought conduce to maintaining order and the status quo and not to attitudes
of effervescence or innovation commonly associated with a "development orientation." In the rapidly developing corpus of analysis of political development by western scholars we find the
same lack of emphasis on the cruciality of legal phenomena. This
is a far different condition from that which we found for an
earlier period with respect to American political development. To
suggest further this significant contrast in attitudes, we can use as
an instructive indicator the series of six studies on political development published under the aegis of the Committee on Comparative Politics of the Social Science Research Council by the Princeton University Press.[11] All six volumes deal with critical influences
on political growth: one deals with communications, one with
education, another with parties, a fourth with bureaucracy; the
remaining two deal generally with modernization in Japan and
Turkey and with construction of a general theory of political
development. One is struck by the fact that there is no volume on
law and political development. Similarly, we search in vain for
analysis of this subject in *Public Policy,* the yearbook of the
Kennedy School of Government of Harvard University where
interest in political development is keen. While the 1966 volume

10. James F. Guyot, "Bureaucratic Transformation in Burma," in Ralph Braibanti and Associates, *Asian Bureaucratic Systems Emergent from the British
Imperial Tradition* (Durham, N.C., 1966), p. 361, n. 12.
11. These volumes are: Lucian W. Pye, ed., *Communications and Political
Development* (1963); Joseph LaPalombara, ed., *Bureaucracy and Political Devel-
opment* (1963); Robert E. Ward and Dankwart A. Rustow, eds., *Political Modern-
ization in Japan and Turkey* (1964); James S. Coleman, ed., *Education and
Political Development* (1965); Joseph LaPalombara and Myron Weiner, eds.,
Political Parties and Political Development (1966); Leonard Binder, James
Coleman, and others, *Crises in Political Development* (1967).

the aristocracy of the robe so extolled by Tocqueville shared the fate of other political and social elites in the new states? In the realm of political analysis, has the once crucial role of legal institutions been eclipsed by other segments of the political system? Does law have any relevance to political growth and, if it has, what is that relevance? Merely to raise these questions is to suggest the impossibility of answering them within the brief compass of this essay. We can only suggest a few reasons for the lesser attention given to law and development, and we make these suggestions with considerable humility, aware as we are that we raise profound and controversial issues and then quickly leave them. First, social science insight applicable to political growth has, in recent years, emphasized functionalism rather than institutions, and insofar as law has been studied as an institution, it has shared the decline of institutionalism generally. To be sure, there is a vigorous functional or behavioral school of jurisprudence, but social science analysis has not conjoined with that approach within law; rather it seems to skirt about the edges of legal scholarship and in so doing encounters its institutional rather than its functional manifestations. It may well be that this is a consequence of or at least related to the condition so well described by Cowan, "It is an astonishing fact of American intellectual life that both law and social science have been able to expand so enormously in the present century without significantly affecting each other."[13] Be that as it may, the dichotomy between institutions and functions is, in my view, a false one. Institutions perform functions, mold behavior and modify themselves. Indeed, the tracing of movement of function as institutions adjust to new demands can best be done by institutional analysis. Political behavior flows imperceptibly into the interstices created by institutions, and its flow is regulated and conditioned by the locus and effectiveness of institutional power. Although institutionalism as a mode of analysis has been eclipsed by functionalism, this eclipse, like all eclipses, is coming rather quickly to an end. The cruciality of institutions in political development has been strikingly

13. Thomas A. Cowan, "What Law Can Do for Social Science," in William M. Evan, ed., *Law and Sociology: Introductory Essays* (New York, 1962), p. 91.

brought to our attention by Huntington in the context of the need for balance between the demands or crises of the social order and the capability of institutions for converting these demands into policy or action.[14] Bertrand de Jouvenel reminds us that the political scientist is an expert on institutions and behavior who must "foretell the adjustments suitable to improve the adequacy of the institutional system to cope with changing circumstances."[15] Pennock neatly stated the case:

Whether political and governmental structures are formal or informal, incorporated in the legal structure or not, it is of greatest importance that they should be institutionalized; and the process of institutionalization is as surely part of development as are specialization of function and differentiation of structure. It is when certain forms and procedures become the accepted ways of doing things that they become effective instruments of stability and of legitimation.[16]

Second, the most spectacular and most pervasive motif in political development has been rapid expansion of political participation—a consequence of popular sovereignty. Such power diffusion has been accomplished largely through political parties or community development structures, both rooted in an ethos of spontaneity and extralegal norms. Third, legal institutions in most new states spring essentially from norms, attitudes, and structures of mature constitutional systems in the West. Since power diffusion derives from indigenous sources, legal institutions come to be regarded not only as alien but even as impediments to the rapid diffusion of public power. Fourth, we are obsessed in the social sciences by the micro-recording of actual behavior. As a consequence, normative concerns have been replaced too often by adulation of what we think we see in man's behavior. When we observe incongruence between law and behavior, we judge law to be the contaminant, despoiling behavior which, simply because we observe it, we judge to be ideal. This relationship overlooks a classic problem in the history of political and legal thought,

14. Samuel P. Huntington, "Political Development and Political Decay," *World Politics*, XVII (1965), 386–430.
15. "Political Science and Prevision," *American Political Science Review*, LIX (March, 1965), 29, 32.
16. J. Roland Pennock, "Political Development, Political Systems, and Political Goods," *World Politics*, XVIII (1966), 418.

namely that there has always been imperfect articulation between law and behavior. This is certainly nothing new nor is it becoming of political anthropology to suggest that lawyers and political scientists have been unaware of this condition. Aristotle set forth the problem and we have pondered it since. In Aristotelian terms, "political society exists for the sake of noble actions, and not of mere companionship." The purpose of statecraft is constantly to adjust behavior of men to legal norms which reflect the state's noble ends. Such adjustment is reciprocal; that is, legal norms and their consequent sanctions modify and direct human behavior, and behavior influences norms and sanctions. If law merely certified man's conduct, some of which derives from his baser nature, then it would have no function except as an instrument to record what we do. This is neither the ideal nor the actual function of law. Law derives its augustness and its power from its perennial struggle to lift men to its own nobility, while at the same time it reflects compassionately man's own ignoble state. If the term "majesty of the law" has any significance, it is that.

There is a fifth reason closely related to the fourth, namely the preoccupation of growing numbers of both legal scholars and political scientists with activist movements, involving physical agitation for immediate change in society. This has commonly been called "confrontation politics." Here we wish to distinguish this phenomenon, which I shall call physical agitation, from two related behaviors: intellectual provocation and legal realism. The former involves influencing the will and searing the conscience so that it compels behavioral change through educative means within the established order in the direction of peaceful innovation. The seared conscience stops and totters precariously on the brink of physical agitation. Legal realism is the intellectual apprehension of actual behavior, the use of empirical evidence, and the awareness of the reciprocal (as against the uni-directional) relationship between law and behavior. Both intellectual provocation and legal realism operate within, indeed are nourished by, the values and the ethos of erudition: caution, prudence, detachment, reflection, and total immersion in a refined and rational thought process tempered by intuition. But physical agitation breaks through the perimeter of the ethos of erudition. We witness on all sides the immoral provocation of eighteen-year-old students to foresake the "sterility and irrelevance" of systematic learning in favor of decision-making beyond their competence or maturity. We witness involvement in party politics and a preoccupation with curbside judicare—a lawyer's secularization of the preacher's social gospel. By serving a master of agitation rather than being mastered by the rigor, order, and beauty of detached analytical scholarship or, what is worse, by attempting to serve both masters, we engender an ethos which distorts the significance of anything which does not appear to be agitation-oriented. Agitation minimizes and eventually corrodes the vitality of law and of institutions. The above are merely five of many reasons which might be related to the present position of law to political development.

III

We propose now to discuss a set of characteristics of political development and to suggest how legal studies may enrich the subsequent construction of a model of political development. In so doing we shall examine five attributes of political growth, and within the context of these attributes, we shall propose a strategy for legal research. The relevance of legal studies to some of these attributes shall be immediately evident and these we shall pass over quickly. Others which may not be so obvious we shall develop at somewhat greater length. The attributes which we have isolated here are not necessarily the same as those singled out by other students of political development. Among such students some of the concepts are the same though the terminology is different. The study of political development is too primitive to allow for common definitions and nomenclature. Huntington has succinctly analyzed the varying lists of criteria as used by Ward and Rustow, Emerson, Pye, and Eisenstadt.[17] He identifies four sets of categories which recur continuously: rationalization, national integration, democratization, participation. He notes that

17. Huntington, "Political Development and Political Decay," p. 387.

the last-mentioned characteristic is given greatest emphasis and he deplores the failure of most definitions to emphasize or even mention political institutions essential for converting demands produced by accelerated participation. Drawing on the works of a larger (some thirty) number of writers (reaching Wilson, Burgess, and Weber), Packenham[18] lists five conditions commonly stressed: a constitution, economic base, administrative capacity, participation, and civic attitudes. Lasswell,[19] reviewing the first three volumes of the Social Science Research Council–Princeton series, alluded to earlier in this chapter,[20] folds them into the context of his own brilliantly conceived six-part model: self-sustaining power accumulation, power-sharing, national independence, a responsible role in world politics, an internal decision-making process conducing to wider participation in all values, and timing of elements in the sequence of development.

Space requires us to eschew the temptation to correlate these summaries or to analyze them in greater depth. For immediate expository convenience, we shall give our list of five attributes of political development and relate certain research possibilities to each.

1. The first attribute is agreement on a fundamental polity of the state, an overarching purpose which gives form, cohesion, and direction to all public action within a sensed community. This is typically embodied in a constitution and in some cases, such as in India and Pakistan most particularly, in segments of the constitution such as the non-justiciable but ideologically crucial directive principles of state policy. The relevance of law to this attribute is obvious. The drafting of constitutions and their subsequent interpretation through judicial case law are classic legal activities to which a moderate amount of research attention has been given. But the research done is excessively exigetical or focuses on textual criticism reminiscent of research in constitutional law in the United States two or more generations ago. What is sorely needed

18. Robert A. Packenham, "Political Development Doctrines in the American Foreign Aid Program," *World Politics*, XVIII (1966), 194–235.
19. Harold D. Lasswell, "The Policy Sciences of Development," *World Politics*, XVII (1965), 286–310.
20. This series is cited in n. 11 above.

is legal analysis of the permeative effect of constitutional law as it confronts antagonistic indigenous norms with its own juridical norms derived from Western systems. The nature of this confrontation and the degree to which it is a factor in maintaining national integration in the face of often overwhelming centrifugal forces is of crucial significance and is almost totally neglected. Another important but critical subject for analysis is the changing pattern of dependence upon indigenous American, British, and other foreign precedent. For example, in Pakistan, the change to a presidential system and a division of powers into enumerated central and reserved provincial requires and, in fact, has resulted in, a shift away from British to analogous American precedent.[21]

Finally, a whole new area of legal research has been dramatically opened by Sec. 201(b) (7) of the Foreign Assistance Act of 1966.[22] Inserted by the Senate Committee on Foreign Relations,[23] this amendment adds a significant criterion which must be taken into account in making development loans. That criterion is the "degree to which the recipient country is making progress toward respect for the rule of law, freedom of expression, and of the press, and recognition of the importance of individual freedom, initiative and private enterprise." The construction of criteria for measuring these qualities, and the question of balance between freedom and order so critical in new states call for the most sophisticated kind of comparative analysis of jurisprudence and the contextual relevance of an ethos of law.

2. A second attribute is the establishment of an institutional apparatus which has the potential for conversion of valid expressions of popular will into actions fairly predictable and consistent with the fundamental polity of the state. Here the role of administrative law is crucial. The problem is that of infusing administra-

21. This phenomenon is developed further in Ralph Braibanti, *Research on the Bureaucracy of Pakistan* (Durham, N.C., 1966), pp. 280–289; Ralph Braibanti, "The Higher Bureaucracy of Pakistan," in Braibanti and Associates, *Asian Bureaucratic Systems Emergent from the British Imperial Tradition,* pp. 209–242, 312–327.

22. Public Law 89–583 (80 Stat. 795).

23. United States Congress, Senate, *Foreign Economic Assistance, Report of the Committee on Foreign Relations . . . on S. 3584,* 89th Cong., 2d Sess., Report No. 1359 (Washington, D.C., 1966), pp. 7–8.

tive action with the spirit and substance of the basic polity. This involves two kinds of compatibility: compatibility of administrative process with the polity—usually a variation of due process of law—and compatibility with the spirit of the statute. This relationship, always difficult to achieve in even mature systems, is much more difficult to attain in new highly unbalanced systems. Here we find that the bureaucracy, long accustomed to near-paramountcy under imperial rule, relies less on statutory sources for its actions and more on its internal resources and on synaptic relations with extra-statutory sources. Such systems may be tottering on the threshold of administrative lawlessness. Ambiguity of function in the whole system, inadequacy of legislative oversight, and other weaknesses allow administrative discretion to flow with minimal reference to the channels—a predicament of which we were well warned in the West as early as 1929 by Lord Hewart of Bury's *The New Despotism*.[24] This kind of despotism is the more dangerous in immature systems. We need research in administrative law to measure the gap between fundamental polity and administrative discretion and to ascertain how law can reduce the gap and render bureaucracy effectively accountable to polity. One is impressed by what a judiciary which is powerful, erudite, and independent can do to regulate this articulation. One of the most influential decisions in Pakistan law was that written by Chief Justice S. M. Murshed in the "Pan case" of 1964. In this historic judgment, Murshed, relying heavily on the Schecter Poultry Company and Panama Refining Company cases, infused into Pakistan law the established doctrines of administrative law essential to curb bureaucratic lawlessness. Commenting on the untrammeled power given bureaucracy by an unsophisticated legislature, he said:

What policy has it laid down? What standard has it formulated? What yardstick has it given? What principles has it formulated? What limitations has it imposed? What guidance has it given? None whatsoever. . . . An effective and efficient legislation could easily be passed to meet the exigencies of the situation within the framework of the Constitution. The Constitution is not unworkable in this behalf. If a

24. (London, 1929.)

valid law had been passed, it could have started functioning from the date on which such law had come into existence. We should not be understood to hold that we do not consider such a legislation to be desirable or expedient, but the essential condition of a valid law is that it must be confined within the limits set by the Constitution. It should not be allowed to 'burst the banks' and the protective barrage set up by our Fundamental Law, namely, the Constitution. There can be selection of commodities for regulation of transport. There may be a specification of means of transport sought to be regulated. Frontiers of regulation may be defined. Standards and norms can be laid down for such regulation of movement. The objects and purposes of regulation can be set out. It would be a salutary provision to require orders in this behalf to be made under public notification. The Constitution requires, and it is possible to do so, that reasonable direction and guidance should be given in various ways under which the Executive may be vested with substantial discretionary powers to work out the details of legislative policies and norms.[25]

While we know much about administrative law in Pakistan, we know very little of it in India and even less in the other developing states. Moreover, we know nothing of the comparative effectiveness of this mode of control of bureaucracy in the former imperial states of France and Britain.

3. The third attribute of political development is the capability of maintaining national integration through orderly and just accommodation of cultural, religious, and similar divisive forces. Here the importance of legal arrangements has not been recognized in research, even though in reality legal means are heavily relied upon to bring about this integration. But the adequacy of differing modes of sanctions and the articulation of sanctions to social stress need to be re-examined in the context of political development. Arens and Lasswell's early study on sanction law[26] needs to be reconsidered in terms of our experience since 1947. Finally, the role of legal sanctions in integration in the British and French imperial traditions should be compared. Within such a comparative context, we may get some glimmer of the differing social effects of codification, non-codification, and blends of both.

25. *Ghulam Zamin v. A. B. Khondkhar* 16 D.L.R. (1964), 486, quotation at 502, 514.
26. Richard Arens and Harold D. Lasswell, *In Defense of Public Order: The Emerging Field of Sanction Law* (New York, 1961).

4. Fourth, a transitional state must have the capacity to blend elements of the popular will in markedly disparate stages of development into an aggregate—an aggregate which must be normatively consistent with the basic polity of the state. Herein lies perhaps the most challenging of research problems for law. The basic polity typically derives from Western sources, but the popular will derives from indigenous sources. The ideological cohesion of the social order may be, and usually is, badly disturbed. Politicization may proceed on the basis of Western constitutional norms often divorced—even in language—from the mainstream of the social order, and within that order even minimal popular comprehension of polity may not exist. In this connection, legal research must re-examine the dynamics of adjustment between indigenous norms and state polity. It may not be possible for the polity to draw into its ambit by osmosis the body of indigenous thought. It may be that legal research will have to find a reconstructed indigenous tradition in which strands of thought equivalent to assumptions underlying Western constitutional systems have been identified, elucidated, and woven into a cohesive doctrine. Or it may be that the role of courts and of administrative law as diffusers and mediators of conflicting norms will have to be strengthened to deal with the gap between behavior and norms which, as stated earlier, always exists everywhere, but which is far more crucial in the bifurcated social orders of emerging states.

Closely related to this question of blending elite and popular wills is the issue of adjustment of spheres of juridical norms. The relationship between tribal, religious, and other indigenous juridical systems and systems of law derived from the West needs further study. Here the work of such pioneers as J. N. D. Anderson, L. C. Green, and S. A. de Smith must be singled out for attention. But there is altogether too little work of this kind. The interaction of spheres of validity bears crucially on the problem of national integration as well as on the problem of blending of wills. A case in point is what has happened in West Pakistan with respect to the effort to extend the *jirga* system of tribal elders in certain criminal cases under the Frontier Crimes Regulation of

1901. What started as an effort to "return" to simple tribal justice ended as an institutional and normative adjustment of two legal systems—tribal law and British criminal law. But what is especially instructive is that the adjustment was far more complex than mere contraction or expansion of spheres. What we find is that the spatial validity of a blend of Western and tribal norms has expanded, but the normative content of that blend has become somewhat more Western than tribal. Thus, it may be that spatial expansion combined with subtle normative modification can serve as a legal mechanism which can be deliberately contrived and effectively used as a means of blending two or more legal systems.

5. Let us now consider the fifth and final (in this tentative listing) attribute of political development. This is the involvement of the entire population in political life—the diffusion of power to the periphery of the social order. Ideologically, this derives from concern for enhancement of human dignity, reflected juridically in the concept of popular sovereignty. We may variously call this power-sharing, power diffusion, politicization, mobilization, or even the participation explosion. Of all five attributes here discussed, this one, at least in its quantitative dimension, has been given the most attention. Virtually no concern has been shown for the quality of such participation, that is, for such factors as literacy, responsibility, understanding of issues, to the quality of civic culture generally.[27] The emphasis has been on the acceleration of involvement—involvement almost indiscriminate and for its own sake. This emphasis is understandable especially because in the past determinations as to the quality of public participation have been used as justification for continued imperial rule, and even now as excuses for authoritarianism. Lest we be misunderstood here, let it be said immediately

27. An exception is the analysis of J. Roland Pennock, cited above in n. 16, who, in the context of "political goods," which he holds to be security, welfare, justice, and liberty, suggests that the substantial universality of these "goods" is tempered by contextual relativity of their implementation. "[H]uman interests are subject to certain natural orderings," he maintains, and the persistence of the political system must take priority over other "goods" (p. 426). A significant effort to relate varying qualities of civic culture to the effectiveness of political systems is Gabriel A. Almond and Sidney Verba, *The Civic Culture* (Princeton, N.J., 1963).

that it is abundantly clear to us that the rapid involvement of large numbers of people—that is to say, the quantitative aspect of power diffusion—is a necessary aspect of development. Only such diffusion can bring about that degree of meaningful participation which enlarges choice and experience, develops responsibility, and enhances human dignity. Moreover, efforts to sedate, repress, or delay such diffusion should be regarded with some wariness since they may be guises for authoritarianism. Nevertheless, we cannot overlook the stress and the crises caused by accelerated power-sharing. The problem can be simply put. New states often simply do not have the institutional strength necessary to convert demands into action. More importantly, they do not have a sufficiently even diffusion of juridical norms to infuse the whole political system with the strength of the basic polity. This is primarily why new systems collapse—not because of corruption, not because of infiltration, not because of institutional weakness —but because of uneven diffusion of norms, and because of the unnatural straining of stronger institutions (such as the judiciary) to take up the slack of the weaker institutions. Let me put the problem in a somewhat more abstract way. The importance of this fifth attribute of power diffusion lies in the fact that rapid diffusion to the perimeters of the social order changes the nature and quantum of political demands, thus increasing the strain on the capability of institutions to convert such demands into effective governmental action.

This condition is aggravated when demands are escalated by the intervention and massive uncontrolled infusion of foreign norms through technical assistance and international entities bent on dissemination of idiosyncrasies without regard to institutional capacity to handle such demands. The possibility of this demand-conversion crisis's being pushed to the brink of political disintegration by foreign ideological inducement makes us wary of the possible effects in developing states of Title IX of the Foreign Assistance Act of 1966.[28] Title IX states that in carrying

---

28. Cited in n. 22 above. The background and theoretical implications of Title IX are explored in greater detail in Ralph Braibanti, "External Inducement of Political Administrative Development: An Institutional Strategy," in Braibanti and Associates, *Political and Administrative Development* (Durham, N.C., forthcoming).

out programs of development assistance, specifically those financed by the Development Loan Fund, and those involving technical co-operation, development grants, the Alliance for Progress, and Southeast Asia multilateral and regional programs, "emphasis shall be placed on assuring maximum participation in the task of economic development on the part of the people of the developing countries, through the encouragement of democratic private and local government institutions." It is clear that the House of Representatives Committee on Foreign Affairs which inserted Title IX in the act feels that "there is a close relationship between popular participation in the process of development, and the effectiveness of this process."[29] The degree of jeopardy in which the demand-conversion dilemma will be placed by Title IX remains to be seen. Much will depend on the means of implementation used by the United States Agency for International Development and on the criteria for and definitions of participation. It is clear that the House Committee on Foreign Affairs "plans to keep close check on the manner in which the intent [of Title IX] is carried out" and that it expects USAID "to develop and use in its next presentation to the Congress, meaningful criteria for judging the results of this effort."[30]

Imbalance between demands and capability is one of the primary—perhaps the primary—causes of the collapse of new political systems. For simplicity's sake, let us call this the demand-conversion crisis. Public bureaucracy is the principal institution for the conversion of such demands. Imbalance can be moderated either by reducing demand incidence, modifying demand content, or by increasing bureaucratic capability to handle the demand-conversion crisis. Where bureaucratic strengthening occurs, it must be done within the general restraints imposed by the polity, and without total retraction of power diffusion if, in fact, diffusion is part of that polity. This delicate balance, extraordinarily difficult to achieve, is crucial to the maturation of political systems. In developing systems, spontaneous adjustment to acute imbalance has assumed various forms. In India, we find contain-

29. House of Representatives, *Foreign Assistance Act of 1966. Report of the Committee on Foreign Affairs on H.R. 15150*, 89th Cong., 2d Sess., Report No. 1651 (Washington, D.C., 1966), p. 27.
30. *Ibid.*, p. 28.

ment, diversion, and sedation of demands by the spatially diffuse and substantively competent single mass party. In Pakistan similar consequences are achieved by indirect elections and by near-paramountcy of juridico-administrative norms. Elsewhere we witness total or partial suspension of participative behaviors and dominance of authoritarian oligarchies, usually military. The elaboration of the process of such adjustment, its contextual relevance, and its ultimate political consequences are crucial research objectives for which the disciplines of political science and law are now ready.

What is the relevance of this demand-conversion crisis to law and to legal institutions? The relevance lies in the adjustment which the system must make to the crisis. Such adjustment may be spontaneous or contrived. We have already mentioned some of the forms which such adjustment may assume. Virtually no systematic studies of the adjustment mechanisms have been made. Many of these adjustments are in the realm of law. One such adjustment which has almost unlimited explanatory power is the construct of ambiguity. Ambiguity is a powerful force. It can be used positively as a device of control and is commonly used in all administration as a means of power. Uncertainty, unease, ambivalence, diffusion of responsibility through alternate invocation of committee jurisdiction and single officer jurisdiction: these and other variations are common even though unhealthy devices of power in church, business, university, and public administration. Ambiguity of polity and structure is and can be used effectively in regulating the demand-conversion crisis. Consider the case of Pakistan. The new political system is suspended between a parliamentary and a presidential system and is based on an ambiguous distribution of legislative powers as between central and provincial governments. Such ambiguity is neatly illustrated by the 1964 preventive detention cases in Pakistan involving Maulana Maudoudi and the ultra-orthodox Muslim group, the Jamaat-e-Islami. Preventive detention is the concern of two levels of government. The Jamaat-e-Islami was disbanded and certain leaders arrested in two provinces under different laws, both central and provincial. Moreover, the ambiguous powers of the governors acting as agents of the president confused the situation. The mixture of actions made it impossible to focus accountability. It demolished the possibility of legislative oversight, since each legislature ruled out discussion of crucial aspects of the case, aspects which it was impossible to separate. It took a woman member of the National Assembly, Begum Shamsum Nahar Mahmood, to identify aptly this confusion of responsibility when she said, "if some question about preventive detention is asked . . . the Central Government refer it to the provincial government . . . if provincial authorities are approached they in turn refer it to the Central Government."[31] In the context of such ambiguity, the role of the judiciary is critical simply because it is the only agency in the whole political system capable of dealing with the totality of such actions and thus spreading an umbrella of normative uniformity over an assortment of actions not otherwise amenable to control and crucially at variance with the basic polity of the state. We have suggested that such structured ambiguity can be beneficial in that it regulates demands by putting them through baffles. But this is probably a short-run benefit. In the long run, excessive ambiguity damages any social system. After all, a mature political system must be characterized by focused accountability, clarity of policy, courageous acceptance of decision-making by officials, and a high degree of rationality. The dangers of spontaneous, whimsical, or capricious action must be balanced not by structured ambiguity but rather by countervailing loci of power, each with enough autonomy to be resilient and gently resistant, and each maintaining boundaries of insulation rather than merging ignominiously into a haze of interlocking structures. The effects of ambiguity may appear as a syndrome: frustration, alienation, withdrawal from political life, violence. The quantum of alienation resulting from ambiguity needs to be measured. It is probably a significant source of counter-productivity in the whole political process. The ultimate danger of structured ambiguity as a regulating device lies in the frustration such ambiguity engenders. Frustration leads to repressed and often simmering animosity against power and eventually to violent action, which may

31. Pakistan National Assembly, *Debates*, July 5, 1962, p. 1066.

then bring crisis to the political system. The evidence for this in political systems is overwhelming. The role of ambiguity both as a regulator and as an agitator of crisis has not been studied. Theoretically, there may be an articulated progression—a gradual decrease of ambiguity as a system matures. Perhaps this is what is occurring in Pakistan. We would need to know why such ambiguity decreases. Do law and the judiciary conduce to its decrease, as we suspect they do, or to its increase? This calls for careful microanalysis of legal and administrative structure and of the substance of all public decisions. It calls for measurement of how much and what kind of ambiguity is desirable and at what point it ceases to be an effective regulator of crisis and becomes instead an agitator of crisis. This kind of study transcends law itself, but it must be rooted in legal analysis if it is to have significance.

There is still another means by which such adjustment can occur. The kind of adjustment we now have in mind is not so much adjustment of the demand-conversion crisis, but rather the infusion of the whole unbalanced political process with juridically impelled values basic to the polity. Imagine for a moment the whole political system as a twelve-cylinder engine, with noisy tappets, gummed-up cylinders, the timing off, and the points and spark plugs inefficient. The engine makes horrible noises and the car bucks like a bronco. Imagine somehow spraying the engine with a penetrating yet thick plastic foam which muffles the noises and somehow evens out the car's motion. Such can be the effect in a new political system. Such has been the effect of the formulary of natural justice embodied in the maxim *audi alteram partem* as interpreted in Pakistan. What we find is a highly uneven diffusion of a standard derived from Western jurisprudence. The judiciary enters a vacuum created by absence or erosion of this norm. It applies the doctrine—spraying it about like foam. It has some good short-term effect—perhaps even good long-term effect. We need to know more about expansive interpretations of such a doctrine of natural justice—how it is related to natural law and to due process of law. Most importantly, how does it relate to judicial self-restraint or non-restraint and how does such application sedate the whole political process—quieting the noises and smoothing the ride. Again, virtually no analysis of this important role of law and political development has been made.

IV

So much for a research agenda in the context of five characteristics of political growth. There is one final item of research which we cannot neatly fit into any of the five categories already discussed; hence we shall deal with it now separately. This is the question of the total impact of the legal community in maintaining some semblance of a constitutional system. We are convinced by our experience in Pakistan that size may be an important positive force. Certainly in Pakistan the size of the legal community has partly made it the most powerful countervailing elite in the system. We estimate the number of legally trained persons at 18,000. From 1954 on, 17 per cent of the total university degrees conferred have been law degrees, the average output of law degrees being 1,000 a year. The ratio of legally trained persons to population would be about one lawyer to 5,500 people; in the United States this ratio in 1960 was one lawyer to 630 people.[32] This comparison will be surprising to many who have assumed that the ratio of lawyers in new states is higher than in old states. Beyond that, we are not certain what these figures mean. But of this we are convinced, we need statistics and ratios on the total number of legally trained persons, not only practicing lawyers, in all systems. If we had that information we could work out some fascinating hypotheses on the relationship of size to influence on political development. But we have these figures only for Pakistan and only scanty, eccentric data for other states. Of another thing we are certain for Pakistan. The sheer size of the legal community, strongly organized into bar associations and closely allied with equally strong courts, has not only been a major source for the diffusion and regeneration of norms generally, but by weight of numbers has enabled the courts to remain strong and

32. This phenomenon is further examined in Braibanti, *Research on the Bureaucracy of Pakistan.* pp. 246–261.

has prevented the rise of administrative lawlessness. There is a curious anomaly here. The legal community, while often antagonistic to government and constraining executive action, is nevertheless closely identified normatively and culturally with the bureaucratic elite. This identification, curiously coupled with healthy antagonism, actually enhances the strength of the legal community. It derives popular support from its ostensible opposition to government, and at the same time elicits bureaucratic support from its command of Western-oriented norms and techniques. Yet it also commands the fearful attention of bureaucracy because of its support in the community at large. It has a network of relationships in rural areas and the cities. A coterie of retainers and para-lawyers such as *munshis, dalals, mukhtars,* clerks, and scribes are dependent on British legal proceedings for a livelihood and serve as linguistic and cultural mediators between lawyers and the vernacularized community at large. Curiously, Tocqueville's description of this phenomenon in early America neatly fits the situation in Pakistan. "Lawyers belong to the people by birth and interest and to the aristocracy by habit and taste; they may be looked upon as the connecting link between the two great classes of society."[33] In short the legal community is a force to be reckoned with. It has challenged the executive during and after martial law, it has defied efforts to restrict court jurisdiction, it has compelled justiciability of fundamental rights, it has forced abrogation of several restrictive enactments. Is this law as an impediment to political development? Is this misallocation of scarce resources in the system? Is this unproductive use of nonproductive manpower? On the contrary, it seems to us that this is the very genius of political development.

Is the experience of Pakistan unique? We do not know. We need careful studies of the impact of the total legal community on development in French-derived and British-derived new states. There may be counter-productivity in some systems. Studies of this kind appear to be the most crucial and the most relevant in establishing a nexus between law and political development.

33. Tocqueville, *Democracy in America,* I, 276.

V

In conclusion, we have tried to suggest only a few of many legal problems for research on political development. In this we have been guilty of at least two distortions. We have deliberately idealized the law and legal institutions. We have also not treated law in the context of economic growth and as a potential generant of social innovation. This is an artificial and risky separation of law from its contextual tissue. Several papers could be written on the impact of law—especially corporation or company law—on the development of entrepreneurship, on the formation of capital, and on the consequent effect of a competing commercial elite balancing the power of government. Further, we have not drawn attention to certain salutary developments in legal research. A few of these might be mentioned. First, the phenomenal rise in interest in the sociology and anthropology of law. Second, a vigorous behavioralism has influenced legal studies in political science and is bound to have the effect of rediffusing juridical studies throughout the discipline. Third, publication of the *Law and Society Review,* the first issue of which appeared in November, 1966, will provide a publishing focus for this rediffusion in the social sciences generally. Fourth, a series of two summer conferences on South Asian law under auspices of the University of Chicago Law School in 1963 and 1967 has accelerated the transfer of juridical research to certain Asian states, especially India. Fifth, the small Conference on Law and Developing Countries sponsored by the Board of Review and Development of the American Society of International Law in Washington, July 16 and 17, 1965, may ultimately generate research interest within the international law fraternity. Sixth, the keen interest of the Rule of Law Research Center of Duke University and of its director, Arthur Larson, in the operational relevance of law as a source of social change (in problems of population control, for example) may lead ultimately to a significant use of legal means in American foreign assistance efforts to induce change. Finally, the continuous emphasis on legal research and on the centrality of institutions which, under the leadership of Robert R. Wilson at Duke University and others, has resulted in a significant corpus of research and in the training of a large number of scholars, is very significant. This conference is one manifestation of such emphasis which has not diminished for more than thirty years.

We are heartened by such indicators as these of a renewed appreciation of law. Unless we re-establish the centrality of legal studies in analysis of political growth, the most important dimension of that process will be lost. Political development is a struggle—perhaps doomed to fail but a struggle nonetheless—to achieve human dignity and a finer aesthetic quality of life. Pope Paul VI in his encyclical of March, 1967, *Populorum Progressio*, put it simply and profoundly in his statement that the basic aspiration of man is "to do more, know more and have more in order to be more."[34] That law can contribute to so majestic and noble an aspiration we must accept as a given. The challenge is that we must reconsider its importance and infuse much of our research with its implications.

34. *Encyclical Letter of His Holiness, Paul VI, Pope. On the Development of Peoples* [*Populorum Progressio*], March 26, 1967 (official translation into English distributed by the United States Catholic Conference, Washington, D.C.), Part I, par. 6, p. 9. There is some controversy as to accuracy of the meaning conveyed in various translations of this encyclical. See New York *Times*, March 29, 1967, p. 1, and *National Observer*, April 3, 1967, p. 5. Apparently, there can be little argument that the English version has correctly transferred the meaning of this particular section. In the official Latin version issued by the Vatican, this expression appears as "hoc est, ut magis operentur, discant, possideant, ut ideo pluris valeant," *Sanctissimi Domini Nostri Pauli Divina Providentia Papae VI, Litterae Encyclicae . . . De Populorum Progressione Promovenda* (Typis Polyglottis Vaticanis, 1967), Part I, par. 6, p. 7. In the official Italian version, the expression appears as ". . . in una parola, fare, conoscere, e avere di piu, per esser di piu . . . ," *Populorum progressio, Lettera Enciclica di S. S. Paolo VI sulla sviluppo dei popoli* published in a special issue of *Quaderni di Ekklesia*, I (1967), 127–172, quotation at 131.

2

The Commonwealth and State Succession

R. Y. Jennings*

The question of state succession is one that has been marked by controversy and doubt to an extent unusual even for international law. It is not that there has been a lack of practice on which to build doctrine; rather the contrary. But the practice, being the product of quite different periods in the history of modern international relations, has been so various as to defy plausible classification. The writers accordingly have had a free field and have enunciated theories ranging from universal succession to the brutal "singular" succession of the late Professor Keith, theories having one quality however in common, that they seemed to be equally ineffective to influence future practice of governments.

The last two decades have seen the realization of a new body of practice with the emergence of an unprecedented number of new states born of the passing of colonial rule. The major sample has been provided by the last stages of the emergence of the Commonwealth. This evolution, moreover, has been relatively homogeneous. Moreover, when it is seen to be linked with the evolution into independence of the older dominions, it is a practice which spans half a century and more. It is proper, therefore, that international lawyers should take stock of this practice to see whether any definite principles seem to emerge from it.

In making a brief attempt at this exercise I should disclaim at once any suggestion of pioneering or of originality: for all the hard work has been done before me by other writers and particularly, of course, by Professor O'Connell, whose massive work in

* Whewell Professor of International Law, Cambridge University.

this field puts everyone who attempts to enter upon it so very much in his debt. I cannot pretend to be able to add anything to what he has already done in works which must be familiar to all here; so I have conceived my task as being simply to collect together a few ideas and suggestions in the hope of provoking a profitable discussion.

It would, I suppose, be usual to begin a discussion on this question of state succession by affirming that we are here thinking of the situation where there has been an actual change of state personalities on the international stage; where a new state has appeared, or an old state has disappeared, or both have happened. We are not here concerned with the situation where there has merely been a transfer of territory from one existing state to another; for that is a quite different situation, however extensive and important the transfer of territory might have been. This distinction is elementary.

And yet, having attempted to make a beginning in this way by stating a familiar and even trite proposition of the law, one is immediately—such is the elusive nature of this subject—assailed by doubts and perplexities. For, after all, is it not the fact in all these cases—even the case of a simple transfer of territory between existing states—that it is the change in the person who exercises sovereignty over *that piece of territory* that is the heart of the problem? If one could imagine a situation in which a new and independent state were created *tout d'un coup* on *terra nullius*, could there then be any question of succession to any existing state? Surely not. For there is not any state to which there could be any succession. Thus it is the transfer of territory from one person to another rather than a mere change in the *dramatis personae* that is the core of the problem of succession. The transfer of territory will always create a succession problem in all circumstances; a change of *personae* merely adds a factor or a complication.

The complication, stated in practical terms, is simply that whereas in a transfer between existing states the problem is limited to questions arising from the transferred territory, the emergence of a new state raises the further problem, not directly connected with the transferred territory at all, of equipping it as it were with a working capital of international legal relationships. And in the modern world this is a very real problem, for a state with the traditional law's "clean slate" for treaty relationships is almost a contradiction in terms. Hence it is that contemporary writers seem to discern a tendency to lean toward succession rather than non-succession. Nevertheless, I am going to suggest that this particular problem of the new state is not really one of succession at all, and that the evolution of legal principles for its solution depends upon recognizing that it is not a question of succession.

For what is that general body of law that we would expect should in any case apply to any new state? To this question the traditional international law gives a somewhat surprising answer. Traditional international law answers by asserting that customary law of course applies to all new states and that it is only in regard to treaty law that a question arises. The answer is surprising because one would expect that the answer would be in terms of the context and purpose of a law rather than of its formal source; especially as so much of the customary law is nowadays at least partly expressed in conventional form.

The reason of course is simply this: that customary law in the international sphere, contrary to the position for example in English law, is the only form in which truly universal law is to be found; on the other hand the treaty is, as Judge Fitzmaurice has pointed out, not really a *source* of law at all, but no more than a source of obligation. Now of course any new person of the law must be subject to the general law in any system; and the traditional insistence that all custom applies to the new state, yet treaties in general do not, merely reflects this legal truism. However, customary law does apply to the new state, not because it is custom, but because it is general law; a local custom or a particular custom might or might not apply to a new state depending upon the circumstances. Furthermore, custom applies to the new state because it is general law and not by way of succession. The fact that the parent state was and is bound by the same rule has nothing whatever to do with the case; what has to do with the case is the legal fact that *every* state is bound.

It is nearly fifteen years since Dr. Jenks pointed out the absurdity of applying the traditional rule to law-making treaties, and the urgent need—in these days when treaty is the legal vehicle by which indeed custom itself is shaped and codified—to recognize that general law-making treaties bind, and are available to, new states in the same way as is general customary law. But there are two major difficulties.

The first is that all treaties, whether law-making or not, are contractual in form—they are strictly sources of obligation and not sources of law—and consequently their efficacy in regard to a new state can only be realized on the basis of a succession of obligation. Thus new states generally have regarded themselves as being parties to the international labor conventions accepted by their predecessor governments; but it would be impossible to say that they were automatically parties to conventions which the predecessor government had not accepted.

The second difficulty is that the law provides no test for a law-making treaty; and indeed many would say that the distinction is not a scientific, nor for that matter a practical, distinction. This is a larger problem than that of state succession. It is certainly not one that can be solved here. But I would say this: the law has got to find a way of distinguishing between treaties that form part of a general law-making process and treaties that are personal. And until it finds such a technique it cannot be said to be a developed law.

The old law did, of course, make one distinction that was based upon the content and purpose of the law and not merely upon the source of it: it was always supposed that dispositive treaties—treaties that directly affected the territory transferred—would always go with the territory. Insofar as this means that treaties having no surviving executive element are not affected by a state succession, it is a truism. But insofar as it is sometimes taken to mean that a continuing arrangement directly affecting territory must survive a succession, it is difficult to see why this should be so. For, as we have already seen, all treaties likely to come in question affect the territory; and to think of those directly concerned with soil and water as being in a different category is merely to exhibit a naïve literal mindedness. Would it not seem odd, for example, that a bilateral treaty concerning the regime of territorial waters should survive, though subscription to the 1958 Geneva Convention on the Territorial Sea would not?

It is of course true that boundary treaties are not directly affected by succession just because these are usually purely dispositive. The same is true for that matter of any other juridical act by which a boundary is defined, e.g., an award. Nevertheless, it is one of the curiosities of recent history, not least within the Commonwealth, that the new nationalisms, born of reaction to colonialism, have been in the main so content apparently with the boundaries—often, in Africa at least, consisting of arbitrary straight lines—originally determined purely for the convenience of the colonial power. The few boundary problems that have arisen, such as that between Somalia and Ethiopia, are special cases and merely emphasize the general absence of difficulty.

And yet, after all, it is not every boundary instrument that the law regards as surviving independence. For some new boundaries are commonly created by the act of independence itself: one need think only of the quite new international boundary between India and Pakistan; or the disappearance of the boundary between Tanganyika and Zanzibar. In the end we have to say merely that boundary dispositions will survive the succession except insofar as they may be changed by the very act that causes the question to be asked. Thus the argument is really circular and the proposition that boundary dispositions are unaffected has to be qualified by adding "except insofar as they *are* affected" by the creation of the new state itself.

Thus, if one may summarize the argument thus far: the one sure proposition is that a new state is bound by and likewise enjoys rights under the general international law, and this is true not because the new state succeeds to any particular state but because it becomes a member of the family of nations subject to international law. This proposition, however, needs adaptation because the only law which is formally general or universal is customary law. The often far more important law which is codified in treaty form is strictly in the form of obligation and therefore the subjection of a new state to it can at present only be expressed in terms of succession to the parent state. It is this general consideration, however, that lies at the root of what seems today to be the tendency toward the succession of treaty law; the true reason for the tendency is not that there is a new attitude to treaties as such, but that much of this stuff forms the necessary stock-in-trade of any state in the contemporary world.

To demonstrate this proposition it is necessary to look merely at the kind of treaty that is usually, though not invariably, regarded by new states as being subject to a regime of continuity. These are analysed for us in the report of the committee on state succession made to the International Law Association at the Helsinki conference in 1966. They are as follows: multilateral conventions of humanitarian, technical, and administrative character; multilateral conventions relating to settlement of disputes by peaceful means; multilateral conventions concerning matters of private law or private international law; bilateral air transport agreements; extradition treaties; technical assistance agreements; commercial agreements; boundary and territorial treaties. Obviously, continuity is sought in these cases merely because of the content and purpose of the treaty. Whether the distinction between these and other kinds of treaties can yet be expressed in terms of legal criteria is more open to doubt. Perhaps the most that can be said is that this tendency, whether realized through devolution or inheritance agreements or otherwise, is one which is at present a political decision but is the stuff from which hard law may yet be made. Certainly, when the law is able to distinguish clearly between law-making and contract-making, it will have taken an important step forward; but it would be a bold spirit who would assert that the stage has already been reached. The important point for present purposes would seem to be, however, that when that stage is reached, those law-making treaties will survive to a new state because they *are* such, and not because of a succession from the parent state; it is precisely because they have at present to be expressed in terms of succession that the decision to continue them is primarily a political one.

Does this suggest then that the rule of the traditional law that treaties as such do not survive independence is still valid, and that the tendency which many see toward survival of treaties is to be explained on grounds other than succession? This is a question which we must now briefly examine.

It is important at the outset to get some idea of the relatively small dimensions of this problem. First, it must always be borne in mind that a large number of treaties can—by notice, denunciation, and so on—be determined by a party anyway, quite apart from any question of succession. And a successor can hardly be more stringently bound than his predecessor. Second, with regard to other treaties, it will almost always be true that a new state's attempt to negotiate a convenient solution of treaty questions is likely to meet with sympathy from third states. So a rule of law is required only for the residuary and occasional case. It is a last resort where better methods of decision have failed. Furthermore, we must beware therefore of drawing inferences about what the legal position is from the facts of political accommodations. The latter are usually entirely without prejudice as to the legal position, and in this perhaps more than most fields of international law, so-called practice is to be approached with caution. There is, after all, nothing so remote from reality and practicality as the realist positivist in search of a precedent. Thus, for example, the attempt sometimes made to draw legal conclusions one way or the other from temporizing declarations such as those made by Tanganyika, Uganda, Kenya, and Malawi does not always take account of the fact that where a new, understaffed, possibly inexpert and certainly inexperienced foreign office is trying to cope with a situation in which even the actual list of treaties in question may not certainly be known, something of the sort is inevitable. No new state can order its treaty relationships on the basis that they must all either survive indefinitely or terminate at a particular hour of the clock on a certain day.

There is another point of some importance: it is astonishing how little attention has been paid on the whole in discussions of succession of treaties to the question of the operation of the *clausula rebus sic stantibus*. Admittedly, this is something of a hot potato that nobody handles if he can avoid it. But since every municipal law except the most primitive has found it necessary to temporize the absolute view of the binding character of contracts, it must be assumed that international law must do likewise, if it is not indeed an a fortiori case. And if then the doctrine of obsolescence means anything at all, what change of circumstances can be more vital than for example the total disappearance of a party to a bilateral treaty and the substitution of a possible inimical one?

All in all, therefore, it is difficult to see even in the new precedents any serious modification of the old rule that treaties do not survive in succession; and the strong tendency to carry over certain categories of treaties seems to be based upon voluntary novation rather than a rule of succession.

But there is a further point to be looked at before we try to draw any firm conclusions about treaties. We have been assuming hitherto that the new state is indeed a new international persona; but of course when we look more closely at this question it turns out to be the most elusive of all.

The well-known case of India and Pakistan provides a good illustration of the difficulties inherent in the basic question, viz. whether there has or has not been a real change in the international persona. There seems to be no decisive reason why it could not have been equally well decided that India and Pakistan were new states both, or that Pakistan was an old state and India a new one, or that both were old states. This question indeed raises an aspect of the problem of state succession in which the Commonwealth experience is particularly rich. For it has been a feature of the Commonwealth that colonial rule has for so long been geared to the idea that independence is the ultimate aim of colonial government and that it constitutes in some measure at least a trust for the colonial peoples themselves. Consequently, the emergence of new independent members of the Commonwealth has always been a more or less gradual process of evolution. In a real sense it is true to say that there are no new states in the Commonwealth.

It would not seem sensible to take no account of this fact in the question of succession of treaties; for what is done for a colonial territory in contemplation of its independence, and a fortiori what was done by a colonial government in virtue of capacities already possessed before independence, ought to continue in operation because there is *pro tanto* a continuing person behind it; and not least because in these circumstances a third state has surely a right to regard the treaty as continuing in force just because it is made in contemplation of the change of personality that has occurred.

Here the evolution of the older dominions seems to provide useful authority and precedent. Now it is of course true that there is a school of thought according to which the history of the older dominions is quite different from the emergence of the new Commonwealth countries after the war; for the dominions were recognized internationally as having achieved a measure of true international personality even before complete independence. This distinction is not decisive, however.[1] At any rate, the advice given by the head of the legal division of the Commonwealth Relations Office in 1960 seems to me to carry a lesson which is by no means confined to the dominions or even for that matter to the Commonwealth:

We start from the premise that though in international law we are engaged in establishing a new State, in fact that State has had, in many respects, a separate identity for a considerable period; in other words, both immediately before and after the moment of independence, we are dealing with exactly the same geographical area, inhabited by the same people and governed by substantially the same government. . . . From this we deduce, as a broad principle, that the country and the government should continue to enjoy the same international rights and be subject to the same liabilities as before independence, though, after the appointed day it is recognized that this position is preserved by a direct link with other countries, instead of through the medium of the metropolitan country. The result is that by achieving complete separation from the Crown in two stages, a mem-

1. See International Law Association, *The Effect of Independence on Treaties* (London, 1965), pp. 144 ff.

ber of the Commonwealth may enjoy succession to treaty rights and obligations in international law. If so, it may be wondered whether the same result may not be achieved when a part of the Commonwealth becomes a separate and independent State at one step.[2]

Thus it would seem sensible, where there has in fact been a gradual evolution of a new country, to allow that there is a succession of those treaties which have been made in contemplation of independence or through the medium of that country's own evolving machinery of government. It will be noted, of course, that this again is not truly a question of succession; for the crux of the matter here is the continuing personality, not the change of personality. Indeed the right municipal law analogy is not succession on death, but the ending of a period of tutelage or guardianship.

However, this principle does not work only in one direction. It will be recollected that as early as the end of the last century the older dominions were finding that the capacity to *withdraw* from treaties, especially those with most-favored-nation clauses, was an essential ingredient of independence; otherwise it was not even possible to grant imperial tariff preferences. Thus, the development of the capacity to make treaties is of little meaning unless it is accompanied by the capacity in proper cases to withdraw from existing treaties.

Perhaps a brief mention should be made here of the old *inter se* doctrine according to which inter-Commonwealth relationships were insulated from international law. In its positive aspect, i.e. as indicating that the *inter se* Commonwealth relationship was a special one governed by the evolving principles laid down at successive Commonwealth conferences and so forth, the *inter se* doctrine was no more than a compendious way of stating a legal fact that was neither anomalous nor in any way irreconcilable with general international law. But in its negative aspect, i.e. as suggesting that the *inter se* relationships were not governed in any way by international law, as for instance is reflected in the usual Commonwealth reservation to the declarations under the optional clause of the Statute of the International Court of Justice,

2. David Davies Institute, *Report of International Conference* . . . (London, 1960), p. 18.

the *inter se* doctrine has been little more than a smoke screen which failed completely to obscure the fact that independence in an international sense can only be achieved in the sphere of international law, and that the attainment of such independence in any degree injects *pro tanto* international law into even *inter se* relationships. The early insistence of Australia and Canada on a right to withdraw from most-favored-nation treaties with third states is an apt illustration of this truth. The need to make the dominions separate high contracting parties to the Warsaw Convention on Carriage of Goods by Air was a later illustration of the same truth.

This consideration of the continuing personality of the new state also suggests the way to approach the vexed question how far a newly independent state is bound by concession contracts. It is, of course, impossible to answer that question at all except after deciding first how far the contracting government itself is bound, quite apart from the complication of succession. It would be foolhardy in an essay of this kind to make any assumptions about the right answer to this question. It is possible to say, however, that insofar as a question of succession may be raised in relation to a concession, it may obviously be pertinent to ask how far the new government itself, in pursuance of already-existing capacities, participated in the negotiation of the concession, as also how far the concession itself contemplated its continuance after the achievement of full independence.

All this may seem to raise doubts about the validity of the traditional distinction between succession of states and succession of governments: a distinction of great importance, for the law has always been clear that succession is complete in the case of the succession of governments; or more accurately, the rights and obligations of a state cannot be changed by a change of government if the state continues to exist. Modern authorities tend toward "an assimilation of the problems of change of sovereigns and of change of governments."[3] Professor O'Connell compares the ready acceptance by the United States that its military

3. D. P. O'Connell, "Independence and Problems of State Succession," in William V. O'Brien, ed., *The New Nations in International Law and Diplomacy* (New York, 1965), p. 12.

bases in a newly independent West Indies would require renego-
tiation, with the fact that "not even Castro's Cuba has, at least
with any conviction, asserted that in virtue of the revolution in
that country the Guantanamo Naval Base Agreement has lapsed.
Yet the social, political, and ideological change in Cuba has been
far more violent than it has in the West Indies, and though in
form it is a change not affecting 'personality,' it is in fact a change
more fundamental than a change of personality."[4]

This argument, with great respect, is fallacious. The existence
of cases that partake somewhat of both governmental and state
succession does not at all mean that the distinction is invalid; on
the contrary it makes it all the more significant. The political fact
that a change of government may be so violent and revolutionary
as to amount to a change in the personality of the state cannot
mean that the legal results of change of government and change
of statehood are to be assimilated; it merely means that what
appeared to be a change of government ought possibly to be
treated as a change of personality. The fact that yellow may in
some lights appear as red does not mean that the distinction
between yellow and red has in general terms ceased to be significant.

Finally, a word should be added about the traditional rule that
there is no succession in matters of delict. In assessing this rule it
must always be remembered that the older cases of state responsibility are concerned with more or less gross violations of personal
liberty and so forth. But when these precedents are sought to be
extended (as for example in Robert E. Brown's Claim) to claims
which are in essence claims to property rights—to what today
would be regarded as a concession—the law is in danger of
contradicting what it says under one rubric by what it says under
the next. Furthermore, the classification of claims as delictual,
proprietary, or contractual is a municipal law system of classification which varies greatly from one system to another. Probably
these earlier precedents arising from cases of conquest may now
be regarded as obsolete and we can say with Professor O'Connell:

4. *Ibid.,* p. 10.

Surely succession cannot be made to depend upon the accidents of municipal-law systems, which may vary in their characterization. In any event, it is surely nonsense to suggest that, although the legal system survives a change of sovereignty, claims of negligence against the Board of Works lapse. For this reason the suggested criterion of liquidated, as distinct from unliquidated claims, when only the former survives the change of sovereignty, is, perhaps, unrealistic.[5]

The conclusions that seem to emerge are therefore these: it would seem that the present tendency found in practice for a succession of rights and obligations from the old state to the new is not in principle at variance with the rule of the traditional law which leans strongly against succession, at any rate, of treaty obligations and rights. For the cases of succession, insofar as they are not to be explained as voluntary novations, illustrate no more than the need to recognize that a new state inherits the ordinary stock in trade of general international law and that this today consists at least as much in treaty as in custom. But since a treaty is still in the form of obligation rather than general law, this need has to be expressed in terms of succession. In addition it has to be recognized also that treaties which were negotiated by or with a government before its independence was fully realized, but in contemplation of its realization eventually, should continue in effect not because there is a case of succession of states but rather because there is *pro tanto* a succession of governments.

5. *Ibid.*, p. 32.

3

Colonial Participation in
International Legal Processes

*David R. Deener**

A few years after the end of World War II, J. E. S. Fawcett observed that "little attention" was being given "to the contemporary treaty relations of British non-self-governing territories," even though British colonies were "participating widely in all manner of treaties and international organizations."[1] Lack of interest after World War II in colonial treaty relations is not surprising. The winds of change, to use a phrase of a British Prime Minister, brought another theme to dominance: the theme of colonial independence. National independence movements in British territories and elsewhere shattered previous patterns of colonial international relations. They relegated colonial participation in the international legal system largely to the realm of history. They turned attention toward the impact of the new, emerging nations on the structure of international law.

The impact of new states, or groups of new states, on the international legal structure has varied from era to era, a variation amply illustrated in the chronicles of the Commonwealth. For the older members of the Commonwealth—the pre-World War II generation—the transition from colonial to independent status was lengthy and gradual. Further, the transition resulted in a

* Professor of Political Science, Newcomb College, Tulane University.
1. "Treaty Relations of British Overseas Territories," *Brit. Year Book Int. Law,* XXVI (1949), 86, 107.

relatively easy accommodation on the part of the older members to the rules and axioms of international law. For most of the newer members of the Commonwealth—the post-World War II generation—the transitional process has been short and abrupt. Moreover, it has resulted in, not ready accommodation to, but persistent questioning of many international legal rules by one after another of the newer Commonwealth nations.

The sharp contrasts in attitudes toward international law as between the older and newer Commonwealth members upon their emergence from dependent to sovereign status serve to underscore two fundamental questions concerning the future of the law of nations. The first is whether the attitudes of the newer Commonwealth states (and of the new post-World War II states in general) represent a repudiation of the basic structure of international law—or merely a temporary set of resentments aimed at the operation of particular rules. The second involves the source of these attitudes, whether colonial experiences with the international legal system contributed importantly to them—or whether the sources of these attitudes lie essentially outside the realm of colonial history.

Commonwealth Attitudes Toward International Law

One of the notable points of contrast between the older and newer Commonwealth members involves attitudes toward state succession, particularly succession to treaty obligations. For the older Commonwealth members, succession to treaty obligations presented no great problem as they assumed independent status in the interwar period. But there appears to have been some premonition, at least in London circles, of possible problems as the newer Commonwealth states began to emerge in the immediate years after World War II. To deal with these, the United Kingdom concluded inheritance or devolution agreements with a number of the newer Commonwealth states. These agreements specified that the rights and obligations of the United Kingdom with respect to the former dependent territory were to devolve upon the new state.[2]

Premonition became prophecy with the position taken by Israel a few years after achieving independence. Israel maintained that "on the basis of generally recognized principles of international law, Israel which was a new international personality, was not automatically bound by the treaties to which Palestine had been a party." Israel further argued that there was "no automatic elevation of a dependent territory to the status of a party to a treaty" merely because the treaty had been made applicable to that territory. Finally, Israel enunciated the doctrine of novation, declaring that she had "acceded *de novo* to a number of international conventions regardless of whether Palestine was formally party to them or whether in some other way their provisions had been made applicable to Palestine."[3]

Some new Commonwealth states followed Israel's lead. For example, Tanganyika (now Tanzania) objected to the so-called Belbase agreements of 1921 and 1951 between the United Kingdom and Belgium, by which the latter obtained transit rights and port facilities in Tanganyika territory. The Prime Minister of Tanganyika pointed out that Tanganyika was a mandate territory and that Britain's authority with respect to it was limited. In denying that the agreements would bind independent Tanganyika, he said that "in appearing to bind the territory of Tanganyika for all time, the United Kingdom was trying to do something which it did not have the power to do."[4] Uganda was more

2. See Agreement of November 11, 1947, with Ceylon, 86 UNTS 25, sec. 6. The precise wording is rather cautious: "All obligations and responsibilities heretofore devolving on the Government of the United Kingdom which arise from any valid international instrument shall henceforth insofar as such instrument may be held to have application to Ceylon devolve upon the Government of Ceylon." Similar arrangements were made with Burma; Treaty of October 17, 1947, 70 UNTS 183, Art. 2. See also n. 6 below.

3. Reply of Ministry for Foreign Affairs, Government of Israel, January 24, 1960, to Questionnaires of the International Law Commission on the Law of Treaties, secs. 24, 25, and 26; UN Doc. A/CN. 4/19; *Yearbook of the Int. Law Comm.*, II (1950), 215–216.

4. See speech of Prime Minister Nyerere, Tanganyika, National Assembly, *Debates*, 37th Sess. (6th Mtg.), November 30–December 2, 1961, p. 10, quoted in Robert R. Wilson, "Some Questions of International Law in Commonwealth Relations," in W. B. Hamilton, Kenneth Robinson, and C. D. W. Goodwin, eds., *A Decade of the Commonwealth, 1955–1964* (Durham, N.C., 1966), pp. 176–177.

cautious. Uganda announced that treaties validly concluded by the United Kingdom on behalf of Uganda or validly applied to her before independence would continue to be applied on a reciprocal basis until a certain date. Thereafter, Uganda would "regard such treaties, unless they must by the application of the rules of customary international law be regarded as otherwise surviving, as having terminated."[5]

Not all of the newer Commonwealth members adopted the strict position embodied in the doctrine of novation. As noted above, several did conclude inheritance agreements with the United Kingdom.[6] In addition, in one or two instances, the treaty succession question was dealt with in the new state's constitution.[7] Nevertheless, the main thrust of the position taken by the emerging new nations is to challenge the notion of state succession to treaty obligations. Or, as one writer from a newer Commonwealth country has put it, to invoke *rebus sic stantibus* freely in the case of previous treaty arrangements deemed disadvantageous.[8]

The contrast with the older Commonwealth members on the point of treaty succession is especially striking. During the latter decades of the nineteenth century, the then developing dominions raised questions concerning the propriety of the Mother Country's automatically extending treaty obligations to their territories. As a result, increasingly wider rights of separate acces-

---

5. Communication to the Secretary-General of the United Nations, dated February 12, 1963; quoted in Wilson, "Some Questions of International Law," p. 178.

6. See n. 2 above. For some other inheritance agreements, see those with Nigeria, Cmnd. 1214; Ghana, 287 UNTS 234; Jamaica, Cmnd. 1918; Cyprus, Cmnd. 1093; Trinidad and Tobago, Cmnd. 1919.

7. See Constitution of Malaya, 1957, Art. 169(a), which stipulates that "any treaty, agreement or convention entered into before Merdeka Day between Her Majesty or her predecessors or the Government of the United Kingdom on behalf of the Federation or any part thereof and another country shall be deemed to be a treaty, agreement or convention between the Federation and that other country." The Constitution of Malaya went into effect on August 31, 1957. On September 12, 1957, Malaya entered into an inheritance agreement with the United Kingdom; *Gazette*, No. 237 of January 22, 1958. For provisions with respect to the Borneo States and Singapore upon the establishment of Malaysia, see sec. 41 of the Malaysia Act, 1963.

8. S. Prakash Sinha, "Perspective of the Newly Independent States on the Binding Quality of International Law," *Int. & Comp. Law Quar.*, 4th ser., XIV (1965), 122.

sion to treaties were granted.[9] When the dominions gained sovereign status, however, they showed little disposition to question treaty obligations imposed before rights of separate accession had been given, or for that matter, to question treaties concluded even before their respective territories came under the British flag. Thus, the *Australian Treaty List* (1956) enumerates treaties dating as far back as 1654 as continuing to bind Australia,[10] a situation also illustrated by Canada.[11]

State succession to treaty obligations illustrates one set of contrasting attitudes on a point of international law as between the older and newer Commonwealth members upon reaching independent status. The range of international law points over which contrasting attitudes have appeared is considerable. As catalogued by one representative of the newer Commonwealth areas, major points of contrast and the attitude taken thereon by the emergent nations include: title to territory (refusal to recognize certain colonial titles even though acquired by discovery and occupation); expropriation (insistence upon relatively unrestricted right to expropriate); territorial sea (broad definition therefor); state responsibility (questioning whether rules and standards governing actually exist); settlement of disputes (emphasis upon negotiation rather than adjudication); territorial integrity (extreme sensitiveness thereover); sovereignty (great emphasis upon discretionary power embodied therein); customary international law (refusal to accept customary rules as a body); and treaty law (claim to invoke *rebus sic stantibus* with wide latitude).[12]

To the above catalogue of points questioned by the new states

9. See nn. 15, 16, below.

10. For examples, the Treaty of 1654 between Britain and Sweden, Treaty of 1656 between Britain and Sweden, Treaty of 1661 between Britain and Denmark, Treaty of 1661 between Britain and Sweden, and Treaty of 1670 between Britain and Denmark. The *Australian Treaty List* referred to is published as the *Australian Treaty Series, 1956*, No. 1.

11. The treaties mentioned in n. 10 are also relevant to Canada, as are, in addition, several more, including the Treaty of Susa, 1629, and the Treaty of Utrecht, 1713; see Senate of Canada, *Proceedings of the Standing Committee on Transport and Communications*, No. 5 (1959), Appendix A. The New Zealand *Treaty List*, 1948 N.Z. *Treaty Series*, No. 11, also lists the treaties of 1654, 1656, and 1661 between Britain and Sweden.

12. This catalogue is drawn from Sinha, "Perspective of the Newly Independent States."

is to be added another element. This is the argument sometimes advanced that the new nations were not necessarily bound by international legal rules upon attaining statehood because they had not participated in their making.[13] Here, again, is a contrast with the older Commonwealth members, for no similar argument accompanied their transition to international statehood.

Standing by itself, the no-participation line of argument has important implications as to the impact of the new states upon the law of nations. But discussion of these implications as well as those posed by the catalogue of contrasting attitudes may be deferred, since the no-participation argument leads more immediately to the subject of colonial experience with participation in the international legal system.

Colonial Experience with International Processes

As Professor Fawcett has observed, British non-self-governing territories were "participating widely in all manner of treaties and international organisations," in the years following World War II.[14] The nature of this participation, its extent and history, bears upon the no-participation argument, just as comparison with that engaged in by the older Commonwealth members prior to their independence bears upon the contrasting attitudes toward international law exhibited by the two categories of Commonwealth states. To Professor Fawcett's areas of participation, treaties and international organization, may be added a third, participation in the customary processes of the law.

Treaty-making. Over the period encompassing the colonial stages of both categories of Commonwealth members the basic international law principle governing responsibility for treaty-

13. For allusions to the factor of colonial non-participation, see J. J. G. Syatauw, *Some Newly Established Asian States and the Development of International Law* (The Hague, 1961), pp. 25, 239; R. P. Anand, "Attitude of the Asian-African States toward Certain Problems of International Law," *Int. & Comp. Law Quar.*, 4th ser., XV (1966), 56; J. Casteneda, "The Undeveloped Nations and the Development of International Law," *Int. Org.*, XV (1961), 38–40.

14. "Treaty Relations of British Overseas Territories," p. 107.

making remained the same. That is, the Mother Country was the internationally responsible person for treaty-making affecting or involving the dependent territories. Further, this principle was embodied in the constitutional law of the empire throughout the period.[15] In practice, however, as noted above, the strict constitutional principle was relaxed, so that from the 1880's on separate rights of adherence and withdrawal were granted to overseas territories with respect to an ever increasing range of treaties.[16] It was out of this practice that the so-called colonial application clause evolved. At first, the separate right of adherence was conceded to then self-governing territories (those which by and large came to form later the older Commonwealth states). From roughly 1900 on, however, the same practice began to appear with respect to the then non-self-governing territories (those which later came to form the newer Commonwealth nations).

Thus, even before World War I both categories of territories were often treated alike at the international level in respect to incurring treaty obligations of various kinds. In some instances, the acceptance of a treaty obligation by the Mother Country did not purport to bind either group of territories. Each territory accepted separately or not, and the acceptance was signified by notice of accession emanating from London. Examples involving both bilateral[17] and multilateral[18] treaties are easy to find. For

15. For exposition of this principle, see A. B. Keith, *Responsible Government in the Dominions* (Oxford, 1912), III, 1102–1108.

16. For discussion of the development of separate adherence and separate withdrawal, see Robert B. Stewart, *Treaty Relations of the British Commonwealth of Nations* (New York, 1939), chaps. 4, 5; Keith, *Responsible Government in the Dominions*, pp. 1108–1114. Separate rights are usually said to have appeared first in connection with commercial treaties, those between Britain and Rumania, March 4–April 5, 1880, and between Britain and Montenegro, January 21, 1882, being landmarks in this respect. However, a case can be made that separate inclusion occurred earlier with respect to international postal conventions; see nn. 39, 40, below.

17. Commencing in the early 1900's, British commercial treaties and arrangements increasingly contained provisions for separate accession or withdrawal by "any of His Majesty's Colonies, possessions, or Protectorates." See Declaration of March 16, 1908, amending Treaty of Commerce with Paraguay, October 16, 1884; 101 *Brit. & For. State Papers* 200.

On March 20, 1907, the British Foreign Office gave notice of the accession of sixteen territories to the Treaty of Commerce with Rumania, October 31, 1905; those acceding included Ceylon, Cyprus, Gold Coast, Malta, Sierra Leone, Straits Settlements, and Uganda; 101 *ibid.* 201.

On the same date, March 20, 1907, the Foreign Office gave notice of accession of thirty-six territories to the Convention relative to the Disposal of Real and

some other kinds of treaties, there was also comparable treatment before World War I. In the case of the Hague Conventions, for example, ratification by the Crown bound the whole empire, self-governing and non-self-governing alike.[19]

In the matter of the implementation of treaty obligations, there was also comparable experience from the legal point of view of both categories of territories. In this matter, the dualist doctrine followed in British practice played an important role. According to this doctrine, treaty provisions requiring an alteration in the law of the land must be incorporated by statute in order to be effective internally.[20] The imperial Parliament possessed, of course, the power to enact a statute applicable to the overseas territories to carry out the obligations of a treaty. On occasion, such as the Extradition Act of 1870, the imperial Parliament did just this.[21] But the usual practice was to leave implementing measures up to the territorial authorities in both the self-governing and non-self-governing areas.

These practices resulted in extensive legal participation in treaty implementation by the older and newer Commonwealth members during their colonial stages. How extensive this participation was on occasion may be seen in the network of measures necessary to make the General Convention on the Privileges and

---

Personal Property with the United States, March 2, 1889. The accession list included Australia, India, and New Zealand as well as most of the territories which have come to comprise the new Commonwealth group; 101 *ibid.* 203.

See also the list of thirty-three accessions to the Treaty of Commerce with Japan of April 3, 1911; 107 *ibid.* 537–538; and list of thirty-five accessions to the Convention of Commerce with Montenegro, January 11, 1910; 107 *ibid.* 541–542.

18. See list of accessions to the International Convention with respect to International Circulation of Motor Vehicles, October 11, 1909; the list included India (except native states), Malta, Northern Nigeria, Southern Nigeria, Sierra Leone; 107 *ibid.* 530. The list of accessions to the International Agreement for the Suppression of Obscene Publications, May 4, 1910, contained Australia, Canada, New Zealand, and South Africa, as well as some thirty-seven other colonies and territories; 107 *ibid.* 531–532.

19. See Stewart, *Treaty Relations of the British Commonwealth*, p. 135; A. B. Keith, *The Dominions as Sovereign States* (London, 1938), pp. 12–13.

20. For a classic statement by Lord Atkin of the dualist doctrine, see the *Labour Conventions Case* [1937], A.C. 326 at 347; also Lord McNair, *The Law of Treaties* (Oxford, 1961), pp. 81–83.

21. 33 & 34 Vict., c. 52. In the 1880's, Canada enacted its own extradition laws, whereupon the British government suspended the operation in Canada of the imperial statute so long as the Canadian law remained in force; see G. V. La Forest, *Extradition to and from Canada* (New Orleans, 1961), pp. 5–7; Stewart, *Treaty Relations of the British Commonwealth*, p. 122.

Immunities of the United Nations effective throughout the British overseas territories.

The General Convention on Privileges and Immunities of the United Nations was approved by the General Assembly on February 13, 1946.[22] The British Parliament did not enact the International Organisations (Immunities and Privileges) Act until 1950.[23] Prior to this date, however, Parliament had acted even before the United Nations itself was founded. In 1944, it enacted the Diplomatic Privileges (Extension) Act.[24] This act provided for extension of privileges, immunities and legal powers to international organizations by Order in Council. Then, in 1946, another Diplomatic Privileges (Extension) Act was enacted.[25] This amended the 1944 act in light of the approval by the General Assembly of the General Convention on Privileges and Immunities of the United Nations; it made specific reference to the United Nations and the International Court of Justice.[26] In 1947, the Diplomatic Privileges (United Nations and International Court of Justice) Order in Council was passed.[27] In the explanatory note to the order, it was stated: "Many of the provisions of the Convention and of the resolution relating to the International Court are provisions which can be fulfilled either by purely executive action under the prerogative or by virtue of powers exercised under Acts of Parliament not necessitating the making of any Order in Council."

The explanatory note also spoke to territorial coverage of the Order in Council: "This Order in Council applies to the United Kingdom only and, for the purpose of fulfilling His Majesty's Government's obligations under the Convention, the Statute or resolution, in respect of colonies, overseas territories, etc., the necessary action will be taken by local legislation in the territories concerned."

The British Diplomatic Privileges (United Nations and Inter-

22. 1 UNTS 15.
23. 14 Geo. 6, c. 14. This act consolidated and repealed earlier legislation on the subject; it provided (sec. 7) that Orders in Council made under the earlier acts should continue in effect if then in force.
24. 7 & 8 Geo. 6, c. 44. An earlier British act was the Diplomatic Privileges (Extension) Act, 1941; 4 & 5 Geo. 6, c. 7.
25. 9 & 10 Geo. 6, c. 66.   26. See Preamble and sec. 2.
27. SRO, 1947, No. 1772.

national Court of Justice) Order in Council, 1947, was made on August 8 and came into force two weeks later. As the order noted, the United Kingdom had acceded to the General Convention on the Privileges and Immunities of the United Nations. Section 34 of the General Convention stipulates that "it is understood that, when an instrument of accession is deposited on behalf of any Member, the Member will be in position under its own law to give effect to the terms of this convention." The British order of 1947 was limited, consistent with dualistic doctrine and empire constitutional practice, to the United Kingdom. Hence, the local action indicated in the note to the order to be taken throughout the various overseas territories was not only a procedure in accord with the dualist doctrine and imperial practice, but also expressly required by the commitment contained in Section 34 of the General Convention.

To make the privileges and immunities specified in the General Convention effective in the overseas areas required local action in over forty separate jurisdictions. The action taken was patterned after that of the United Kingdom. A local act or ordinance was enacted which empowered the local executive to designate international organizations and declare their entitlement to the privileges and immunities specified in the act or ordinance; later, an order or declaration would be issued designating the United Nations. Such procedure was followed in territories large and small, east and west, such as Nigeria,[28] Tanganyika,[29] or Uganda,[30] as well as in places such as Swaziland,[31] Mauritius,[32] Tonga,[33] and

28. Nigeria, Diplomatic Privileges (Extension) Ordinance, 1947, No. 25 of 1947; Diplomatic Privileges (United Nations and International Court of Justice) Order in Council, No. 27 of 1948.

29. Tanganyika, Diplomatic Privileges (Extension) Ordinance, No. 16 of 1947; Diplomatic Privileges (United Nations and International Court of Justice) Order, G.N. 140 of 1948.

30. Uganda, Diplomatic Privileges (Extension) Ordinance, No. 10 of 1948; Diplomatic Privileges (Extension) (Declared Organisations) Order, L.N. 215 of 1950 (lists the UN and ICJ in its Schedule, along with the ILO, FAO, UNESCO, ICAO, IRO, and WHO). There was an earlier order applying only to the UN and ICJ; L.N. 40 of 1949.

31. Swaziland, Diplomatic Immunities and Privileges Proclamation, No. 17 of 1948; High Commissioner's Notice, No. 267 of 1949.

32. Mauritius, Diplomatic Privileges Ordinance, 1947, No. 4 of 1947; Diplomatic Privileges (United Nations and International Court of Justice) Order, 1948, G.N. No. 113 of 1948.

33. Tonga, Diplomatic Privileges Act, 1948, No. 7 of 1948; United Nations and International Court of Justice (Immunities and Privileges) Order, 1948, G.N. 9 of 1950.

Zanzibar.[34] Thus, in overseas territories tiny as well as huge,[35] the legal steps necessary to implement the General Convention were very similar to those taken in the United Kingdom,[36] or for that matter, in other Commonwealth states.[37]

One further similarity may be noted. The time span from the early 1880's, when separate rights of adherence to particular types of treaties were granted to the now older Commonwealth members, to the mid-1920's, when their independence is recognizable, is 40–50 years.[38] There is virtually the same time span from the early 1900's, when separate adherence began to appear for the now newer Commonwealth members, to the late years of the 1940's, when the first members of the newer group obtained full independence. With respect, then, to the major aspects of treaty-making, the incurring of treaty obligations and their implementation, the colonial experiences of the two groups of Com-

34. Zanzibar, Diplomatic Privileges (Extension) Decree, 1948, No. 10 of 1948; Diplomatic Privileges (United Nations and International Court of Justice) Order, 1948, G.N. 119 of 1948.

35. It is not clear whether some territories were covered by an order. Such appears to have been the case with, appropriately enough, Inaccessible Island. It also appears that the United Nations and the International Court of Justice were not covered in Southern Rhodesia, although several specialized agencies were; see Diplomatic Privileges Extension Act, No. 29 of 1949, and Proclamations Nos. 49–54 of 1949 covering IRO, ICAO, UNESCO, ILO, WHO, and FAO. The Federation of Rhodesia and Nyasaland enacted an Immunities and Privileges Act in 1956 (No. 31 of 1956), but, as of July, 1962, no orders had been issued to cover the UN, ICJ, or specialized agencies.

36. In one instance, too similar. The order issued by Mauritius, cited n. 32, above, actually reprinted the note appended to the British Order of 1947, with the result that the Mauritius' order is stated to apply to the United Kingdom only.

37. See Australia, International Organizations (Privileges and Immunities) Act, 1948, No. 72; International Organizations (Privileges and Immunities) Regulations, 1959, Stat. Rules 1959, No. 20; Canada, Privileges and Immunities (United Nations) Act, 1947, *Can. Stat.* 1947, c. 69; Order in Council P.C. 3946 of October 1, 1947; New Zealand, Diplomatic Immunities and Privileges Act, 1957; Diplomatic Privileges (United Nations) Order, 1959. Texts of the above are given in United Nations, *Legislative Texts and Treaty Provisions concerning the Legal States, Privileges and Immunities of International Organizations*, Vol. I (1959), ST./LEG/Ser.B/10.

One further point concerning the British action may be mentioned. As noted earlier, sec. 34 of the convention required a state to be "in a position under its own law to give effect" to the convention's terms. Britain acceded on September 17, 1946, but almost all of the implementing action in the territories came well after that date and after the date of the British Order of 1947, which applied only to the United Kingdom. This raises the question whether Britain was "in a position" to give effect to the convention throughout the territories for which she was internationally responsible.

38. The percise date when the older British dominions attained international independence is not easily ascertained, but it happened sometime between World Wars I and II. Herbert W. Briggs, ed., *The Law of Nations* (2nd ed.; New York, 1952), p. 66, indicates 1939 as the date.

monwealth states were, from a legal point of view at least, rather more comparable than otherwise.[39]

International Organizations. As noted above, separate rights of adherence to particular kinds of treaties were granted to the now older Commonwealth states in the 1880's. Actually, instances of separate participation in international organizations by British dependencies occurred earlier. For example, the General Postal Union Convention of 1874 made provision (Art. 17) for entry into the union of "countries beyond the seas." Under this provision, India entered the union on January 27, 1876.[40] Indeed, in the Universal Postal Union Convention of 1878, a number of British colonies as well as Canada and British India were designated as parties to the convention; among these colonies were Ceylon, Straits Settlements, Hong Kong, Mauritius, Bermuda, Jamaica, and Trinidad.[41] A distinction was drawn, however, between membership in the union (or being a party to the convention) and voting rights in postal congresses. With respect to voting, Great Britain was assigned one vote and India was assigned one vote; and one more vote was given to all the rest of the participating British colonies.[42] This distinction between membership and voting continued. In 1920, for example, Britain received one vote, the dominions received four votes, and one vote went to the "whole" of the British colonies.[43]

39. Thus, in another area, the dominions (as well as other territories) continued to be included in British extradition treaties until after World War I. In extradition treaties after World War I, the dominions were not automatically included, although other territories were. See Stewart, *Treaty Relations of the British Commonwealth*, pp. 121–127.

40. 67 *Brit. & For. State Papers* 549; see also Stewart, *Treaty Relations of the British Commonwealth*, p. 117. It should be noted, however, that British territories had concluded separate postal conventions prior to the 1880's. For example, see the Postal Convention between the Postal Department of the United States of America and the Postal Department of the Dominion of Canada, dated June 8 and 23, 1875 (20 *U.S. Stat.* 673); Postal Convention of March 25, 1851, between Canada and the United States (16 *U.S. Stat.* 1095); Postal Convention of Aug. 10, 1867, between the United States and the Colonial Government of Hong Kong (15 *U.S. Stat.* 563).

41. See Preamble and Art. 21 of the convention (text at 20 *U.S. Stat.* 734); and Final Protocol, sec. IV (text at 20 *U.S. Stat.* 748).

42. See Arts. 19 and 21 of the Convention of 1878. Single votes each were also assigned to the "whole" of the Danish, Spanish, French, Netherlands, and Portuguese colonies.

43. See Convention of November 30, 1920, Arts. 27 and 29 (text at 42 *U.S. Stat.* 1971). The convention was signed by representatives of Great Britain and the

Developments in the fields of telegraph and radio took paths somewhat similar, albeit with a few turnings here and there, to that followed in the postal area. The convention of 1865 establishing the International Telegraphic Union was limited to European countries, but the question of participation by non-European countries soon arose.[44] In 1875, the convention was altered to permit "different Administrations" of the same government to be represented and vote.[45] Beginning with the conference of 1879, colonial administrations sent separate delegates, and the number of colonial votes gradually rose.[46] As a result, in the conference of 1925, the "British Empire" had a total of seven votes, distributed to Britain herself, four dominions, and two other British territories, and other "empires" also had several votes because of the participation of colonies; the French, indeed, had ten.[47] The international telegraphic conferences came to an end, however, in the thirties, when they merged with radio.

International radio developments began in 1906 with the conference which produced the Radio Telegraph Convention of that year. The 1906 convention provided for the adherence thereto of colonies, but stipulated that the number of votes for an imperial system could not exceed six.[48] The same provision appeared in the Radio Telegraph Convention of 1912.[49] At the conference of 1932, the question of colonial votes touched off a lengthy debate. No provision concerning the question was placed in the resulting convention, but the internal regulations for the conference allotted a vote each to Great Britain, British India, and the "whole" of British colonies, as well as to the Union of South Africa, Australia, Canada, and New Zealand. Other colo-

---

British colonies, British India, Australia, Canada, New Zealand, and the Union of South Africa. However, New Zealand was not specified to have a separate vote (although India and the other dominions were), but the vote specified for the other British colonies was assigned to New Zealand. See Louis B. Sohn, "Multiple Representation in International Assemblies," *Am. Jour. Int. Law,* XL (1946), 80–81.

44. For example, at the conference of 1872, India was allowed a separate vote; see Sohn, "Multiple Representation," p. 85.

45. See Art. 16 of the convention, 57 L.N.T.S. 217.

46. Sohn, "Multiple Representation," p. 85.

47. *Ibid.,* p. 86.   48. Art. 12.

49. Art. 12.

nial clusters also were allotted a separate vote, but the "six vote" rule of the earlier conventions was abandoned.[50]

The postal, radio, and telegraph fields were not the only areas of international organization in which there was colonial participation prior to World War II.[51] Developments in the three fields do, however, illustrate the general pattern of colonial participation and one important distinction which emerged in the general pattern. This is the distinction between mere membership in an international organization and the right to vote in proceedings, or, perhaps phrased differently, between legal participation and political participation. Non-self-governing territories (with the exception of British India) were generally not accorded a full voting membership, but self-governing territories frequently were. The Versailles Conference of 1919 and the League of Nations Covenant dramatized the distinction with the provision for separate voting participation on the part of India, Canada, Australia, New Zealand, and the Union of South Africa as well as the United Kingdom.[52]

The distinction between legal membership in international organizations and voting participation which was applied to territories later to become the newer Commonwealth states carried over into the post-World War II period. Except for India, no new Commonwealth member played a role in the formation of the United Nations in any way comparable to that of the older Commonwealth states in the Versailles Conference and the drafting of the League Covenant. Indeed, the status of legal membership but

50. See Sohn, "Multiple Representation," pp. 90–97. In general, the number of votes was cut down. Britain, excluding the Commonwealth votes, had three; France received three.

51. Other examples include: Convention concerning the Formation of an International Union for the Publication of Customs Tariffs, 1890 ("Great Britain and sundry British colonies, the Dominion of Canada, the colonies of West Australia, the Cape of Good Hope, Natal, New South Wales, New Zealand, Queensland, Tasmania, Newfoundland and Victoria" were actually named as contracting parties; Art. 14 made provision for accession of "States and colonies"); a procès-verbal attached to the International Sanitary Convention of 1903 stipulated (in sec. III) that the convention was not applicable to the colonies, possessions, or protectorates of His Britannic Majesty except by special accession; the Convention Creating the International Agricultural Institute, 1905 (Art. 10 provided for accession of colonies under the same conditions as independent states).

52. For an account of dominion participation, see Stewart, *Treaty Relations of the British Commonwealth*, pp. 136–158.

less-than-full voting participation was explicitly spelled out in many post-World War II international organization documents. For example, the International Telecommunications Convention of 1947 authorized a single membership with one vote for the "whole" of the British overseas territories.[53] But it also went on to establish an associate membership for any territory not fully responsible for the conduct of its international relations, with the stipulation that associate membership did not carry voting rights.[54] A decade later, to give another example, the Convention on the Intergovernmental Maritime Consultative Organization of 1958 provided for associate membership in much the same terms.[55]

On the whole, then, while there were some similarities in the legal experience of the two groups of Commonwealth states during their colonial stages with membership in international organizations, there was also a significant difference. This difference concerned full voting participation, a kind of participation frequently denied to the territories now comprising the newer Commonwealth states, and, furthermore, denied in explicit legal terms.

Custom. One spokesman from the new states has summed up their attitude toward international custom rather succinctly: "For not all the rules of customary international law are acceptable to them."[56] In contrast, there was little disposition on the part of the older Commonwealth members to question the customary law upon their attainment of statehood. One factor behind the attitude of the new states toward custom, so the spokesman quoted above intimates, is that the new states did not participate in international customary processes while they were in the colonial status.[57] This intimation invites comparison of the colonial legal experiences of the older and newer Commonwealth members with the customary law of nations.

53. Art. I(2), and Annex I(19); text of convention at 63 *Stat.* 1397.
54. Art. I(4), and Art. I(6).
55. See Arts. 9 and 10; for text, see TIAS 4044.
56. See Sinha, "Perspective of the Newly Independent States," p. 122.
57. *Ibid.*

Perhaps the first point to be investigated is whether customary international law was part of the local law of the two groups of Commonwealth members when they were in the colonial stage. According to the doctrine of dualism followed in the British system, international law is not per se part of municipal law. It must be incorporated or received into domestic law. It is possible, of course, that customary international law was incorporated into the colonial law of the territories now comprising the older Commonwealth members, but was not incorporated into the law of the territories of the newer members when they were in a dependent status. Thus, at the moment of independence, one group of Commonwealth members would have had a history of direct legal contact with customary international law, while the other would not.

Universal agreement is lacking as to the precise principle by which customary international law is incorporated or received into municipal law in the English system.[58] One doctrine that has its advocates holds that the customary law of nations is part of the common law and hence part of the law of the land. On the logic of this doctrine, if English common law extended to a colonial territory, then customary international law must also have extended. English common law—or the laws of England, as it is sometimes phrased—reached colonial territories through a variety of means: settlement, express imperial act or order, or local adoption.[59] By these means and over the centuries from the seventeenth to the twentieth, the common law spread widely and generally throughout British overseas territories and to both the areas later to comprise the older Commonwealth members and the newer.[60] And, a fortiori by the doctrine, the customary law of

58. See Robert R. Wilson, "Reception of Norms," in Wilson *et al., The International Law Standard and Commonwealth Developments* (Durham, N.C., 1966), pp. 75–81; J. E. S. Fawcett, *The British Commonwealth in International Law* (London, 1963), pp. 18, 35–55, 73–74.

59. See Charles J. Tarring, *Chapters on the Law Relating to the Colonies* (4th ed.; London, 1913), pp. 3–7; Henry Jenkyns, *British Rule and Jurisdiction beyond the Seas* (1902), pp. 5–6.

60. See Wilson, "Some Questions of International Law," pp. 187–189. In some areas, French civil law (Quebec, Mauritius) or Roman-Dutch law (Ceylon, parts of South Africa, Southern Rhodesia) rather than the common law took root.

nations reached the territories of both categories of members during the colonial stage.

A contrasting approach to the problem of reception of international law, one which does not rest upon the common-law theory, has been elaborated by Professor Fawcett. This approach takes as a premise that if "there is one thing clear in the United Kingdom, and in the legal systems derived from it, it is that there is no general adoption or incorporation of international law so that it makes sense to speak of it as 'part of the law.'"[61] Instead, only particular customary rules, "which have been duly established and recognised, are observed and applied." English courts simply adopt and apply generally accepted international rules directly as *lex fori,* "making no distinction in the process between them and municipal law."[62] This approach sees the English court rather than the English common law as the avenue for reception of customary international law. Yet this approach may not have discarded the common law entirely, for the peculiar authority of the English court to apply international law directly as *lex fori* may well stem from the common-law concept of the court and judicial power. Regardless of the intrinsic differences between the English court and the English common-law approaches, their effects on customary international law and colonial territories are about the same. For English-type courts (and English-trained judges) like the common law spread widely throughout British colonial areas. And during the colonial periods of both the older and newer Commonwealth members, the English-type local court wherever it existed stood as a potential instrument for reception of the customary law of nations.

At any rate, both the common-law theory and the English court approach seem to underlie a line of reasoning advanced to explain the application of customary international law by Indian courts after independence. The reasoning runs that English law which included customary international law was applied by Indian courts before independence; the Indian constitution pro-

61. Fawcett, *The British Commonwealth,* p. 18.
62. *Ibid.,* pp. 73–74.

vided that the law in force immediately prior to independence was to continue in effect after independence; hence English law and thus customary international law could be applied by Indian courts after independence.[63]

There are other evidences that the customary law of nations reached British overseas territories without categorical distinction as between the two groups which later became the older and newer Commonwealth states. Such evidences include the widespread location of foreign consulates throughout British territories,[64] the phraseology of certain imperial statutes,[65] and the implications of various judicial decisions.[66]

Comparable as the colonial legal experiences of the two groups of Commonwealth members may have been in their contact with customary international law, this aspect is not, really, the main target of the no-participation argument. The main thrust of the argument is non-participation by the newer Commonwealth members in the processes by which existing customary rules were formulated. But in this respect, the colonial legal experience of the newer Commonwealth states was not much different from the experience of the older. In legal theory, both international and imperial, no colonial territory had a direct role in the custom-making process. Whatever part a colony may have played, it was not a direct legal part, but one of influence upon the policies of the imperial government.

63. See S. K. Agrawala, *International Law: Indian Courts and Legislature* (Bombay, 1965), pp. 12–13.

64. See, for example, the listings of United States consular officers stationed in colonial areas in *Register of Officers and Agents, Civil, Military, and Naval, in the Service of the United States on the Thirtieth September, 1859* . . . (1859), and *Regulations Prescribed for the Use of the Consular Service of the United States* (1888), at pp. 523–526.

65. For example, the Territorial Waters Jurisdiction Act, 1878, defined (sec. 7) the "territorial waters of Her Majesty's dominions" as "such part of the sea adjacent to the coast of the United Kingdom, or the coast of some other part of Her Majesty's dominions, as is deemed by international law to be within the territorial sovereignty of Her Majesty."

66. For example, the rhetorical question asked by the Privy Council in *Croft* v. *Dunphy* [1933], A.C. 156, 164–165, whether the English Parliament in the British North America Act had authorized the Canadian Parliament to legislate in contravention of the principles of international law. Also, given the origins of the cases, *West Rand Central Gold Mining Co.* v. *The King* [1905], 2 K.B. 391, and *Chung Chi Cheung* v. *The King* [1939], A.C. 160, are relevant. See also the statements of Chief Justice Duff of Canada in *Reference re Tax on Foreign Legations* [1943], 2 D.L.R. 481.

Impact on the Law of Nations

Both the older and the newer Commonwealth states came to participate widely during their colonial stages in international legal processes. In treaty-making, in international organization, and with respect to the processes of the customary law, the colonial participation of the two groups of members from the strict legal point of view was on the whole comparable rather than otherwise. How, then, does the comparability of their colonial legal experiences square with their differences in attitude toward international law following independence? This question may be approached in various ways. One approach will attach more weight to colonial legal experience than another and will lead to different conclusions as to the results of the impact of the new states upon the international legal system.

For example, one approach may take as a starting point the fact of the differences in attitudes toward international law on the part of the older and newer Commonwealth states. Since comparable colonial legal participation did not produce similar attitudes, this approach may assign little weight—perhaps even insignificance—to legal experience, and possibly, too, little weight to historical experience in the narrow sense. Instead, this approach focuses on the vast differences between the older and newer states as regards color, race, religion, and culture. It suggests that existing international law is not international law at all, but rather a European law, or more broadly, a public law of Christendom. It sees, then, the impact of the new states as essentially a collision of worlds, worlds of different cultures and values. This approach, akin to that of cultural relativism in the social sciences, raises ultimately the crucial questions whether there can be any universal values, values not culture-bound, and whether there can be a universal international law.

A second approach may take the colonial legal experience of the two groups of Commonwealth states as a starting point, but ask, what was involved in those experiences despite their comparability that produced the differences in attitudes toward international law. One element has already been indicated by the distinction made between legal membership in international organization and full voting participation therein, the latter having been much more often accorded to the older Commonwealth states than to the newer during their respective colonial periods. This distinction suggests that the element of political responsibility was importantly involved in colonial participation and that it was much more likely to have accompanied colonial legal participation on the part of the older Commonwealth members than by the newer. In fact, for the older Commonwealth members, increasingly wide participation in international legal processes came after the development of responsible local government. For the newer Commonwealth members, the reverse is largely true. Legal participation came first; responsible local government came later, in some cases much later. Indeed, as late as 1949, only Southern Rhodesia and Malta among some forty British overseas territories operated under responsible government, and only one or two of the now newer Commonwealth members (not counting India, Pakistan, and Ceylon, then fully independent) enjoyed even representative government in the sense of having fully elective local legislatures.[67]

For the older members operating under responsible government, colonial participation meant direct and responsible experience on the part of local political leaders with international legal processes. For the newer members, however, colonial participation meant little direct, and even less responsible, experience with international law on the part of local leaders, for colonial government remained in most cases largely in the hands of a British bureaucracy during most of the colonial period.

The approach which takes colonial participation as a starting point may borrow from the political behavior field of political science and emphasize the process of political socialization. It would then interpret the period of colonial participation as a process of political socialization into the international legal system. The socialization process was successful and relatively com-

67. See Fawcett, "Treaty Relations of British Overseas Territories," p. 88.

plete in the case of the older Commonwealth members, but unsuccessful and clearly incomplete in the case of the newer members.[68] This aproach views the impact of the newer nations upon international law as the problem of a non-socialized group within the political system. The question this approach poses is whether full political participation by the newer states after independence will result finally in socialization into the international legal system or only further alienation.

A third approach may take the simple presence of the new states as a starting point. It would not attach fundamental importance to the differences in attitudes toward international law as between the old and new states, nor to colonial participation. In fact, this approach may not be concerned with the new states because they are new, but because they are states. For this approach could be based on the so-called pragmatic realism of the sociological school of jurisprudence and the followers of Roscoe Pound. It would then accept as a basic fact that a participant in the legal and political system will have certain interests and voice certain demands. It would conceive the function of the legal system to be the furtherance of interests and the realization of demands. It would view the impact of the new states upon international law as simply the insertion of another set of interests and demands alongside of and in competition with those already existing. The question this approach raises is one of means, whether the means can be devised so that the international legal system can satisfy the interests and demands of the new states and at the same time continue to accommodate all those of other participants.

As to which of the various approaches to the question of the impact of the new nations on international law may possess the greatest validity, events through the mid-1960's hardly permit

68. The efforts of Canadian officials in attempting directly to negotiate treaties with a number of foreign countries in the latter half of the nineteenth century provide a good example of a socializing experience. If any Canadian officials were starry-eyed about the realities of direct participation in international affairs and the responsibilities to the local electorate resulting therefrom, they must have been disabused by the negotiations on commercial and other matters with the United States ranging from the Reciprocity Treaty of 1854 to its ill-fated successor of 1911; see G. P. deT. Glazebrook, *A History of Canadian External Relations* (New York, 1950), pp. 55–73, 110–164, 187–192.

any definitive conclusion. Certainly, insofar as the particular approaches sketched above are concerned, there is no basis as yet for dismissing any of them. Consequently, in theory, a wide range of possibilities exists as to the ultimate impact of the new states upon the structure of the law of nations.

Perhaps the approach utilizing the concept of political socialization will prove to be correct, and the leadership in the new states will become socialized. This leadership would then presumably come to accept the system of international law pretty much *in toto*, and begin using the system to better their country's position within it.[69] Of course, alienation of the leadership is also a possibility, which would result in a continued criticism of the international system.

Again, the pragmatic realists may be right. Perhaps a legal means can be devised, possibly in the area of economics and the relationships of the capital-exporting (industrialized) states and capital-importing (non-industrialized) states, to satisfy the demands of the new nations and also preserve the interests of the older.[70] This might entail some radical reworkings of one area of the law, but leave the main body intact. Such a means may not be found, however, and the international body politic will be left gnawing, as it were, at its own entrails.

Finally, the cultural relativist may hold the key. If so, the very structure of an international law may disappear, to be replaced by several regional and culture-bound political systems, with relations between them essentially bilateral and based in each case on separate *modi vivendi* of uneasy coexistence.[71]

---

69. Thus, the extreme "clean slate" position on the question of state succession to treaties appears to have been taken only by two or three new states; and, in practice, considering the number of treaties involved, the number of disputes over particular treaties has been remarkedly small. Doctrinal positions seem to have been softened by practical experience; see Hugh J. Lawford, "Some Problems of Treaty Succession in the Commonwealth," paper delivered at a Regional Meeting of the American Society of International Law, East Carolina University, Greenville, N.C., April 25, 1967.

70. An example of this appears in another area of the law, treaty law and the doctrine of *rebus sic stantibus*. Here, the doctrine is being rendered increasingly obsolete by the simple means of inserting termination provisions in an increasing number of treaties.

71. There appear, indeed, to be overtones of a cultural conflict in the Arab-Israeli and Hindu-Muslim confrontations.

On the other hand, there may prove to be, as modern international law has insisted from its very beginnings, a set of universal values, whether deriving from natural law, the nature of mankind, or the immutable facts of social existence. Here, too, is the basis for an approach, the international law approach. It would agree that the principles of international law may well express those universal values only imperfectly. The international law approach would see the advent of the new states as the first opportunity in history to refine its principles in the light of the reason of all men to a greater and more universal perfection.[72] There is no reason to dismiss this approach, either.

Theories and approaches may suggest various alternative limitations, and prospects as well, for the future of human affairs. Which of these alternatives shall come to pass lies in the history yet to be made. For the social scientist, then, the decades of the 1970's and 1980's promise to provide a historical laboratory in which the applicability to the international scene of various theories of societal change can be put to the test of unfolding events as the impact of the new nations inexorably runs its course. Whether revolutionary or evolutionary, peaceful or no, the emergence of the new states presages a period of international societal change whose roots reach back to the colonial era. The relevance of that era to the future cannot be dismissed lightly either. As a commentator from the emerging new states has put it, "although colonies did not constitute a separate subject of international law, their participation as separate units in international affairs has been unduly minimized and underestimated."[73]

72. The trend toward universal recognition of human rights and of the individual as a subject of international law may serve as examples of principles, latently present in the pre-World War II body of international law, receiving polish and shape with the expansion of the international legal system after World War II.
73. Syatauw, *Some Newly Established Asian States*, p. 27.

4

The Impact of Islamic Law on Commonwealth Legal Systems

*J. N. D. Anderson**

This title must, I think, be understood to cover the way in which Islamic law has been incorporated into the composite legal systems of different countries in the Commonwealth. In a considerable number of territories the imported English law has been superimposed both on Islamic law and on customary law, just as the Islamic law, in its turn, had previously infiltrated into areas where indigenous customary law formerly prevailed. As a result the three systems—the English, Islamic, and customary—have had to co-exist and have inevitably impinged upon each other.

On the one hand, Islamic principles have profoundly modified and transformed the customary law of many parts of the Commonwealth. On the other, customary practices have survived even in those areas where Islamic law is regarded as dominant, and has materially influenced the way in which that law has been applied by the courts. It would not be correct to say that the Islamic law has influenced English law as such, or vice versa; but it is certainly true that "English" or statute law has radically restricted the extent to which, and the way in which, Islamic law is applied, and that Islamic law has both influenced, and formed the subject matter of, many statutory enactments.

For the rest, Islamic law has retained for itself a distinct sphere in the legal systems of almost all those countries in which there is

* Director, Institute of Advanced Legal Studies, and Professor of Oriental Laws, School of Oriental and African Studies, University of London.

a significant number of Muslims. Even in this sphere, moreover, the application of Islamic law in the Indian subcontinent—and, indeed, elsewhere under the influence of India—by personnel trained in English law, under rules of evidence which are substantially English, and under the doctrine of *stare decisis,* has resulted in the emergence of a system of law which has been aptly termed "Anglo-Mohammedan law" in recognition of the significant degree to which it has parted company with the Islamic law of the classical texts.

This is a vast subject, so it seems best to concentrate attention in this brief paper on three parts of the Commonwealth in which the influence of Islamic law has been particularly strong— namely, the Indian subcontinent, Zanzibar, and Northern Nigeria. And I shall accord the predominant pride of place and emphasis, on this occasion, to India.

The Indian Subcontinent

Muslim influence in India dates right back to the Arab occupation of Sind in A.D. 711. It was, indeed, at that early date that the Muslims were forced to take an absolutely fundamental decision: whether to treat the Hindu population as idolators, and therefore present them with the bleak alternatives of Islam or death, or to give them the third alternative of paying tribute and accepting the status of *dhimmis,* or protected non-Muslims, as provided in the Qur'an for those non-Muslims who possess a Scripture based on divine revelation. This question had first been posed by the Zoroastrians of Persia, who certainly had a Scripture which they themselves believed to be divinely given. The Hindus too, of course, indubitably had Scriptures of a sort, although the popular form of that religion could scarcely be described as other than idolatrous. But, however that may be, the more lenient view prevailed; and Abu Hanifa subsequently taught that the sterner view should be confined to the idolaters of Arabia. In any case, no other solution was, of course, practicable politics in India.

At a somewhat later date the raids of Mahmud al-Ghazni led to the occupation of Lahore, although it was only under the "Slave Kings" of Delhi that permanent Muslim rule may be said to have been established. The invaders were mostly Turks, and therefore Sunni Hanafis at a time when the Hidaya had recently been compiled; but there were also Persian Shi'is, who established two kingdoms in the Deccan, while Arab traders, who were mostly Sunnis of the Shafi'i school, settled on the southwest coast. What is quite clear, however, is that the Hindu population was largely left to follow their own law in civil matters. The *jizya,* or tribute, was sometimes collected, and sometimes not; disputes between themselves were normally settled by Brahmin judges with the threat of excommunication as a sufficient sanction; and disputes between Hindus and Muslims were sometimes taken before a Muslim *qadi* under Islamic law, sometimes before a lay official under customary law (*'urf*). But in the sphere of criminal law the Shari'a was applicable to all (with the proviso that that law itself makes exceptions in certain respects for non-Muslims) insofar as it can be said to have been consistently applied at all in such matters. And this, in its turn, varied greatly from time to time, according to the personality of the ruler and his local officials.

Space forbids any consideration here of the profound modifications in the law introduced by Akbar in 1579, or the sweeping reaction under Aurangzib after 1659. It was, indeed, under the latter that a famous book of legal decisions (the *Fatawa 'Alamgiriya*) was compiled.

Up till 1765 the responsibility of the East India Company for the administration of law in India was confined to the three Presidency towns of Madras, Bombay, and Calcutta, where its "factories" had been established. The company had come to exercise authority there from 1639, 1668, and 1698, respectively; but it was not until 1726 that "Mayors' Courts" were set up. These were courts not of the company but of the English Crown, and the law to be applied was, by implication, the law of England. It was, however, provided under a charter of 1753 that these courts were not to try cases between Indians except by consent of both the parties—and this represented, no doubt, existing practice.

Outside the Presidency towns it was not until 1765, and in

Bengal, that Clive received the grant of the Diwan, or fiscal administration and civil jurisdiction, from the puppet Moghul Emperor in Delhi. And at much the same date the company took over or usurped the Nizamat, or criminal jurisdiction. But this was exercised, at first, very much under indirect control.

Civil jurisdiction, under Warren Hastings, was exercised under Regulation II of 1772, which expressly provided that Hindus and Muslims were to be governed by their own laws in "suits regarding inheritance, marriage and caste and other religious usages and institutions."[1] No specific directions were given regarding the law applicable to them in other matters; but in 1781 Sir Elijah Impey added the word "succession" to "inheritance" and—much more important—declared that where no specific directions were given, judges should act "according to justice, equity and good conscience."

The points which need emphasis about the system of civil justice thus instituted are, first, that English law was not made applicable as such to the Indian provinces (by contrast with the Presidency towns); second, that in civil cases Hindus and Muslims were put on an equal footing and both left to follow their own laws; and, third, that no law at all was prescribed except for certain topics (and the judges, in any case, were not professional lawyers), so cases of contract and debt were largely handled by arbitration, while in cases under Islamic or Hindu law the advice of "law officers" (*maulawis* and *pandits*) was called in aid.

The next development was in 1781, when an act of Parliament gave civil jurisdiction even over Indian inhabitants of Calcutta —i.e., one of the Presidency towns—to the Supreme Court, with the proviso that "their inheritance and succession to land rents and goods and all matters of contract and dealing between party and party" should be determined, in the case of Muslims and Hindus, by their respective laws and, where only one of the parties was a Muslim or a Hindu, then "by the laws and usages of the defendant." Curiously enough, no specific mention was made of marriage; but this was regarded as included under the word "contract"—which was accurate enough insofar as Muslims, but

1. Art. 27.

not Hindus, were concerned. These principles were, moreover, soon extended to Madras and Bombay, with the result that the broad distinction between the law applicable in the Presidency towns, on the one hand, and the provinces, on the other, was that the *residual* law in the former was the law of England, and in the latter "justice, equity, and good conscience." A further difference, in theory, was that in the company's courts the Islamic and Hindu laws of contract, and the Islamic law of gifts and "pre-emption," were applied, naturally enough, under the umbrella of justice, equity, and good conscience, while in the Presidency towns it was somewhat more difficult to extend Islamic and Hindu law beyond the terms of the act of 1781. In practice, however, the family laws of the two communities came to be as fully respected here as in the provinces—although it must be observed that it is exceedingly difficult, to say the least, to give any sensible meaning, in many cases, to the "law of the defendant."

In Madras Regulation III of 1802 followed Hastings' formula of 1772. But Bombay Regulation IV of 1799 was somewhat more detailed, and provided[2] that in every claim to personal or real right and property "the cause is to be decided, so far as shall depend on the point of law, by that of the defendant" in regard to Muslims and Hindus; and "with respect to Portuguese and Parsee inhabitants, when they are defendants, the Judge is to be guided by a view to equity in his decisions, making due allowance for their respective customs as far as he can ascertain the same." But in all cases whatsoever he was to see if there was not "an unwritten yet ascertained common law" (i.e., usage or custom) "and whether this be not usually applied to cases like the one before him, whether the claim be by a Hindu or a Mussulman." And the same sequence—i.e., usage before the ancient texts, then the law of the defendant, and finally justice, equity, and good conscience—reappeared in Regulation IV of 1827 for the Province of Bombay, and was subsequently applied in Aden, in the British courts in Zanzibar, and in parts of the mainland of East Africa.

How then, it may be asked, did English law come to assume

2. Art. 16.

the place it occupies in the Indian subcontinent today? The answer must be that the situation in the provinces, as outlined above, was far from satisfactory. The judges were untrained, so the rule about justice, equity, and good conscience was, no doubt, inevitable. But it was equally inevitable that this phrase should be interpreted, to an ever increasing degree, in terms of such English law as they knew. All the same, this could, at best, be little more than a rough and ready rule of decision. What, moreover, of the personal laws of others than Muslims and Hindus? And what of Europeans? There was a manifest need for greater uniformity and certainty, and for the filling of "gaps and interspaces." So, after much argument, recourse was had to codification. In this the influence of Bentham and Fitzjames Stephen was not far to seek. But the attitude that prevailed can, perhaps, best be summarized in words used by Lord Macaulay in the second reading of the Charter Act of 1833:

We do not mean that all the people of India should live under the same law; far from it, . . . we know how desirable that object is but we also know that it is unobtainable. . . . Our principle is simply this—uniformity where you can have it; diversity where you must have it—but in all cases certainty. . . . A code is almost the only blessing—perhaps it is the only blessing—which absolute governments are better fitted to confer on a nation than popular governments.

But the need for such action was even more obvious in the field of criminal law, for here it was Islamic law which was applied, both to Muslims and Hindus, except only in Bombay, and in criminal matters the company's title was distinctly questionable and its control exercised through Muslim officials. Under Warren Hastings, moreover, even impalements were permitted. Then, in 1790, criminal justice was taken over by the company, and the courts were presided over by one of the company's servants as judge, assisted by Muslim law officers. The practice was for a *fatwa*, or legal opinion on the case, to be written at the bottom of the record by the Muslim *qadi* (judge) or *mufti* (jurisconsult). It was then the duty of the company's judge to consider this carefully and, provided that it seemed to him consonant both with Islamic law and with natural justice, to pass sentence accordingly and issue a warrant to the magistrate for execution (except in regard to any sentence of death or perpetual imprisonment, which required confirmation by the Sadr Nizamat Adalat, or court of criminal appeal, which was later combined with the Sadr Diwani Adalat, or court of civil appeal, under the title of Sadr Adalat). If, on the other hand, the *fatwa* seemed to be contrary either to natural justice or Islamic law, it had to be transmitted to the court of appeal together with the judge's objections; and if the court of appeal considered the *fatwa* to be in accordance with Islamic law, but contrary to natural justice, they would accept it if in favor of the prisoner, but recommend pardon or mitigation of sentence if it was against him.

Next, progressive modifications were made in the Islamic criminal law—or, rather, in the way in which this was administered by the courts. In 1790 the right of the heirs of blood to pardon a murderer was taken away, and the test of "deliberate" homicide was transferred from the weapon used to an abstract consideration of whether the prisoner intended to kill. In 1791 mutilation of the hand for theft, and of two limbs in the case of highway robbery, was abolished, and seven and fourteen years imprisonment, respectively, substituted therefor. Then, from 1793 onward, reform was achieved, and the consciences of the Muslim law officers saved, by the device of asking them to give their *fatwas* on certain assumptions. Where, for example, the heirs of blood had refused to prosecute, had pardoned the murderer, or had commuted his offense, they were asked to say if the death penalty would have been applicable on the assumption that the heirs had claimed it. Where, again, talion was not in fact applicable under Islamic law because of the relationship between the murderer and his victim, or because one of several accomplices was for some reason exempt, they were asked if the death penalty would have been applicable had the circumstances been otherwise. Where a case against a Muslim rested on the evidence of non-Muslims (which, under the strict application of Islamic law, is not eligible testimony in such circumstances), they were asked to give a *fatwa* on the assumption that the witnesses had been Muslims. And where the evidence was not enough for the imposition of one of the prescribed penalties (*hudud*), they were asked to give their opinion on the assumption that it had in fact reached the exceedingly exacting standard that the Islamic law here requires.

It may be noted in passing that in 1811 the sale of slaves was made a criminal offense, and that the practice of *sati* was first restricted and then, in 1829, made totally illegal. In 1832, moreover, non-Muslims were granted the right to claim exemption from being tried under the Islamic criminal law—although no other law was provided to take its place! This meant, of course, that the Islamic law, however mutilated, had now ceased to be the general law of crime. In 1837 Lord Macaulay submitted a draft "Indian Penal Code"; in 1843 slavery was made illegal; and in 1860 the Indian Penal Code was promulgated. With this the period of codification began, and legislation such as the Code of Criminal Procedure, the Indian Succession Act, the Indian Evidence Act, the Indian Contract Act, the Indian Majority Act, and the Transfer of Property Act soon followed.

In the preceding period two principles had prevailed: to change existing laws as little as possible and, where change seemed essential, to apply the maxim of justice, equity, and good conscience. The first of these principles was persuasively stated by Sir William Jones in 1788, when he claimed that nothing could be wiser than "to assure the Hindu and Mussulman subjects of Great Britain that the private laws, which they severally hold sacred, and violation of which they would have thought the most grievous oppression, should not be suppressed by a new system, of which they could have no knowledge, and which they must have considered as imposed on them by a spirit of rigor and intolerance." As for the second of these principles, it seems in fact to have been accepted without much opposition—partly, perhaps, because the influence of religious beliefs in secular matters had begun somewhat to wane, even in India, and partly because the Muslim administrators themselves were convinced of the need for reforms. Even so, the Muslim law officers would frequently add, at the end of their *fatwas*, a reference to the will of the ruler (*hakim*), which could alter punishments. But the posi-

tion just before the promulgation of the Penal Code was summarized by Sir George Campbell in these words:

> The foundation of our criminal law is still the Mahomedan Code
> [*sic*]; but so altered and added to by our regulations that it is hardly to
> be recognised; and there has, in fact, by practice and continual emenda-
> tive enactments, grown up a system of our own, well understood by
> those whose profession it is, and towards which the original Mahome-
> dan law and Mahomedan lawyers are really little consulted. Still the
> hidden substructure on which the whole building rests is this Ma-
> homedan law, take away which and we should have no definition of or
> authority for punishing many of the most common crimes.[3]

On this situation the Penal Code made a decisive impact. In
1861, moreover, the different courts for the provinces and the
Presidency towns, respectively, were unified; and in 1864 the
services of the law officers—both Muslim and Hindu—were dis-
pensed with. Henceforth Islamic law, where applicable, would be
applied by the court itself, without the advice of those trained in
the ancient texts, and the field was set for the development of the
system of "Anglo-Mohammedan law" to which reference has already been made.

So the position in the Indian subcontinent for the last hundred
years is that Islamic law is expressly excluded by statute law from
all such spheres as those of crime, evidence, and procedure; is
applied under the principle of justice, equity, and good conscience insofar as the law of pre-emption is concerned, except
only in Madras, to Muslims and to those Hindus who have accepted pre-emption into their customary law; and is still applicable as of right to Muslims in the field of family law, succession,
gifts, and *waqfs*—although even here its application has been
considerably restricted by statute law and modified by both customary law and by case law.

Examples of its restriction by statute law may be found in such
legislation as the Caste Disabilities Removal Act, of 1850, which
abolished, *inter alia,* the civil disabilities which the pure Islamic
law attached to apostasy from Islam by declaring that no right to
inheritance of property should henceforth be lost to anyone by

3. *Modern India* (London, 1852), p. 464.

reason of his renunciation of, or exclusion from, the communion of any religion. Similarly, the minimum age for marriage was modified by the Child Marriage Restraint Act, 1929 (as subsequently amended), while the consummation of marriage at a very tender age was made a criminal offense under the Penal Code. A further example can be found in the changes introduced by the Evidence Act in the rules which govern the legitimacy of a child born to a married couple during the first six months of their marriage, or to a widowed or divorced wife after her marriage has ended.

Outstanding examples of its restriction by custom, on the other hand, are provided by the history of such sects as the Cutchi Memons and the Khojas. These communities, which largely consist of converts from Hinduism, for many centuries retained by custom the Hindu law of inheritance and succession. But now, since the Shariat Act of 1937 and the Cutchi Memons Act of 1938, the Cutchi Memons have been governed by Hanafi law in all respects and the Khojas by "Islamic" law in intestate succession and, *optionally* only, in regard to testamentary dispositions. But the proviso must be added that such legislation does not extend to agricultural land, which is within the exclusive competence of the legislatures of the different states.

Examples of the way in which the Islamic law itself, as understood and applied in the Indian subcontinent, has been modified by case law may be found in the law of intestate succession, where Mr. Justice Mahmud's decision in Jafri Begam's case[4] runs radically counter to the Hanafi law which he presumably believed himself to be applying; and in the law applicable to "paternity by acknowledgement," where the judgment of the same learned judge in *Muhammad Allahdad* v. *Muhammad Ismail*[5] represents the strangest mixture of accurate and totally inaccurate comment on the relevant principles of the pure Islamic law. The most outstanding example of all, however, is provided by the law of *waqf*, where the judgment of the Judicial Committee of the Privy Council in *Abul Fata* v. *Russomoy*[6] represented such a departure from pure Islamic principles that a not altogether successful attempt had to be made, in 1913, to obviate the effect of

4. *Jafri Begam v. Amir Muhammad Khan* (1885), 7 All. 822.
5. (1888), 10 All. 289.   6. (1894), 22 I.A. 76.

this, and certain similar decisions, by the Mussulman Waqf Validating Act. Even so, this unfortunate decision has been regarded as binding by the courts of Aden, Zanzibar, and Kenya, with the result that legislative amendments have had to be promulgated in all these countries, and even now the position is far from satisfactory.[7]

It is also instructive to note that reforms in the Islamic law as administered by the courts have been introduced in the subcontinent, in recent years, by legislative enactments somewhat, but not wholly, along the lines of similar reforms in the Ottoman Empire in 1917 and subsequently in many of the Arab countries. Thus in 1939 the Dissolution of Muslim Marriages Act was passed in what was then British India, and this gave Muslim wives the right to a judicial divorce in a wide range of circumstances in which this is not available in the pure Hanafi law which previously prevailed, although it is permitted in one or more of the other Sunni schools. This corresponds closely in principle with a large number of reforms in the Middle East, most of which are based on the right of the ruler to confine and define the jurisdiction of his courts, and thus to order them to abandon the dominant view of their particular school of law, where the public interests so require, in favor of some other view propounded by another school or jurist. The difference is that the Indian legislation does not conform nearly so closely to the precise dicta of the Maliki or other jurists as do the reforms introduced in the Arab countries.

Nothing further has yet been effected in India[8] since Independence, but in Pakistan the Muslim Family Laws Ordinance, 1961, has attempted to grapple with the problems of polygamy, di-

---

7. See J. N. D. Anderson, "Waqfs in East Africa," *Jour. of Afr. Law*, III (1959), 152–164; also "A Recent Decision of the Judicial Committee of the Privy Council," in *Arabic and Islamic Studies in Honour of Hamilton A. R. Gibb*, ed. George Makdisi (Cambridge, Mass., 1965), pp. 53 ff.

8. In *Saiffudin Saheb* v. *State of Bombay* (A.I.R. 1962 S.C. 853) the court held that it is not open to the legislature to interfere with a religious precept or practice, since this would be contrary to Art. 26(b) of the constitution, which empowers every religious denomination to manage its own affairs. In this case, an act of the Bombay Legislature, which prohibited the excommunication of a member of a religious faith, was held to be void. The religious faith involved was the Da'udi Bohra Community, which belongs to the Musta'li subsect of the Isma'ili Shi'is. The court appears to have ignored Art. 25(1) of the constitution, which guarantees to every person the right to profess, practice, and propagate a religion, since this right *might* be regarded as contravened by a power to excommunicate.

vorce, and inheritance in a forthright and courageous manner. Yet it must be observed that the reform it has effected in the law of inheritance does not seem nearly so judicious as the corresponding reforms in several of the Middle Eastern countries, that the provisions relating to divorce appear to present a major challenge to conservative opinion without commensurate amelioration of the position of an unwanted wife; and that a severe restriction of a man's right to contract a polygamous marriage, without any corresponding restriction of his right to repudiate the wife he has already married, is scarcely likely to benefit the latter.

Zanzibar[9]

The most unusual feature in the legal and judicial system of Zanzibar, prior to Independence, was the "dual jurisdiction" exercised by the British and the Zanzibar courts respectively. In brief summary, the British Court had jurisdiction in all cases in which any plaintiff or defendant, accused or complainant was a British subject, a British "protected person," a subject (etc.) of any of the foreign powers which had agreed thereto, a subject of any other Christian power not represented by a consul in Zanzibar, or a person in the regular service of any of the above. In addition, the British Court alone had jurisdiction under certain decrees concerning which the Sultan had made a complete surrender of jurisdiction. The Zanzibar Court of His Highness the Sultan, on the other hand, had jurisdiction in all other cases, i.e., in criminal cases where both all the accused and all the persons against whom an offense was alleged to have been committed were either subjects of His Highness or of some non-Christian power, and in civil suits where all the plaintiffs and defendants fell into one of these two categories—except, of course, where the Sultan had expressly surrendered his jurisdiction.

Both the organization and personnel of the courts which exer-

---

9. This section of my paper reproduces—with omissions, additions, and other changes—certain paragraphs in the relevant chapter of my *Islamic Law in Africa* (London, 1954).

cised the jurisdiction belonging to Her Britannic Majesty and to His Highness the Sultan respectively had, however, been completely assimilated by the British Subordinate Courts Order, 1923, and the Zanzibar Courts Decree of the same date (as repeatedly amended), and appeals from both courts went to the Court of Appeal for Eastern Africa and thence to the Privy Council. As a consequence of this assimilation, therefore, the same judge would sit sometimes as the British Court exercising the jurisdiction of Her Britannic Majesty and sometimes as the Zanzibar Court exercising the jurisdiction of His Highness the Sultan. This must have been somewhat confusing, but an effective safeguard for any error had been provided in the Jurisdiction Decree, 1934, Section 5, which enacted (in effect) that should Her Majesty's courts through inadvertence exercise jurisdiction in a case which should have been taken by His Highness' courts, their judgment would not on that account be liable to appeal or revision!

What, then, was the difference in the law they administered? In effect, not very much; for an enormous proportion of the law they both administered, whether substantive or adjective, was covered by the Sultan's decrees which, when countersigned by the British Resident, were equally binding on all courts, while any Order of Her Majesty in Council, and any acts of the Parliament of the United Kingdom which applied to Zanzibar, were of recent years automatically applicable in the Sultan's courts as well as the British courts—with the solitary qualification that Imperial Enactments were not to be construed as applying to His Highness' subjects "where a contrary intention appears." Thus the penal and other decrees contained the whole of the criminal law applicable in Zanzibar. Similarly, the Criminal Procedure and Evidence Decrees almost entirely covered their respective subjects. And it is worth noting, in this context, that the Evidence Decree, Section 2, expressly excluded the Islamic law of evidence from any court in Zanzibar; while on the civil side the Rules of Court, the Civil Procedure Decree and Rules, together with the Evidence and Limitation Decrees, governed procedure in both sets of courts. This was also true of the Oaths Decree.

It was only in the substantive law applicable to civil proceedings, therefore, that the distinction remained of any great practical importance. Here, too, legislation covered much of the field: but the difference remained that, for the rest, the *corpus juris* in the Sultan's courts consisted of Shari'a law, as locally applied, while in the British courts it consisted of the common law and doctrines of equity, together with that application of Islamic, Hindu, and Buddhist personal law (in regard to matrimonial matters and questions of inheritance) which the British courts in Zanzibar inherited from those of Bombay under Regulation IV of 1827. In matters of inheritance, moreover, this was expressly reinforced by the Succession Decree, 1917, Section 7 whereof provided that Muslims, Hindus, Buddhists, and "exempted persons" should be governed by their own personal law in this respect. It should also be observed that the British courts would apply Shari'a law in any suit concerning land not covered by any special enactment, on the common law principle of the *lex loci rei sitae*—for, however many encroachments had been made by statute law since 1908, Section 7 of the Courts Decree of 1923 still declared that "in civil matters the Law of Islam is and is hereby declared to be the fundamental law of the Protectorate."

All the same, this "fundamental law" had been ousted by the decrees of the Sultan, as has been noted, to an enormous extent. Nothing whatever of the Islamic criminal law or law of evidence and procedure officially remained, except, perhaps, such of the latter as may have been indirectly preserved under the Oaths Decree of 1917. But this did not mean that the *qadis*, in Zanzibar as elsewhere in East Africa, did not in fact follow the basic rules of evidence and procedure laid down in the Shari'a, from reasons both of conscience and training; and in practice their judgments were only quashed or varied on this account on appeal where some miscarriage of justice or flagrant breach of the law seemed to have occurred. Again, the Contract Decree and the Transfer of Property Decree, both of 1917 and countersigned, largely covered matters of contract and commerce, but Section 1 (2) of the former provided that "nothing herein contained shall effect . . . any usage or custom of trade, nor any incident of any contract, not inconsistent with the provisions of this Decree," while Sections 2 and 116 of the latter enacted that nothing in certain specified parts of this decree "shall be deemed to affect any rule of Hindu, Mahommedan, or Buddhist law." Even in theory, therefore, cases might still come before the courts regarding contracts made under the Shari'a, although such cases, except those concerning gifts, seem to have been increasingly rare and unimportant. In addition, moreover, cases properly covered by the above decrees were sometimes decided without reference thereto. But in general the application of "the law of Islam" seems largely to have been limited, before Independence, to actions in tort before His Highness' courts and questions of Muslim family law (including, of course, testate and intestate succession), gifts, *waqfs,* and certain real property cases under the respective jurisdiction of both sets of courts.

Even in these matters, however, the provisions of certain decrees had restricted or otherwise affected the law to be applied. Among relevant legislation may be mentioned the Slavery Decree, 1909, the Marriage (Solemnisation and Registration) Decree, 1915, the Succession Decree, 1917, the Penal Decree, 1934, the Juvenile Offenders Decree, 1935, and the *Wakf* Validating Decree, 1946, etc.

The immediate effect of the advent of Independence was, of course, the abolition of the British courts and the unification of all jurisdiction in the Zanzibar courts. Unhappily, however, I do not know what has happened since the revolution; but I have no reason to think that Islamic law is not applied to the same extent, and in substantially the same way, as it was previously. Whether the two *qadis,* the Shafi'i and the Ibadi, still both sit in adjoining rooms in the same court building and administer each the law of their respective school, I do not know. That a Shafi'i *qadi* still administers the law seems highly probable; but whether many Ibadis are left on the island today is somewhat dubious.[10]

10. I understand, unofficially, that the Ibadi *qadi* no longer holds office.

Northern Nigeria

When we turn to Nigeria we find that, right up until 1956, the position with regard to Islamic law was almost the direct opposite from that which prevailed in Zanzibar. In the latter, as we have seen, the Islamic law was expressly stated to be the "fundamental law" in the courts of the Sultan, but had been unequivocally excluded from all criminal matters, from the law of evidence, and from much else. In Nigeria, on the other hand, the only express mention of Islamic law in the statute book prior to 1956 was an incidental reference to "Mohammedan law" in the Sheriffs and Enforcement of Judgments and Orders Ordinance, 1945. Yet the Islamic law was in fact applied in Northern Nigeria at that time more extensively than anywhere else in the world outside the Arabian peninsula, even (within certain limits) in matters of homicide, theft, and other crimes. This extensive application of Islamic law was, however, under the comprehensive umbrella of "native law and custom," which was interpreted as meaning law which closely approximated to that of the pure Maliki texts in the staunchly Muslim areas, pagan customary law in those areas into which Islam had never penetrated, and an amalgam of the two in those areas of more mixed or equivocal allegiance. Yet even in the most rigidly orthodox areas the law which the courts actually applied was not by any means exclusively that of the classical texts, which had in fact been modified or even excluded in a number of different respects by the customary law of the area.

It might well be objected by the purist, of course, that there is something fundamentally inappropriate about a highly sophisticated system of law, which had been developed in meticulous detail in the Middle East and in Spain, being applied as the "native law and custom" of African tribes today. Yet, insofar as this law had in fact been accepted by them in substitution for their previous customary law, it could—in one sense at least—be so regarded. And this attitude on the part of legal draftsmen and others had two palpable advantages: first, that it allowed a law which differed greatly from area to area to be applied under the same legislative enactment; and, second, that it gave no countenance whatever to any attempt by a rigorist to impose the law of the classical texts when this had not in fact become the law recognized and followed in the area concerned.

Another highly significant point in regard to Northern Nigeria was the extent of the jurisdiction of the "native courts." Partly because of the highly developed condition of some of these courts at the time when the British protectorate was instituted, partly because of the system of "indirect rule," and partly because of the vast extent of the territory they had to cover, they handled more than 90 per cent of all litigation. Not only so, but some sixteen of the leading emirs greatly prized the "power of life and death"—i.e., the competence to try capital cases—which their courts enjoyed. As a consequence, these courts even entertained accusations of murder, and decided them according to "native law and custom," or the Maliki school of Islamic law as locally applied.

This, in its turn, gave rise to complex problems. If a Northern Nigerian committed a homicide, he might well be tried before the High Court under the Nigerian Criminal Code, or he might equally well be tried before the court of the local emir under Maliki law—and the final result might be diametrically different according to which way this initial decision regarding jurisdiction had gone. Nor was this only a matter of procedure or of detailed rules of law; on the contrary, the basic definition of capital homicide in Maliki law is considerably wider than that of the code, while the Maliki law also allows the heirs of blood to choose, in such cases, between demanding talion, commuting the offense, or pardoning the offender; and it also precludes the demand for talion altogether, in most cases, should the accused be a Muslim and his victim a non-Muslim.[11] It is obvious, of course, that this might have given rise to serious injustice; but this was usually avoided, during the "colonial" regime, either by the exercise of a British administrative officer's right to transfer cases from the

11. This is because the blood of a Muslim is regarded as worth so much more than that of a non-Muslim. In many parts of Northern Nigeria a pagan's heirs of blood could claim only one-fifteenth of the blood money payable in respect of a dead Muslim!

native courts to the High Court, by means of appeal, or by the exercise by the Governor of the Royal prerogative of mercy.

Reference has already been made to the year 1956, but only because two enactments then promulgated—the Moslem Court of Appeal Law and the Native Courts Law—both differentiated, for the first time insofar as statute law was concerned, between "Muslim law" and "native law and custom." But far more important than this were the problems posed by the differences between the English and Islamic criminal law, particularly in homicide cases, and the apprehensions of non-Muslims about the possible application—and even extension—of Islamic law after Independence.

It was in these circumstances that the Northern Nigerian government appointed a "Panel of Jurists," on which I had the honor to serve, to advise them on all such matters. Our chairman was the Chief Justice of the Sudan, himself a Sudanese Muslim, and the other members were the then chairman of the Pakistan Law Reform Committee (a judge of the Supreme Court who was a pious Muslim), three Northern Nigerians, and myself. But I must content myself in this context with observing that as a result of our recommendations—but to everyone's surprise—the Northern Nigerian government agreed to replace the Islamic law in all matters of crime, whether substantive or adjectival, in favor of new codes based substantially on those Indian codes[12] to which reference has already been made—although it should be observed in passing that they insisted on including a clause which makes it a criminal offense, for a Muslim only, to partake of any alcohol at all except for medicinal purposes, and another which made illicit sex relations a criminal offense if committed by anyone whose religious or customary law so regarded them.

As a result, the Islamic law as such is now applicable in Northern Nigeria only insofar as the personal and family law of Muslims is concerned, although it may also, on occasions, be applied as the law under which a contract was in fact decided or as the law of tort traditionally accepted in the locality concerned.

12. Or, more accurately, on the adaptations of those codes which had been promulgated in the Anglo-Egyptian Sudan.

5

The Common Law and Native Systems of Law

L. C. Green*

When I reflect upon the spread and acceptance of our common law principles throughout the United States and Canada and Australia and New Zealand, may I not say that nothing has left a deeper or more beneficent impression upon the Western World than the Common Law of England. Its work can never be undone. Its spirit and its ideals must ever live. If this country were to sink to-morrow beneath the waves, the record of the Common Law of England would stand for ever on the noblest pages of history.

Mr. Justice McCardie, The Law, The
Advocate and the Judge (London, 1927), p. 17.

With such content as we may, we must even believe that our lady the Common Law, like many other good-natured people busied with more matters than they can attend to in person, allowed herself to be put upon and her customers harassed by fussy, greedy and sometimes dishonest underlings.

Sir Frederick Pollock, The Genius of
the Common Law (New York, 1912), p. 37.

Perhaps one of the least objectionable features of British imperialism has been the introduction into colonial territories of the English concept of the rule of law. This stems from the fact that, as is probably known to the veriest tyro in the legal world, when an Englishman goes abroad he takes his law with him. As long

---

* Professor of International Law and Organization, Department of Political Science, University of Alberta; formerly Dean, Faculty of Law, University of Singapore.

ago as 1693 Holt C.J. pointed out: "In case of an uninhabited country newly found out by English subjects, all laws in England are in force there."[1] The extent of this incorporation was reduced somewhat by the Master of the Rolls thirty years later: "If there be a new and uninhabited country found out by English subjects, as the law is the birthright of every subject, so, wherever they go, they carry their laws with them, and therefore such new found country is to be governed by the laws of England; though, after such country is inhabited by the English, acts of parliament made in England, without naming the foreign plantations, will not bind them."[2]

Basing himself upon these two judgments, but at the same time restricting the scope of English law still further, Blackstone wrote that

colonists carry with them only so much of the English law as is applicable to their own situation and the condition of an infant colony; such, for instance, as the general rules of inheritance, and of protection from personal injuries. The artificial refinements and distinctions incident to the property of a great and commercial people, the laws of police and revenue, . . . the jurisdiction of spiritual courts, and a multitude of other provisions, are neither necessary nor convenient for them, and therefor not in force. What shall be admitted and what rejected, at what times, and under what restrictions, must, in case of dispute, be decided in the first instance by their own provincial judicature, subject to the revision and control of the king in council.[3]

As Blackstone pointed out, this situation only prevailed in territories which had not been formerly occupied by a recognized sovereign. Insofar as ceded or conquered territory was concerned, English common law recognized that the already-existing law prevailed until such time as it was amended by the King. This practice reflected convenience, for an immediate abrogation of existing law could easily produce anarchy. Moreover, where a *lex loci* already existed, the local residents, unlike their English conquerors, would be unacquainted with English law, but would be accustomed to a legal system that was already operating.[4] This

1. *Blankard* v. *Galdy*, 2 Salk 411.   2. *Anon.* (1722), 2 P. Wms. 75.
3. 1 *Commentaries* (10th ed.; London, 1787), p. 108.
4. *Freeman* v. *Fairlie* (1828), 1 Moo. Ind. App. 305, 324.

attitude underlies the judgment of Chief Justice Marshall in *Worcester* v. *Georgia*[5] insofar as the North American Indians are concerned: "America, separated from Europe by a wide ocean, was inhabited by a distinct people, divided into separate nations, independent of each other and of the rest of the world, having institutions of their own, and governing themselves by their own laws." This approach was confirmed by the Supreme Court in *Ex parte Crow Dog*,[6] holding that an Indian who had murdered another Indian on a reservation was not amenable to federal criminal law, but only to tribal law. This situation was altered by statute two years later.[7] Further, in most cases conquered territories were acquired from Christian rulers, and a different approach was adopted to fellow Christians as distinct from barbarians.[8] Newly discovered territories possessed no recognized legal system; it was therefore obvious that the new settlers would apply the law to which they were accustomed, although some of its manifestations might differ from the law as known and practiced in the Royal Courts of Justice. It was unlikely, for example, that the settlers would be unduly concerned with the intricacies of land law as it had developed in England expressing itself in such rules as that in Shelley's case, for this rested on "reasons affecting the land and society in England and not reasons applying to a new colony."[9]

It should not be thought that it was only the English who took their law with them when they went into foreign climes. A somewhat similar practice operated in ancient Rome, for in classical law the inhabitants of conquered territories did not become citizens: "The vast majority of Roman subjects are, so far as her law is concerned, *peregrini*, 'foreigners,' outside the pale of the strict law and only entitled to such rights as all free persons have under the *ius gentium*," with the *ius civile* applying only to citizens.[10]

5. (1832), 6 Pet. 515, at 542.   6. (1883), 109 U.S. 556.
7. 1885, 18 U.S.C.A. sec. 548.
8. See, e.g., *Calvin's Case* (1608), 7 Co. Rep. 1a; *Campbell* v. *Hall* (1774), 1 Cowp. 204; *Adv.-Gen. of Bengal* v. *Ranee Surnanoye Dossee* (1883), 9 Moo. Ind. App. 391.
9. *In re Simpson's Estate* [1927], 3 W.W.R. 534, 539 (Alberta).
10. Herbert F. Jolowicz, *Historical Introduction to Roman Law* (3d ed.; Cambridge, 1961), pp. 71, 101.

Bryce's description of the situation is similar to that of Blackstone concerning English possessions and the rights of the inhabitants:

> [*Peregrini*] had their own laws or tribal customs, and to them Roman law was primarily inapplicable, not only because it was novel and unfamiliar, so strange to their habits that it would have been unjust as well as practically inconvenient to have applied it to them, but also because the Romans, like the other civilised communities of antiquity, had been so much accustomed to consider private legal rights as necessarily connected with membership of a city community that it would have seemed unnatural to apply the private law of one city community to the citizens of another. . . . Each province was administered by a governor. . . . The governor's court was the proper tribunal for those persons who in the provinces enjoyed Roman citizenship, and in it Roman law was applied to such persons. . . . No special law was needed for them. As regards the provincials, they lived under their own law, whatever it might be, subject to one important modification. Every governor when he entered his province issued an Edict setting forth certain rules which he proposed to apply during his term of office, . . .

but when the distinction between citizens and provincials disappeared, Roman law became applicable throughout the empire and to all its inhabitants.[11]

The Dutch, too, took their law with them and the principles of Roman-Dutch law were introduced into their territories. Thus, "when Van Riebeck and his band of pioneers settled at the Cape in 1652, they introduced the general principles and rules of law prevailing at that date in the Netherlands,"[12] but "the first settlers carried with them only those laws which were applicable to the circumstances of this country."[13] The purity of Roman-Dutch law as the common law of those Dutch colonies which were conquered by the British was affected by the fact that, for the main part, English-trained lawyers and judges were called upon to apply it. Insofar as Ceylon is concerned, it has been said that "the Roman-Dutch law, as applied by the British, was like an old

11. James Bryce, *Studies in History and Jurisprudence* (Oxford, 1901), pp. 77–78.

12. George Wille, *Principles of South African Law* (2d ed.; Capetown and Johannesburg, 1961), p. 38.

13. *Seaville* v. *Colley* (1891), 9 S.C. 39, *per* De Villiers C.J., at 42. See also *Wijekoon* v. *Gunawardena* (1892), 1. S.C.R. 147, 149 (Ceylon).

kadjan roof; as it got older it let in the outside elements, and they were mainly English law."[14] The same criticism has been made by the courts in South Africa:

Here we have a phenomenon that appears all too often in our jurisprudence. A Roman Dutch legal rule is compared with its English counterpart; with pleasure, if indeed not with joy, it is stated that there is no difference, and then the door is wide open for the reception of English law. . . . Gradual adaptation to new circumstances and problems is a type of development that leads to strength; uncontrolled development on the other hand leads to malignant growths and decay.[15]

In fact, it has been stated that it was because of the wrong interpretation of Roman-Dutch law and the grafting thereon of English principles by the Judicial Committee of the Privy Council in *Pearl Assurance Co.* v. *Union Government*[16] that South Africa abandoned appeals to that body.[17]

Apart from the introduction of some system of common law—for in South Africa, Southern Rhodesia, Basutoland, and Ceylon, Roman-Dutch law is the common law—by settlers or conquerors, it may happen that a territory expressly adopts an alien system of common law. Thus, in British Guiana "an Ordinance to codify and to substitute the English common law and principles of equity for the Roman-Dutch common law" was enacted. In Liberia, which has never been a British colony, similar legislation has been passed. In 1820 "the common law, as in force and modified in the United States and applicable to the situation of the people" was introduced, but in 1824 this was widened to include "the common law and usages of the courts of Great Britain and the United States," to which there was added in 1839 "such parts of the common law as set forth in Blackstone's *Commentaries* as may be applicable to the situation of the people." Finally, the 1956 code provides:[18]

14. W. I. Jennings and H. V. Tambiah, *The Dominion of Ceylon* (London, 1952), p. 198.
15. *Preller* v. *Jordan* (1956), (1) S.A. 483 (A.D.), *per* van den Heever J.A., at 504.
16. [1934], A.C. 570, *per* Lord Tomlin, at 585.
17. Aquilius, "Immortality and Illegality in Contract," *So. Afr. Law Jour.*, LX (1943), 468, 476.
18. Title 16, chap. 3, sec. 40.

Except as modified by laws now in force and those which may hereafter be enacted and by the Liberian common law, the following shall
be, when applicable, considered Liberian law: (a) the rules adopted
for chancery procedure in England, and (b) the common law and
usages of the courts of England and of the United States of America,
as set forth in case law and in Blackstone's and Kent's *Commentaries*
and in other authoritative treatises and digests.[19]

Insofar as British colonial territories are concerned, after the
initial introduction of the English common law, legislation has
tended to be introduced specifying what parts of English law are
to be applied in the territory in question, and indicating an
operative date. In the Gold Coast, for example, the relevant
ordinance provides that "the common law, the doctrines of equity, and the statutes of general application, which were in force
in England at the date when the colony obtained a local legislature, that is to say, on the 24th day of July, 1874, shall be in force
within the jurisdiction of the court,"[20] together with the law and
practice in divorce which is in force in the Probate, Divorce, and
Admiralty Division of the English High Court.[21] This has resulted
in the invidious consequence that "when a principle or doctrine
of the English common law has been abolished by a post-1874
British statute of general application in the United Kingdom, but
which has not been expressly or implicitly applied to Ghana, the
old principle or rule must still be followed in Ghana until altered
by local legislation."[22]

There are some colonial territories where no calendar date is
specified, reference being made merely to the coming into force
of the particular ordinance, and occasionally it is specified that
the common law is only introduced into a specific field of law.
Insofar as Malaysia is concerned, the Civil Law Enactment of
1937[23] provided that the "common law of England, and the rules
of equity as administered in England at the commencement of

19. A. N. Allott, *Essays in African Law* (London, 1960), p. 12.
20. Sup. Cts. Ord. No. 4, 1874; Cts. Ord. 1951, sec. 83.
21. T. O. Elias, *Ghana and Sierra Leone* (London, 1962), p. 116.
22. *Ibid.* (citing *Mensah* v. *Konongo*). See also *Brand* v. *Griffin* (1908), 9
W.W.R. 427, in which it was held that since the operative date in Alberta is
1870, a statute of 1874 is inapplicable.
23. F.M.S. No. 3, sec. 2(1).

this enactment, other than any modifications of such law or any such rules enacted by statute, shall be in force." This was amended some twenty years later, so that

save in so far as other provision has been made or may hereafter be made by any written law in force in the Federation or any part thereof, the Court shall apply the common law of England and the rules of equity as administered in England at the date of the coming into force of this Ordinance; provided always that the said common law and rules of equity shall be applied so far only as the circumstances of the States and Settlements comprised in the Federation and their respective inhabitants permit and subject to such qualifications as local circumstances render necessary.[24]

It is further provided that in commercial cases "the law to be administered shall be the same as would be administered in England."[25] A somewhat similar situation prevails in Singapore, where

in all questions or issues which arise or which have to be decided in the Colony with respect to the law of partnership, corporations, banks and banking, principals and agents, carriers by air, land and sea, marine insurance, average, life and fire insurance, and with respect to mercantile law generally, the law to be administered shall be the same as would be administered in the like case, at the corresponding period, if such question or issue had arisen or had to be decided in England, unless in any case other provision is or shall be made by statute.[26]

It may also happen that the system of prevailing law to which reference is made is not English alone, but also the law which operates in some other part of the Commonwealth. This is the position in Kenya, where the civil and criminal jurisdiction is, so far as circumstances allow, in conformity with Indian acts in force in East Africa, and

so far as the same shall not extend or apply, shall be exercised in conformity with the substance of the common law, the doctrines of equity, and the statutes of general application in force in England on August 12, 1897. . . . Provided always that the common law, doctrines of equity and statutes of general application shall be in force in the protectorate so far only as the circumstances of the protectorate and

24. Civil Law Ord. 1956 (No. 5 as amended by No. 41), sec. 3(1).
25. Sec. 5.   26. Civil Law Ord., sec. 5.

its inhabitants and the limits of H.M.'s jurisdiction permit and subject to such qualifications as local circumstances render necessary.[27]

This provision was commented upon by Denning L.J. in *Nyali Ltd.* v. *Att. Gen.*[28] after he had pointed out that the Crown's prerogatives applied within the protectorate since they were "the very substance of the common law":

Just as with an English oak, so with the English common law. You cannot transplant it to the African continent and expect it to retain the tough character which it has in England. It will flourish indeed but it needs careful tending. So with the common law. It has many principles of manifest justice and good sense which can be applied with advantage to peoples of every race and colour all the world over; but it also has many refinements, subtleties and technicalities which are not suited to other folk. These off-shoots must be cut away. In these far off lands the people must have a law which they understand and which they will respect. The common law cannot fulfill this role except with considerable qualifications. The task of making these qualifications is entrusted to the judges of these lands.

This realistic approach should be compared with *Welbeck* v. *Brown*[29] in which the Chief Justice of the Gold Coast held that "according to the principles of English jurisprudence" a local custom must date back to 1189, a view which was rejected in *Mensah* v. *Winabob*,[30] and which had never operated in Singapore, for "the history of Singapore began in 1819, more than 600 years after 1189, and that in itself concludes the matter."[31]

The tendency to apply principles of English law because they are those best known to English judges is well illustrated by the award of Lord Asquith of Bishopstone in *Petroleum Development (Trucial Coast) Ltd.* v. *Sheikh of Abu Dhabi*. The learned arbitrator had to determine the proper law of a contract, conceding that

27. E. Africa Order in Council, 1902 (S.R. & O. 1902, No. 661, amended 1911, No. 243). For the position in West Africa see W. C. E. Daniels, *The Common Law in West Africa* (London, 1964), chaps. 4, 6.

28. [1955], 1 All.E.R. 646, 652, 653 (affirmed [1956], 3 W.L.R. 541).

29. (1882), Sar(bah) F(anti) C(ustomary) L(aws) 172.

30. (1925), Div. Ct. Judgments 1921–25, 172 (Elias, *Ghana and Sierra Leone*, p. 119).

31. *Anguillia* v. *Ong Boon Tat* (1921), 15 S.S.L.R. 190, 193.

if any municipal system of law were applicable, it would prima facie be that of Abud Dhabi. But no such law can reasonably be said to exist. . . . Nor can I see any basis upon which the municipal law of England could apply. . . . The terms of [the contract] . . . prescribe the application of principles rooted in the good sense and common practice of the generality of civilized nations—a sort of 'modern law of nature.' . . . But, albeit English municipal law is inapplicable *as such,* some of its rules are in my view so firmly grounded in reason, as to form part of this broad body of jurisprudence—this 'modern law of nature.' . . . [While] the rigid English rules have been disregarded, . . . the English rule which attributes paramount importance to the actual language of the written instrument in which the negotiations result seems to me no mere idiosyncracy of our system, but a principle of ecumenical validity. Chaos may obviously result if that rule is widely departed from: and if, instead of asking what the words used mean, the inquiry extends at large to what each of the parties meant them to mean, and how and why each phrase came to be inserted.[32]

The desire to apply and occasionally to limit English common-law doctrines in a foreign environment may be illustrated by reference to India and Ghana. Ever since the charter given by Charles II to the East India Company in 1683, judges in India have interpreted their function as being to judge in accordance with "justice, equity and good conscience." These concepts were "generally interpreted to mean the rules of English law if found applicable to Indian society and circumstances,"[33] and in 1937[34] Stone C.J. was of the opinion that

in considering what is today consonant to justice, equity and good conscience, one should regard the law as it is in England today, and not the law that was part of England yesterday. One cannot take the common law of England divorced from the statute law of England and argue that the former is in accordance with justice, equity and good conscience. . . . The doctrine of common employment would not apply, not because the case would fall outside the common law doctrine of common employment, but because it would fall inside the Employer's Liability Act.[35] What I desire to point out is that when I find a rule has been abrogated by legislation, that rule becomes an

32. *Int. Law Rep.*, XVIII (1951), 144, 149.
33. *Waghela Rajsanji* v. *Shekh Masludin* (1887), 14 Ind. App. 89, *per* Lord Hobhouse, at 96.
34. *Sec. of State* v. *Rukhminibai,* A.I.R. [1937] Nag. 354.
35. 1880, 43 & 44 Vict., c. 42.

unsafe guide. Even when, as in this case, the rule remains but its practical applicability is by statute very greatly reduced, one is entitled and bound to view it more critically than would be the case if it remained in full force and effect. When one finds it criticised by competent jurists in the country of its origin and followed not because of its infrangible logic but because of its authority, and authority derived from an earlier age when circumstances were different, one is also justified in treating it as an unsafe guide.

No such hesitation was shown in Ghana in 1948 when the doctrine was accepted in *Mensah* v. *Konongo Gold Mines Ltd.*[36]

The courts in Ghana have also shown a conservative attitude in connection with contributory negligence. In *Amoabeng* v. *Mills*[37] contributory negligence was held to be a complete defense, and despite the passage in England of the Law Reform (Contributory Negligence) Act, 1945,[38] the court followed *Radley* v. *London and North Western Railway.*[39] The law was, however, changed by the Ghana Civil Liability Act, 1963. The Privy Council, too, has felt constrained to apply the common-law rule to an overseas territory even though it has been abrogated in England. When dealing with a case concerning wagering in India, Lord Campbell said: "We are bound to consider the common law of England to be that an action may be maintained on a wager, . . . and I rejoice that it is at last constitutionally abrogated by the Legislature. . . . The Statute does not extend to India, and although both parties on the record are Hindoos, no peculiar Hindoo law is alleged to exist upon the subject: therefore this case must be decided by the common law of England."[40]

A case in which English law applied despite the existence of native law was decided in Uganda in 1920. Guthrie Smith J. was dealing with succession to immovables and held that

in the absence of any enactment we must fall back on what English law decides as to its own application to newly acquired territories. . . . Taking into consideration the general effect of the Uganda Act, 1900, I think I may say we adopted much the same course as was done

---

36. Unreported (cited in Daniels, *Common Law in West Africa*, p. 240).
37. [1956], 1 W.A.L.R. 210.   38. 8 & 9 Geo. 6, c. 28.
39. (1876), 1 App. Cas. 754.
40. *Ramloll Thackoorseydass* v. *Soojanmull Dhoondumull* (1848), 4 Moo. Ind. App. 339, 348–349.

in the settlement of India which is described in *Freeman* v. *Fairlie*[41] as follows: "The course actually taken seems to have been to treat the case in a great measure like that of a newly discovered country for the Government of the Company's servants, and other British or Christian settlers using the laws of the mother country, so far as they were capable of being applied for the purpose and leaving the Mohammedan and Gentoo inhabitants to their own laws and customs but with some particular exceptions that were called for by commercial policy or the convenience of mutual intercourse." If we substitute "Natives of the Protectorate" for the words "Mohammedans and Gentoo inhabitants" . . . we shall have a correct description of how the matter has been treated in Uganda. Therefore, apart from the Succession Ordinance, 1906, the law of inheritance for immovables was English law . . . as far as regards foreigners and native customs as far as regards Natives of the Protectorate. There is no room anywhere for the application of Mohammedan law to land and it would lead to hopeless confusion if the course of descent of land depended both on tribe and religion. The conclusion is that this case falls to be determined according to the English rules of succession.[42]

The learned judge made no attempt to explain why confusion would be caused by deciding succession cases affecting Mohammedans in accordance with Mohammedan law, while it would apparently not be so caused by applying native custom in the case of Natives. This decision was not cited in *Re Abdulhusen Abhai decd.*[43] nor in *Re Cookman Mugnal Imam Din decd.*,[44] in which it was pointed out that it was "unreasonable to suppose that if the legislature had seen fit to exempt Muslims from an alien system of intestate succession under the Act, it had done so only to make them subject to an equally alien system under the law of England."

It is particularly in the field of public policy, and especially with regard to morality and marriage, that the strange consequences of the interplay between common and native law become most marked, with judges waxing almost lyrical on repugnancy, barbarism, and civilization. An example of this arose

41. See n. 4 above.
42. *Re Mohd Habash, Vasila* v. *Worsta Sophia* (1920), 3 U.L.R. 20, 26.
43. (1941), 6 U.L.R. 89.
44. (1949), cited in H. F. Morris and J. S. Read, *Uganda* (London, 1966), p. 401.

recently in an English court. The parties, although Christians, had gone through a customary form of marriage in Nigeria in 1949, and in 1953, in order to obtain a certificate, had followed it by an English register office marriage. At the time of the marriage, Nigeria permitted polygamy, and Wrangham J. held:

> Whatever might be the effect on the marriage for other purposes and in other courts of the parties being Christians, in this court and for this purpose the Nigerian marriage must be regarded as a polygamous marriage over which this court does not exercise jurisdiction. I therefore pronounce a decree nisi for the dissolution not of the Nigerian marriage but of the marriage in London. I am told that, in fact, that will be effective by Nigerian law to dissolve the Nigerian marriage; but that forms no part of my judgment. That is for someone else to determine and not for me.[45]

The learned judge did not deal with the situation that would have arisen had Nigeria not recognized the validity of the English decree. In such a case the parties would have been in the strange position of finding that though the English marriage had been dissolved, since English law recognizes a polygamous marriage as creating the status of husband and wife (a matter which became greatly significant in *M* v. *K*),[46] an attempt by either to enter into a second monogamous marriage in England would have produced a null effect,[47] though it might not have grounded an action for bigamy.[48]

A case in which English colonial judges approached native custom in a similarly cavalier fashion, and one which is still being applied by the courts of the territory in question, is the *Six Widows* case.[49] Here, English judges introduced into Singapore a concept of Chinese law not previously known and which is still not recognized in China.[50] The case concerned the status of Chinese "concubines," and Hyndman Jones C.J. accepted that

---

45. *Ohochuku* v. *Ohochuku* [1960], 1 W.L.R. 183, 185.
46. The *Times* (London), March 29, 1968.
47. *Baindall* v. *Baindall* [1946], P. 122. See also *Thynne* v. *Thynne* [1955], P. 272.
48. *R.* v. *Sarwan Singh* [1962], 3 All E.R. 612.
49. (1888), 12 S.S.L.R. 120, 187, 209.
50. Information supplied to the writer by senior Chinese members of the Supreme Courts of Singapore and Malaya.

the evidence is very contradictory, but I am disposed to think that when it is intended to take a woman into a man's household as a concubine for the purpose of securing a succession, or at all events as more than a temporary mistress, there is some sort of ceremonies; although these ceremonies, in some districts and among some classes are of a more or less perfunctory character, and always much less elaborate than those adopted in the case of taking a t'sai [principal wife].

Braddell J., whose knowledge of Chinese law was apparently no better than that of the Chief Justice, declared, "I entirely adopt the exposition of the Chinese law given in the judgment of the Chief Justice and concur with him in the conclusion to which he has arrived, namely, that concubinage is recognized as a legal institution under the law, conferring upon the t'sip [secondary wife] a legal status of a permanent character." The anxiety of Singapore judges to assert the existence of the marriage bond was recognized by the Privy Council in affirming *Penhas* v. *Tan Soo Eng*[51] in which a form of ceremony was conducted by a Chinese between a Chinese Christian woman and a Jewish man in a house before witnesses, with each of the parties offering prayers in his own way. In the view of the Privy Council, although

it is not suggested that either of the parties is a Christian[,] . . . the evidence as it stands sufficiently proves a common law monogamous marriage. The wishes expressed by the respondent and her mother for a Church marriage, the reason why a modified Chinese ceremony was substituted, the presence of Jewish friends at the ceremony, the words spoken by the Chinese gentleman who performed the ceremony as to a lifelong union, the cohabitation as man and wife which followed and continued until the husband's death, and the introduction to a Christian pastor of the respondent as his wife, and last but not least the baptism of their children as Christians, with the approval of their father, all indicate that the spouses intended to contract a common law marriage.

While it may be true that the parties did indeed intend to effect a lifelong marriage and that this was rendered respectable by the common law's being introduced to modify the rigors of the local law, a similar effect might have been obtained had the court

51. [1953], A.C. 304, 318, 319–320.

adopted the words of Lord Phillimore, that "in deciding upon a case where the customs and the laws are so different from British ideas a Court may do well to recollect that it is a possible jural conception that a child may be legitimate, though its parents were not and could not be called legitimately married."[52]

It should not be thought that the desire to sustain a marriage if that should be possible has been confined to native systems of law. In January, 1967, Browne J. was called upon to decide upon the validity of a will, and his decision turned on the question of the subsistence of a marriage put forward by a surviving husband who could not remember the name of the Scottish town in which the ceremony was performed. Mr. S. stated that when he returned from a walk

he was informed by the deceased that she had arranged a marriage for the following morning. The next morning they went to a chapel which was in a village hall. The interior resembled a church, with pews, altar rail, dais, combined lectern and pulpit, and a table with a candle and Bible upon it. The priest, who had been expecting them, wore black and conducted a very short service during which S. and the deceased agreed to take each other as husband and wife respectively. Both signed a large book and the deceased was given a certificate which some years later she destroyed after a row with her family. That account of the ceremony was highly improbable, the arrangements were incredibly casual, and grave doubts were necessarily aroused by the failure to remember the date or place of the ceremony, the absence of any record, and the account of the destruction of the certificate. It was clear that if S.'s case rested on his own account alone the Court would have no hesitation in holding the marriage was not proved. [In *Penhas* v. *Tan Soo Eng*, however, the Court accepted equally questionable proof.] On the other hand the Court was satisfied from independent evidence that for the 14 years after the marriage the defendant and deceased had lived together, and were known as Mr. and Mrs. S. and accepted as a married couple. The deceased always wore a wedding ring and there was strong evidence to suggest that it was not in keeping with the deceased's character to be living in sin.

Since, however, a common-law marriage will today only be assumed to exist by the English courts in exceptional circumstances,

52. *Khoo Hooi Leong* v. *Khoo Hean Kwee* [1926], A.C. 529, 543.

the marriage was upheld on the basis of repute from cohabitation.[53]

An up-to-date attitude to marriages performed in accordance with native law is shown by a Queen's Bench Divisional Court in March 1968. Justices had committed a fourteen-year-old Nigerian girl to the care of a local authority as being exposed to moral danger and in need of care, protection, and control. The girl was living with a twenty-eight-year-old Nigerian man, having married him by Nigerian law in Nigeria where they were both domiciled. The magistrates wrongly concluded that since the marriage was potentially polygamous it could not be recognized in England. The Court held that in so far as the girl's status was concerned the marriage would be recognized and she would, therefore, be a wife. The Lord Chief Justice accepted the decision in Baindail v. Baindail,[54] and recognized the possibility that even a wife might be the subject of a fit person order.

The question was whether the evidence justified such an order. The justices had found that before the marriage the [man] had lived with a woman and had had three illegitimate children, and that after the marriage at a time when his wife had almost certainly not reached puberty, he had had intercourse with her. After the marriage he had contracted gonorrhoea from a prostitute, but he was now cured and intended to resume intercourse with his wife. The justices had found that the continuance of the association between the girl and the appellant would be *repugnant to any decent minded English person.*

Lord Parker was convinced that

they had misdirected themselves and that they were considering the *reactions of an Englishman regarding an English man and woman in the western way of life. A decent Englishman realising the way in which a Nigerian man and woman were brought up would not say it was repugnant.* They developed sooner and there was nothing abhorrent in a girl of 13 marrying a man of 35. To say the girl was in moral danger would be *ignoring the way of life in which she and her husband had been brought up.* It had been suggested that every time the appellant slept with his wife in England, he was committing a criminal offence under the Sexual Offences Act, 1956, s.6,[55] which made it an

---

53. *Rumsey* v. *Sterne* (1967), *Times* (London), January 12, 1967.
54. See n. 46 above.   55. 4 & 5 Eliz.2, c. 69.

offence for a man to have unlawful intercourse with a girl between 13 and 16. . . . [The Lord Chief Justice did] not think the police could properly prosecute in cases where a foreign marriage was recognised in England. . . . Intercourse between a man and wife was lawful. . . . Where a husband and wife were recognised as validly married according to the laws of England, His Lordship would not say the wife was exposed to moral danger because she carried out her wifely duties.[56]

An enlightened approach to the native law of marriage and the consequential rejection of English law was shown by Witman J. when called upon to decide whether a marriage between Indians in Canada's Northwest Territories, and contracted in a form which would have been valid before the introduction of English law in 1870, was to be recognized. He asked:

[A]re the laws of England respecting the solemnisation of marriage applicable to these Territories *quoad* the Indian population? I have great doubt if these laws are applicable to the Territories in any respect. According to these laws marriages can be solemnised only at certain times and in certain places or buildings. These times would be in many cases most inconvenient here and the buildings, if they exist at all, are often so remote from the contracting parties that they could not be reached save with the greatest inconvenience. I am satisfied however that these laws are not applicable to the Territories *quoad* the Indians. The Indians are for the most part unchristianised; they yet adhere to their own particular marriage customs and usages. It would be monstrous to hold that the law of England respecting the solemnisation of marriage is applicable to them. . . . A marriage between Indians by mutual consent and according to Indian custom since 15th July 1870, is a valid marriage, providing that neither of the parties had a husband or wife, as the case might be, living at the time. . . .[57]

The learned judge could have reached the same conclusion by holding that a common-law marriage had been created, but he preferred to apply the native law, even though he insisted on monogamy.

In the case of American Indians, marriages contracted in accordance with native custom have been upheld, even though they have been polygamous.[58]

56. *M. v. K.*, The *Times* (London), March 29, 1968. (Italics added.)
57. *Reg. v. Nan-E–Quis–A-Ka* (1885), 1 *Terr. Law Rep.*, 211, 215.
58. *Kobogum v. Jackson Iron Co.* (1889), 43 N.W. 602, at 605, *per* Justice Campbell.

[A]mong these Indians polygamous marriages have always been recognized as valid, and have never been confounded with such promiscuous or informal temporary intercourse as is not reckoned as marriage. While most civilized nations in our day very wisely discard polygamy, and it is not probably lawful anywhere among English speaking nations, yet it is a recognized and valid institution among many nations, and in no way universally unlawful. We must either hold that there can be no valid Indian marriage, or we must hold that all marriages are valid which by Indian usage are so regarded. . . . We have here had marriages between members of an Indian tribe in tribal relations, and unquestionably good by the Indian rules. The parties were not subject in those relations to the laws of Michigan. . . . We cannot interfere with such marriages without subjecting them to rules of law which never bound them.

A similar view of the inapplicability, if not irrelevance, of the technicalities of English law was taken by the Privy Council in *Amodu Tijani v. Secretary, Southern Nigeria:*[59]

In interpreting the native title to land, not only in Southern Nigeria, but in other parts of the British Empire, much caution is essential. There is a tendency, operating at times unconsciously, to render that title conceptually in terms which are appropriate only to systems which have grown up under English law. But this tendency has to be held in check closely. As a rule, in the various systems of native jurisprudence throughout the Empire, there is no such full division between property and possession as English lawyers are familiar with.

The Privy Council's attitude has, however, been inconsistent when dealing with terms in colonial legislation which are the same as or similar to terms in English law. Thus, in *Nadarajan Chettiar v. Walaawa Mahatmee*[60] the Council pointed out that Section 2 of the Ceylon Moneylenders' Ordinance was the equivalent of Section 1 of the Moneylenders' Act, 1900, and commented that

it is one thing to presume that a local legislature, when re-enacting a former statute, intends to accept the interpretation placed on that statute by local courts of competent jurisdiction with whose decision the legislature must be taken to be familiar; it is quite another thing to presume that a legislature, when it incorporates in a local act the

---

59. [1921], 2 A.C. 399, 402–403, *per* Lord Haldane.
60. [1950], A.C. 481, 491–492, *per* Sir John Beaumont.

terms of a foreign statute, intends to accept the interpretation placed on those terms by the courts of the foreign country with which the legislature may or may not be familiar. There is no presumption that the people of Ceylon at the relevant date knew, or must be taken to have known, decisions of the English courts under the Moneylenders' Acts, there is no basis for imputing to the legislature an intention to accept those decisions. . . . In *Trimble v. Hill*[61] the Board expressed this opinion ". . . in colonies where a like enactment has been passed by the legislature the Colonial Courts should also govern themselves by it [a decision of the Court of Appeal]." This, in their Lordships' view, is a sound rule, though there may be in any particular case conditions which make it inappropriate. It is not suggested that any such conditions exist in the present case, and the Courts in Ceylon acted correctly in following the decision of the English Court of Appeal.

Local conditions were recognized, however, in *Adegbenro* v. *Akintola*,[62] for,

while it may well be useful on occasions to draw on British practice or doctrine in interpreting a doubtful phrase whose origins can be traced or to study decisions on the Constitution of Australia or the United States when federal issues are involved, it is in the end the wording of the Constitution itself that is to be interpreted and applied, and this wording can never be overriden by the extraneous principles of other Constitutions which are not explicitly incorporated in the formulae that have been chosen as the frame of this Constitution.

Once again the position concerning Indian custom in the United States is more enlightened than tends to be usual with the interplay of English and local law. The Supreme Court refused to uphold a South Dakota prosecution for adultery when the parties were Sioux and the offense was alleged to have taken place on a Sioux reservation. In *U.S. v. Quiver*[63] Justice Van Devanter stated:

At an early period it became the settled policy of Congress to permit the personal and domestic relations of the Indians with each other to be regulated, and offenses by one Indian against the person or property of another Indian to be dealt with according to their tribal customs and laws. . . . [T]he act of June 30, 1834, ch. 161, sec. 25, 4 Stat. at L.729,733, while providing that "so much of the laws of the

61. [1879], 5 App. Cas. 342, 344, *per* Sir Montague Smith.
62. [1963], A.C. 614, 632, *per* Lord Radcliffe.
63. (1916), 241 U.S. 602, at 603–605.

United States as provides for the punishment of crimes committed within any place within the sole and exclusive jurisdiction of the United States shall be in force in the Indian country," qualified its action by saying, "the same shall not extend to crimes committed by one Indian against the person or property of another Indian!" That provision with its qualification was later carried into the Revised Statutes as Secs. 2145 and 2146. . . . There is [no statute] dealing with bigamy, polygamy, incest, adultery or fornication, which in terms refers to Indians, these matters always having been left to the tribal customs and laws and to such preventive and corrective measures as reasonably could be taken by the administrative officers.

It is perhaps unfortunate that judges in colonial territories, who are called upon to apply native law and to examine its interconnection with the common law far more frequently than the Privy Council, appear to be more reticent in recognizing local needs and abandoning English concepts. This is the case with Wilson J. in Tanganyika, who held[64] that "a Turu custom whereby the property of a father might be seized in compensation for a wrong done by his son was so repugnant to British ideas of justice and morality that it should not be endorsed in the High Court. It would, however, almost certainly have succeeded in a local court, to which such ideas of vicarious liability would not be so difficult to accept."[65] Similar attitudes are evident in Nigerian decisions, where

the repugnancy doctrine has also been applied in the field of customary family law. In *Joshua Chawere* v. *Hannah Aihenu*[66] it was held that any native custom to the effect that a wife who committed adultery ipso facto of the adultery became the wife of the male adulterer would be repugnant and unenforceable. And in this same field, the English common law concept of "public policy," which would forbid the encouragement of promiscuous intercourse,[67] has been suggested[68] as capable of striking down the now well-established[69] customary rule that an originally illegitimate child

---

64. *Gwao bin Kelimo* v. *Kisunda bin Ifuti* (1938), 1 *Tanganyika Law Reports* (R) 403.

65. J. S. R. Cole and W. N. Denison, *Tanganyika* (London, 1964), p. 131.

66. 12 N. L. R. 4.

67. See "The Ladies' Directory Case" (*Shaw* v. *D.P.P.* [1961], 2 W.L.R. 897).

68. *In re Sarah Adadevoh* (1951), 13 W.A.C.A. 304, *per* Verity C.J., at 310.

69. *Savage* v. *Macfay* (1909), Ren. 504; *Re Sapara* (1911), Ren. 605.

whose paternity is acknowledged and recognized by its father thereby acquires the same status as a child born legitimate.[70]

Perhaps one of the most glaring instances of trimming native customary law to the moral code of the English common law is to be seen in *Re GM (An Infant)*.[71] A Kikuyu orphan child had been placed by the local authorities in a state of *de facto* adoption with a respectable woman, against whom the deceased father's brother brought an action on the ground that by Kikuyu law and custom he had "the right of custody as against all strangers." Miles J. found that it was in the infant's interest to stay with the respondent, and that by English law this was the test to apply in a contest between strangers or between parents. As between a parent and a stranger, however, he held that the parent must prevail unless this would be inimical to the child. He decided that English law applied, but that in determining the child's welfare it was necessary to look to native custom and habits:

I am entitled to inquire what the position of the applicant is under native law and then to inquire what would be the rights of a person in that position under English law. . . . The applicant cannot be said to be a "parent." It is also clear on the evidence that the applicant is, under Kikuyu law, in the position of a guardian with surely all the obligations of a parent. He has greater obligations than a guardian under English law who is not bound to support a child except out of the child's estate. [Since the respondent was a stranger, and the applicant a blood relation] under English law the latter would be held to have a legal right as against all strangers.

It would seem that the learned judge assimilated a "guardian" in Kikuyu law with a "parent" under English law.[72]

It is decisions such as this which make one feel that Maine's comment in 1871 is still valid:

The higher courts, though they openly borrowed the English rules from the recognized English authorities, constantly used language which implied that they believed themselves to be taking them from some abstract body of legal principles which lay behind all law; and

70. F. A. Ajayi, "Interaction of English Law with Customary Law in Western Nigeria, II," *Jour. of Afr. Law*, IV (1960), at 98, 104–105.
71. [1957], E.A. 714, 716.
72. A. N. Allott, note, *Jour. of Afr. Law*, III (1959), 72, at 74.

the inferior judges, when they were applying some half-remembered legal rule learnt in boyhood, or culling a proposition of law from a half-understood English textbook, no doubt honestly thought in many cases that they were following the rule prescribed for them, to decide "by equity and good conscience" whenever no native law or usage was discoverable.[73]

One would like to hope that judges faced with assessing whether native customary law was applicable despite its apparent inconsistency with the common law would adopt the reasoning of Lord Atkin:

The more barbarous customs of earlier days may under the influence of civilization become milder without losing their character as custom, so as in that form to regulate the relations of the native community *inter se.* In other words, the court cannot itself transform a barbarous custom into a milder one. If it still stands in its barbarous character it must be rejected as repugnant to "natural justice, equity and good conscience." It is the essence of a native community that gives a custom its validity, and, therefore, barbarous or mild, it must be shown to be recognized by the native community whose conduct it is supposed to regulate. . . .[74]

The Chief Justice of Gambia has recently shown that the concept of "barbarism" is relative and that customs which might not be approved by Christian missionaries are not necessarily contrary to "natural justice." Thus, in *Koykoy Jatta* v. *Menna Camara*[75] he held that female circumcision "is your custom but can only be your custom in your own tribe and applied to your own people."

The problems involved when an outsider is called upon to assess native customary law are also evident in the attitude of Indian Bureau officials of the United States

who disapproved of the "uncivilized" practices of the Indians and sought to substitute a "civilized" system of "courts of Indian offenses" in which the superintendent of the reservation claimed the right to act as lawmaker, chief of police, prosecutor, witness, and court of appeal. This allegedly "civilized" system of justice was in force on a number of reservations from 1884 until 1935, when it was superseded by a more

73. H. J. S. Maine, *Village Communities in the East and West* (London, 1871), pp. 298–299.
74. *Eshugbayi Eleko* v. *Govt. of Nigeria (Officer Administering)* [1931], A.C. 662, 673.
75. (1961), *Jour. of Afr. Law*, VIII (1964), 35.

liberal system which made the so-called Courts of Indian Offenses responsible to the Indian tribes and terminated the reservation superintendent's power to control proceedings in these courts.[76]

In Ceylon, Roman-Dutch common law has had to give way before the customary law of a particular community, for while

no Court would recognize as reasonable a custom which deprived a section of the community of its common law rights in the freedom which the custom is supposed to regulate, it must be remembered that in Ceylon there are customary laws governing people, and if it could be proved that such customary laws enunciate principles which are in derogation to the general principles of Roman-Dutch law, it is the customary law which would govern such a matter to the exclusion of Roman-Dutch law.[77]

Where Roman-Dutch law happens to be the common law, problems sometimes arise not only because of the relevance of native law, but also because the concept being examined is also known in England and the judges are frequently English trained. Mr. De Silva, delivering judgment on behalf of the Privy Council, dealt with this problem insofar as it affected accessories after the fact of murder:

Under section 2 of the General Law Proclamation[78] the common law of Basutoland "shall, as nearly as the circumstances of the country will permit, be the same as the law for the time being in force in the Colony of the Cape of Good Hope." . . . The determination of the question before their Lordships depends on the Roman-Dutch common law, which is the common law of the Cape of Good Hope and is also the common law in force in South Africa. . . . It does not necessarily follow from the fact that the term "accessory after the fact" has been adopted from the English law that it has the same meaning in the law of South Africa as it has under the English law. No doubt it would retain much of the connotation which it possessed under the English law, but its meaning in the country of its adoption could naturally and properly be influenced by the system of law prevailing in that country, namely the Roman-Dutch law. This was almost inevitable, as the term had to be used in relation to, and in the course of administration of that law.[79]

76. Felix S. Cohen, "Indian Rights and the Federal Courts," *Minn. Law Rev.*, XXIV (1939/40), 145–200, at 153.
77. *Fernando v. Fernando* (1920), 22 N.L.R. 260, per Bertram C.J.
78. Laws of Basutoland, chap. 26.
79. *Nkau Majara v. The Queen* [1954], A.C. 235, 240–241.

In the instant case, while the accused was not guilty under English law, he was guilty under the Roman-Dutch common law by which the case was governed.

The importance of South African decisions in determining the meaning of Roman-Dutch law (for those areas in which it is the common law) remains, even though South Africa has become a republic outside the Commonwealth. This is illustrated by the comments of Lord Donovan on behalf of the Privy Council in *Mapolisa* v. R.:

> The common law in force in the Cape of Good Hope (now part of the Republic of South Africa) on the date specified [by the High Court Act of Southern Rhodesia, 1893] was, and remains, Roman-Dutch law. Under that law a *socius criminis* [accomplice] is not regarded as committing the self-same crime as the principal perpetrator but as committing instead the offence of aiding and abetting that crime. . . . Even if the Roman-Dutch common law regarded the *socius criminis* as committing the very crime perpetrated, it did so only in relation to crimes which were offences created by that common law. Since Roman-Dutch law is the common law of Southern Rhodesia, judicial decisions given in the courts of what is now the Republic of South Africa have relevance in Southern Rhodesia and are applicable subject to any statutory modification of the law in Southern Rhodesia. The Appellate Division of the Supreme Court of South Africa served until recently as a Court of Appeal for Southern Rhodesia. During that period its decisions were binding in Southern Rhodesia, and while this is technically no longer so, those decisions continue to have persuasive authority.[80]

It is to be hoped that the reduction of South African appellate decisions to a level of persuasive rather than binding authority will not result in the elevation of decisions of the English Court of Appeal on similar causes to the level of compulsive authority.

From what has been said it is clear that while the introduction of the common law into native societies has undoubtedly led to some modification of local native customs which were not acceptable to Western Christian society, and has resulted in the expansion of the scope of the rule of law as understood in such society, it remains true that too often the judges called upon to

80. [1965], A.C. 840, 857–858.

apply the one or the other or an admixture of the two have tended to disregard local conditions or susceptibilities, and have frequently stretched English concepts as if their task lay in creating replicas of the English legal system wherever English or English-trained judges held sway. This situation was condemned by Sir Frederick Pollock insofar as India was concerned in 1912:

> One may find indeed that imitation is now and then carried to excess. Not only the decisions of Indian superior courts and of the Judicial Committee on appeal therefrom, but those of English courts, are cited wholesale throughout British India, frequently by advocates who cannot know much of the common law and by judges or magistrates who may know as little; and the citations, one suspects, are too often not even from the report but at second hand from textbooks. Even technical rules of English real property law have been relied on by Indian courts without considering whether they had any reasonable application to the facts and usage of the country. Some Indian judges, even in the superior judgment seats of the High Courts, have forgotten that the law they administer . . . is not English law as such, but "justice, equity and good conscience" interpreted to mean as much of English jurisprudence as appears to be reasonably applicable, and no more. Blind following of English precedents according to the letter can only have the effect of reducing the estimation of the common law by intelligent Indians to the level of its more technical and less fruitful portions and making these portions appear, if possible, more inscrutable to Indian than they do to English lay suitors.[81]

It would appear that the underlying basis of these comments was true, insofar as the Privy Council is concerned, even as recently as 1955. In *Leong v. Lim Beng Chye*[82] the issue concerned the validity of restraints on marriage in Penang, and the opinion of the Board was delivered by Lord Radcliffe:

> The considerations which have influenced the Court of Appeal can be plausibly restated in the proposition that the rule of English law ought

---

81. Frederick Pollock, *Genius of the Common Law* (New York, 1912), p. 92. On the position of Indian law generally, see Motilal Setalvad, *The Common Law in India* (London, 1960), chap. 1. See, however, Setalvad, *The Role of English Law in India* (London, 1966), in which the learned author examines the suitability or otherwise of English law under Indian conditions, and forecasts the emergence of Indian legal thought as a contributing force to Anglo-Saxon jurisprudence.

82. [1955], A.C. 648, 665–666.

not to be applied by the courts in Malaya, having regard to the differences of race and social custom that separate the one country from the other. Something like this proposition was indeed advanced by the respondent's counsel in his argument on the appeal. The rule in question, it was said, was a rule of construction only, which, originating in an attempt to correct a social malady that prevailed in one period of the Roman Empire, had found an ambiguous and rather restricted lodging in one part of the law of England. It would be wrong to resort to it when dealing with the construction of wills made by residents of Malaya, many of whom inherit customs and traditions very different from those of the English race. Their Lordships are far from denying that there is force in an argument on these lines. It is very natural to see something anomalous in the introduction into Malaya of a special rule of English law of this kind. But English law itself has been introduced into Penang . . . "so far as it is applicable to the circumstances of the place";[83] and while so much of that law as can be said to relate to matters and exigencies peculiar to the local condition of England and to be inapplicable to the conditions of the overseas territory is not to be treated as so imported, their Lordships are of opinion that the process of selection cannot rest on anything less than some solid ground that establishes the inconsistency. And it is any solid ground of that sort which is lacking in this case; not the less when it is recalled that the testator made the will in the English language, and employed in it forms and legal conceptions that are wholly derived from English law [this is to ignore the fact that the language of the testator was almost certainly English as it is with so many Straits Chinese; that the lawyer who drafted the will was English-trained; and that the language of the law in Malaya at that time was English]. In fact, if the English law was so far imported into Penang as to nullify through the rule against perpetuities a Chinese lady's testamentary disposition relating to a family burying place and a house for performing religious ceremonies to the memory of her dead husband,[84] it would be very hard to say why there was not also imported the English rule as to the effect of conditions of partial restraint of marriage. . . . This rule . . . is not merely a rule of construction, since its history shows that it owes its existence to a particular conception of what public policy required, even though that conception never prevailed in the English law as a whole. Yet there is nothing that is peculiar to the local conditions of England or, for all that appears, anything necessarily inappropriate to the circumstances of Malaya, in a reluctance on the part of the courts of law to allow a

83. *Yeap Cheah Neo* v. *Ong Cheng Neo* (1875), L.R. 6 P.C. 381, 393.
84. *Ibid.*, p. 393.

person's decision whether or not to enter the state of matrimony to be overhung by [such] a condition.[85]

A somewhat different approach by non-native judges is to be found in the treatment of North American Indians: "Where [federal] statutes do not reach, Indian custom is the only law. As a matter of convenience, the regular courts (white men's courts) tacitly assume that the general law of the community is the law in civil cases between Indians, but these courts will apply Indian custom where it is proved."[86]

Addressing the International Commission of Jurists in 1966, Judge Vivian Bose remarked that "in developing countries the rule of law is often being equated with the former foreign domination. . . . These new nations must be shown that law was not a western product, but something grounded in their own traditions. Institutions rooted in their own customs could be raised and moulded to modern forms."[87] An early recognition of the need to acknowledge the existence of native institutions of law was shown by Lord Sumner who pointed out in 1919 that

the estimation of the rights of aboriginal tribes is always inherently difficult. Some tribes are so low in the scale of social organization that their usages and conceptions of rights and duties are not to be reconciled with the institutions of the legal ideas of civilized society. Such a gulf cannot be bridged. It would be idle to impute to such people some shadow of the rights known to our law and then to transmute it into the substance of transferable rights of property as we know them. . . . On the other hand, there are indigenous peoples whose legal conceptions, though differently developed are hardly less precise than our own. When once they have been studied and understood they are no less enforceable than rights arising under English law.[88]

With the rise as new independent states of territories which were formerly colonies, and the feelings of national pride which

---

85. See, however, *Adeyinka Oyekan* v. *Musendiku Adele* [1957], 1 W.L.R. 876, in which Lord Denning remarked that in Nigeria government grants of land "do not convey English titles or English rights of ownership. The words 'his heirs, executors, administrators and assigns forever' are to be rejected as meaningless and inapplicable in their African setting" (p. 882).

86. W. G. Rice, Jr., "The Position of the American Indian in the Law of the United States," *Jour. of Comp. Leg.*, 3d ser., XVI (1934), 78–95, at 90.

87. *Times* (London), October 1, 1966.

88. *In re Southern Rhodesia* [1919], A.C. 211, 233–234.

their people enjoy, together with the gradual replacement of expatriate lawyers and judges and the retreat from the Judicial Committee of the Privy Council as the supreme court of appeal, we are on the threshold of a new relationship between the common law and native systems. Those English judges who remain, and the English lawyers who have gone out to staff the law schools, are conscious of the realities that surround them. While there is still the need to supplement the law and realization that what has been past practice cannot be abandoned, there is growing recognition that the local people will not be satisfied with the example of their former rulers and that, in any case, local needs require more than a slavish adoption of the common law. Further, the principles of public policy and concepts of civilization understood in such native societies are no longer seen as inferior to those of another legal system, as was realized in the United States, insofar as Indians on the reserves are concerned, a generation ago.[89] The common law has served the purpose of making the basic principles of a Western view of the rule of law understood and appreciated. If it is to continue to play a role, (English) common lawyers must be prepared to see its adaptation and rejection in issues where, in the past, it might have been adopted either in full or in amended form. In addition, if they do not adapt themselves to this view and continue to look down upon "barbaric" and "uncivilized" systems, they may find that there is a reaction which results in a total rejection of the influences of the common law, instead of its being but one of the various systems of law that nationalist lawyers and judges seeking to serve the needs of their people are prepared to investigate and adapt as their requirements demand.

89. See n. 72 above.

· 6 ·

International Rendition in United States–Commonwealth Relations

Alona E. Evans[*]

International rendition of fugitive offenders is an appropriate subject for discussion in the context of a conference on international and comparative law of the Commonwealth, if only for the historic reason that it was a Canadian fugitive whose "wanted" picture shown on the first international transmission by the Early Bird Satellite led to his arrest in Florida the next day on a "tip" from a television fan who recognized him as a local resident.[1] That Early Bird telecast dramatically points up the problem of control of international fugitive offenders in an age of speedy transportation and communication. At the same time many common-law countries are concerned today about the problem of protection of the accused in criminal proceedings. As international rendition of fugitive offenders is an ancillary part of such proceedings, this concern properly extends to it.

There is more than one way for a state to acquire custody of an international fugitive offender whom it wishes to bring to trial or to restore to prison, depending upon the stage of the legal process which the fugitive has chosen to avoid in favor of a foreign asylum. "International rendition" is the generic term for the process of acquiring such custody, whether by resort to formal proce-

[*] Professor of Political Science, Wellesley College.
1. Case of Georges Lemay. *Immigration and Naturalization Service Annual Report* (Washington, D.C., 1965), p. 9. The present essay was completed in October, 1966.

dures, such as extradition, or to informal or irregular procedures. Formal procedures comprehend extradition by treaty or by statute as well as rendition in pursuance of penal provisions which are found, for example, in United States practice, in certain treaties dealing with conservation of natural resources of the sea, jurisdiction over military personnel in foreign bases, and with desertion of naval vessels.[2] Informal methods include the substitution of the civil law procedures of exclusion and expulsion for the criminal law procedure of rendition, as well as irregular methods of rendition such as kidnapping. This essay is a brief examination of certain features of international rendition under extradition treaties and in pursuance of informal methods as illustrated in the relations of the United States with some of the independent members of the Commonwealth.

Treaty Relations

It is possible to speak of "international extradition law" as a distinctive and well-developed aspect of international law, for such rules as double criminality, specialty, proscription of rendition for political offenses, as well as procedural rules as to arrest, detention, surrender, costs, and third party claims, can be said to be relatively "standardized," making due allowance for variations arising from differences among the legal systems of states. Whether these extradition rules are embodied in treaties or in municipal law or both,[3] rendition under such rules is a formal

2. E.g. Art. VI, Interim Convention on Conservation of North Pacific Fur Seals, 1957, 314 U.N.T.S. 105, see Marjorie M. Whiteman, *Digest of International Law* (Washington, D.C., 1965), IV, 1004–1005. (1965); Art. VII (5)(a), Agreement between the Parties to the North Atlantic Treaty Regarding the Status of their Forces, 1951, 199 U.N.T.S. 67; Art. XXIV, Treaty of Friendship and General Relations with Spain, 1902, 33 *Stat.* 2105, see *United States ex rel. Martinez-Angosto v. Mason*, 232 F. Supp. 102 (S.D.N.Y. 1964), rev'd. 344 F. 2d 673 (2d Cir. 1965). Cf. Westberg case in which British authorities surrendered a Swedish seaman to Sweden for an offense committed on a Swedish ship in British territorial waters. L. C. Green, "Recent Practice in the Law of Extradition," *Current Legal Problems*, VI (1953), 274–296, at 287. A similar incident in Australia involving a Dutch seaman is reported by I. A. Shearer, "Extradition and Asylum in Australia," in D. P. O'Connell, ed., *International Law in Australia* (Sydney, 1965), p. 567.

3. Although extradition treaties have been held to be self-executing in the United States (see *United States v. Robins*, 27 Fed. Cas. 825 [D.S.C. 1799]), the

process which provides some protection of the interests of all parties concerned. Extradition in pursuance of treaty terms, however, provides both the fugitive and the asylum and requesting states with more standing to protect their respective interests than would be likely under municipal law rules alone, for in the former situation, questions may be raised as to the existence of a treaty under which extradition may be had; as to whether the offense charged is a treaty offense; and as to the procedure followed before, during, and after extradition. The United States, for its part, is barred by law from extraditing a fugitive in the absence of a treaty; and as a matter of practice, this country is not disposed to ask for extradition where reciprocity cannot be granted.[4] The principal British Extradition Act of 1870, presumes the existence of an "arrangement" or treaty for extradition relations with a foreign state, as do the recent extradition acts of Ghana, India, New Zealand, Sierra Leone, and Uganda.[5] The 1952 Canadian Extradition Act, however, specifically provides for extradition in the absence of a treaty. This provision is qualified by the requirement that it takes effect only when it has been extended to a particular state by proclamation of the Governor General. According to La Forest, there is no instance of such extension.[6]

The United States has extradition relations with twenty-two

---

issue has been obviated by the enactment of an extradition law. In the Commonwealth countries, extradition treaties are usually transformed into municipal law by statute or special order, e.g., Extradition Act, 1870, 33 & 34 Vict., c. 52, sec. 2; Ghana, Extradition Act, 1960, sec. 1(1)(2).

4. 18 U.S.C. sec. 3184. See, Arguelles case (1864), John B. Moore, *Digest of International Law* (Washington, D.C., 1906), IV, 249; *United States v. Paroutian*, 299 F. 2d 486 (2d Cir. 1962), aff'd. 319 F. 2d 661 (2d Cir. 1963), in which accused was extradited to the United States pursuant to Lebanese law (Art. 30, code pénal). Where the Soviet Union requested the surrender of a former employee of the Soviet Trade Representative in Mexico who had found asylum in the United States, the Department of State took the view that "it is a well-established principle of international law that no right to extradition exists apart from treaty" (*Dept. State Bull.*, XVI [1947], 212).

5. Ghana, Extradition Act, 1960, sec. 1; India, Extradition Act, 1962, No. 34 of 1962, secs. 2, 3; New Zealand, Extradition Act, 1965, No. 44, sec. 3; Sierra Leone, Extradition Act, 1962, Supplement to Sierra Leone *Gazette*, XCIII, No. 91 (October 11, 1962), sec. 2(3); Uganda, Extradition Act 1964, Act 16 of 1964, sec. 1. Australia's Extradition Act, 1903–1950, is effective as part of the Imperial Extradition Acts, and a treaty is assumed. Shearer, "Extradition," pp. 562, 569.

6. R.S.C. 1952, c. 322, Part II, secs. 35, 37. G. A. La Forest, *Extradition to and from Canada* (New Orleans, 1961), p. 13.

independent Commonwealth countries.[7] Actually, the United States is party to one agreement, the 1931 Extradition Treaty with the United Kingdom, which also binds seventeen other Commonwealth states. Article X of the Webster-Ashburton Treaty of 1842, and three other extradition treaties concluded with the United Kingdom between 1889 and 1905, are in force with Canada and New Zealand; in addition the United States and Canada are parties to the supplementary extradition treaties of 1922, 1925, and 1951.[8] A question was raised in a Canadian extradition case in 1953 as to whether that country was bound by treaty commitments antedating the Statute of Westminster. The court held that the Webster-Ashburton Treaty (and presumably the others) was binding until Canada chose to abrogate it.[9] Canada did conclude a new treaty with the United States in 1942, but the treaty was never perfected.[10]

The addition of many new independent members to the Commonwealth system during the past decade has brought into sharp focus the legal problems of state succession. Where extradition treaties are concerned, the determination of succession is particularly important because this is a point which is likely to be litigated. Twelve of the new members with which the United

7. Australia, Botswana, Canada, Ceylon, Cyprus, Ghana, Guyana, India, Jamaica, Kenya, Malawi, Malaysia, Malta, New Zealand, Nigeria, Pakistan, Sierra Leone, Singapore, Tanzania, Trinidad and Tobago, United Kingdom, Zambia. Department of State, *Treaties in Force. A List of Treaties and Other International Agreements of the United States in Force on January 1, 1966* (1966), Letter of Oct. 21, 1966, from Charles I. Bevans, Assistant Legal Adviser, Department of State.

8. Canada and New Zealand: Webster-Ashburton Treaty, 8 *Stat.* 572; Extradition Convention, 1889, 26 *Stat.* 1508; Supplementary Extradition Convention, 1900, 32 *Stat.* 1864; Supplementary Extradition Convention, 1905, 34 *Stat.* 2903. Canada: Supplementary Extradition Convention, 1922, 42 *Stat.* 2224; Convention to Provide for Extradition on Account of Crimes or Offenses against Narcotic Laws, 1925, 44 *Stat.* 2100; Supplementary Convention to 1900 Convention, 1951, 206 UNTS 319. The 1908 Treaty with Canada Providing for Reciprocal Rights in Matters of Conveyance of Prisoners and Wrecking and Salvage permits the conveyance of extradited persons through the territories of the parties. United Kingdom: Extradition Treaty, 1931, 47 *Stat.* 2122. It may be added that Ireland is bound by the agreements of 1842, 1889, 1900, and 1905. Burma is bound by the 1931 treaty.

9. *Ex parte O'Dell and Griffin,* 105 *Can. Crim. Rep.* 256 (Ont. High Ct. 1953). Note Art. 18, 1931 treaty.

10. State Dept. MS. File No. 211.42/204. See La Forest, *Extradition to and from Canada,* p. 125. Australia continues to be bound by extradition treaties concluded by the United Kingdom before 1939 but has not acceded to any British treaties concluded since 1945. Shearer, "Extradition," p. 560.

States has extradition relations have committed themselves to "devolution" or inheritance agreements whereby they have accepted in general or explicit terms the treaty commitments by which they were bound before independence.[11] Five others have made what O'Connell calls "temporising declarations" in one form or another whereby treaties concluded before independence continue in force for a fixed period of time after independence, subject to automatic abrogation if notification is not given as to their continuation. The Zambian variation on this formula, followed also by Guyana, regards such treaties as existing for an unlimited period of time or until formal notification of abrogation is made.[12] These temporizing declarations are rather penumbral in character, leaving the issue of the succession of the new states to the treaty or the recognition of such action by the other party unsettled until questioned in actual extradition proceedings. The Department of State files indicate that in a recent case in which the United States extradited a fugitive to Zambia on a forgery charge, the department certified to the extradition magistrate that in its opinion the 1931 treaty with the United Kingdom which had been in force with Northern Rhodesia continued to be in force for the successor state.[13]

Reference has been made to the United States treaties with twenty-two independent members of the Commonwealth, whereas a count as of October 4, 1966, indicates that twenty-five states may be so classified. The status of United States extradition relations with Uganda, The Gambia, Guyana, Botswana, and Lesotho is not entirely clear. The protectorates of Uganda, The Gambia, and Bechuanaland were covered by the 1931 treaty.[14]

11. E.g. Federation of Nigeria, International Rights and Obligations, Exchange of letters assuming obligations and responsibilities of the United Kingdom under valid international instruments thereof, October 1, 1960, Cmnd. 1214 (1960). The states are Botswana, Ceylon, Cyprus, Ghana, India, Jamaica, Malaysia, Nigeria, Pakistan, Sierra Leone, Singapore, and Trinidad and Tobago. See D. P. O'Connell, ed., *Interim Report* of the Committee on the Succession of New States to the Treaties and Certain Other Obligations of their Predecessors, International Law Association, 4 ff. (1966). Cf. *Re Westerling*, 17 *Int. Law Rep.*, 82 (High Ct. Singapore 1950). See Whiteman, *Digest* (1963), II, 936 ff.

12. Guyana, Kenya, Malawi, Uganda, Zambia. See, O'Connell, ed., p. 6. Letter of Oct. 21, 1966, from Charles I. Bevans.

13. *Re Zwamgendaba Jere*, D.D.C., March 29, 1966.

14. S.R. & O. 1935, No. 574 (Rev. IX, 421), Art. 16.

Uganda made a temporizing declaration in February, 1963, to the effect that preindependence treaties would continue in force until the end of December but would be presumed to have lapsed if parties were not notified to the contrary at the end of this period or any extension thereof.[15] In December, 1963, this declaration was extended for another year. No further communication apparently ensued. The Department of State does not list an extradition treaty with Uganda in the 1966 edition of *Treaties in Force*; however, Uganda's Extradition Act of 1966 suggests that the 1931 treaty continues in force.[16] The Gambia and Lesotho have not informed the Department of State of their intentions regarding the 1931 treaty.[17]

Treaty Relations in Practice

Although there are nine agreements to be taken into consideration in an examination of extradition relations between the independent Commonwealth countries and the United States, for purposes of discussion of practice thereunder, the four treaties with New Zealand and the eight with Canada will be regarded as constituting one agreement each, which can be compared with the 1931 treaty in effect with the United Kingdom and at least nineteen other independent Commonwealth members. The 1889 treaty combined with Article X of the Webster-Ashburton Treaty and the 1931 treaty constitute "principal" treaties or general treaties which define the conditions under which extradition will be granted. All are of indefinite duration; the 1931 agreement, however, provides for termination on notice of six months to one year.

The 1931 treaty has the most comprehensive list of offenses, adding eight to those which are included in the Canadian and New Zealand agreements. The New Zealand treaty has the shortest list, the most notable omission in terms of the other two agreements being offenses in connection with traffic in narcotics.

15. Whiteman, *Digest*, II, 1001.
16. Letter of Oct. 21, 1966, from Charles I. Bevans.
17. *Ibid.*

The Canadian agreement includes three offenses which do not appear in the other two. The 1922 supplementary treaty with Canada takes cognizance of the facilitation of one aspect of the "poor man's divorce" by reason of the long border and makes wilful desertion or wilful non-support of minor or dependent children an extraditable offense.[18] The supplementary treaty of 1951, representing the culmination of almost two decades of effort by the United States to find a way to limit the use of Canada as a haven for persons accused of violations of the Securities Act of 1933, spells out the offense of "obtaining money, valuable securities or other property by false pretenses" by providing a broad definition of fraud and including the offense of use of the mails to defraud.[19]

The treaties with Canada, New Zealand, and the United Kingdom expand their lists of offenses by providing for "participation" in the offenses listed but with the proviso that participation must be punishable by the laws of both parties. There is no general clause in these treaties regarding conspiracy; however, statutory provisions may supply the deficiency. In a 1962 case, an Ontario extradition judge held that as conspiracy to traffic in narcotics is an offense under the laws of Canada and the United States relating to the suppression of this trade, it might be considered an extraditable offense within the purview of the 1922 supplementary treaty despite the fact that conspiracy as such is not found in that treaty.[20]

The British tradition of protection of the individual accused of

18. *Commonwealth of Massachusetts* v. *Stebbins* [1949], *Ont. Weekly Notes* 741.

19. Sec. 17(a), 48 *Stat.* 84, 15 U.S.C. sec. 77 q (a); 18 U.S.C. sec. 1341. The analogous Canadian fraud provisions, adopted in 1948, appear in *Can. Crim. Code 1953–54*, c. 51, secs. 323(1)(2), 324. See William H. Timbers and Irving M. Pollack, "Extradition from Canada to the United States for Securities Fraud: Frustration of the National Policies of Both Countries," *Fordham Law Rev.*, XXIV (1955), 301–325; Louis Loss, *Securities Regulation* (2d ed.; Boston, 1961), III, 1995–2004; John P. Williamson, *Securities Regulation in Canada* (Toronto, 1960), pp. 381–385.

20. *Re Brisbois*, 133 *Can. Crim. Cas.* 188 (Ont. High Ct. 1962). *Can. Crim. Code 1953–54*, c. 51, sec. 408(1)(d). Sierra Leone lists conspiracy among the offenses for which extradition is possible to the foreign states listed in the extradition law. Extradition Act, 1962, Schedule IV, No. 28. The Indian Extradition Act of 1962 was amended in 1963 to provide for conspiracy. This clause applies to non-treaty states and Commonwealth states. No. 167 of 1963, *Gazette of India*, Extraordinary, Part II, sec. 3(1).

political offenses is written into the 1870 Extradition Law which is the prototype for those references to this aspect of extradition to non-Commonwealth states where found in the laws of Canada, Ghana, India, New Zealand, and Sierra Leone; and it is reflected in the proscription of extradition of political offenders found in the principal treaties of the United States with Canada and New Zealand of 1889 and with the United Kingdom of 1931.[21] In United States practice, as extradition can be granted only in pursuance of a treaty, and all United States treaties contain a clause exempting the political offender from extradition, equivalent protection is provided. Specific reference is made to the political offense in only one section of the American extradition law concerning the surrender of a fugitive from a foreign country or territory under United States occupation or control.[22]

When it comes to defining the "political offense," however, the treaty or statutory provisions offer little guidance. In British practice the term may comprehend a political activist involved in an uprising against an incumbent government or a political dissident who seeks to escape from the control of an oppressive regime; but it does not comprehend the situation in which the common crime element is dominant.[23] Political activism appears to be the distinguishing characteristic of the political offense in judicial and administrative treatment of the matter in the United States.[24] Although the determination of whether an extradition request is political in character is at the discretion of the asylum state, the

---

21. Art. II, 1889 treaty; Art. VI, 1931 treaty. Extradition laws: Canada, secs. 21, 22; Ghana, secs. 2(a), 7(1), 9(1), 23; India, secs. 7(2), 31(a); New Zealand, secs. 5(1)(b), 6, 9 (1)(d); Sierra Leone, sec. 16(b). See Shearer, "Extradition," pp. 559–560. Extradition before the nineteenth century was designed primarily for the purpose of securing custody of political offenders. L. F. L. Oppenheim, *International Law*, ed. H. Lauterpacht (8th ed.; New York, 1957), I, 696 ff.

22. 18 U.S.C. sec. 3185.

23. *Re Castioni* [1891], 1 Q.B. 149; *Ex parte Kolczynski* [1955], 1 Q.B. 540; *R. v. Governor of Brixton Prison, ex parte Schtraks* [1962], 3 All.E.R. 529. Shearer is of the opinion that Australia would follow the United Kingdom in the matter, 583. See Evans, "Reflections upon the Political Offense in International Practice," *Am. Jour. Int. Law*, LVII (1963), 1.

24. *United States ex rel. Karadzole v. Artukovic*, 170 F. Supp. 383 (S.D.Cal. 1959) on remand from Supreme Court, 355 U.S. 393 (1958); *In re Gonzalez*, 217 F. Supp. 717 (S.D.N.Y. 1963); *Matter of K (Family)*, 4 I. and N. Dec. 108 (1950–1953). See Green H. Hackworth, *Digest of International Law* (Washington, D.C., 1943), IV, 45 ff.

decision does involve some sensitivity as to relations with the requesting state which courts do not undertake to assume lightly.[25] The importance of executive discretion in this matter was vigorously stated by the Australian Prime Minister in 1956, with regard to extradition to Eastern European countries:

[Australia] will exercise its discretion under the Extradition Acts and will not grant extradition *unless it is thoroughly satisfied that such a move is not being sought for political purposes*. . . . The Australian Government *has to be convinced* before agreeing to extradition that the application from Eastern European countries is *bona fide* and not a pretext to obtain custody of an individual for other purposes.[26]

This policy was inspired by the Petrov case in 1955 and practiced with regard to the Zielinski case in 1961.[27] These problems of definition and of discretion are particularly troublesome for the new Commonwealth members, especially in Africa where political evolution has different growth rates. Balzac's wry comment that "les conspirateurs vaincus sont des brigands, victorieux ils sont des héros,"[28] is particularly apt in the African context, for these states as with others elsewhere in which political instability is a threat if not a commonplace, concern for the political offender is ambivalent at best.

Rendition under the British Fugitive Offenders Act of 1881 falls somewhere between extradition in international law terms and interstate rendition as practiced in the United States. This paper does not extend to an examination of intra-Commonwealth rendition, but some comment with regard to recent developments is pertinent. In certain of the independent Commonwealth members, the act has been superseded by extradition laws which reflect its terms but attempt to remedy its deficiencies, particularly with regard to the protection of the political offender.[29] The

25. *Re Government of India and Mubarak Ali Ahmad* [1952], 1 All.E.R. 1060.
26. Quoted by Shearer, "Extradition," p. 583 (emphasis Shearer's).
27. *Ibid.*, 592–593.
28. Quoted by Pella, "Draft Code of Offences against the Peace and Security of Mankind," *Yearbook of the Int. Law Comm.*, II (1950), 290.
29. Intra-Commonwealth rendition is still largely governed by the Fugitive Offenders Act, 1881, as amended in 1915, 44 & 45 Vict., c. 69, 5 & 6 Geo. 5, c. 39. Extradition laws: Ghana, sec. 3(1), India, chaps. ii, iii, Sierra Leone, part II. See *Re K.R.P.L. Chockalingam Chettiar*, 1960 Cri.L.J. 1625 (High Ct. Madras). See also, *Re McDougall*, 53 W.W.R. 618 (B.C. 1965). See generally, Clute, "Law and Practice in Commonwealth Extradition," *Am. Jour. Comp. Law*, VIII (1959), 15.

Extradition Act of Sierra Leone contains special provisions regarding Guinea, which taken with the Judicial Convention with Guinea, amount to a bilateral "Fugitive Offenders Act." Rendition of political offenders is recognized; however, this act has a saving clause whereby rendition of a fugitive to Guinea, the Commonwealth states, or non-Commonwealth states may be denied if in the opinion of the appropriate administrative authority rendition "would be contrary to the public policy of Sierra Leone. . . ."[30] In the recent Armah case, Ghana, invoking the Fugitive Offenders Act, sought the rendition from the United Kingdom of an individual charged with corruption and extortion committed while he was a member of the government. Appeal from a dismissal of Armah's application for a writ of habeas corpus was allowed by the House of Lords on two issues, one of which concerned the effect of Ghana's "undertakings" that specialty would be observed, in particular that no political charges would be considered in any trial of the accused. In allowing the appeal, the Judicial Committee noted that on the evidence before the magistrate probable cause had not been established; the majority took a poor view of the use of "undertakings" for special treatment of a fugitive as the price of rendition.[31]

The Enahoro case was instrumental in bringing sharply to public attention the fact that the Fugitive Offenders Act is an anachronism as far as the relations of the independent Commonwealth members are concerned.[32] Apart from unilateral changes in the application of the act as between certain independent members and the United Kingdom,[33] joint action by the independent members looking to new rules of rendition within the Commonwealth was initiated by the Commonwealth Law Minis-

30. Secs. 15(a)(b), 16. See statement of "Objects and Reasons, No. 4" accompanying the act.
31. *Armah* v. *Government of Ghana*, Times (London), August 13, 1966, p. 6, col. 1, reversing [1966] 3 W.L.R. 23.
32. *R.* v. *Brixton Prison Governor, ex parte Enahoro* (No. 2) [1963], 2 Q.B. 455. See Robert R. Wilson, "Some Questions of International Law in Commonwealth Relations," in W. B. Hamilton *et al.*, *A Decade of the Commonwealth, 1955–1964* (Durham, N.C., 1966), pp. 185–186. For a personal account, see Anthony Enahoro, *Fugitive Offender* (London, 1965).
33. Paul O'Higgins, "Recent Practice under the Fugitive Offenders Acts," *Crim. Law Rev.* (1965), p. 133.

ters in 1965. Their 1966 meeting produced a scheme consisting of principles which have been recommended to the members as the bases for new legislation on intra-Commonwealth rendition.[34] The scheme appears to be a compromise between common extradition rules and the provisions of the Fugitive Offenders Act. Although it can hardly be described as innovative in most of its provisions, the scheme does go beyond ordinary extradition treaties or statutes in its definition of the political offense:

> The return of a fugitive offender will be precluded by law if it appears to the competent judicial or executive authority—
> (a) that the request for his surrender although purporting to be made for a returnable offence was in fact made for the purpose of prosecuting or punishing the person on account of his race, religion, nationality or political opinions, or
> (b) that he may be prejudiced at his trial or punished, detained or restricted in his personal liberty by reason of his race, religion, nationality or political opinions.[35]

These provisions would seem to offer clear opportunities for judicial originality in the matter of interpretation. One agrees with O'Higgins that an attempt to improve the present system of intra-Commonwealth rendition is to be commended; however, if the independent Commonwealth members were subsumed to foreign states under the 1870 Extradition Law or their own extradition laws, the desired result could be effected without resort to new legislation under the terms of the scheme.

The treaties under discussion do not contain general provisions regarding double criminality although they do qualify certain offenses with the phrase, "made criminal by the laws of both countries."[36] In extradition practice, however, the rule of double criminality provides a useful argument on behalf of the accused, particularly where, as in the United States, criminal law is under concurrent federal and state jurisdiction. The Factor case is the *casus classicus* of an attempt to take advantage of this situation by

---

34. Scheme Relating to the Rendition of Fugitive Offenders within the Commonwealth. Cmnd. 3008 (1966).

35. Paul O'Higgins, "The Reform of Intra-Commonwealth Extradition," *Crim. Law Rev.* (1966), 361, 365.

36. 1889 treaty, Art. II(4)(10) and participation; 1905 treaty, Art. I(14)(15); 1931 treaty, Art. II(6) and participation; 1951 treaty, Preamble. The Sierra Leone extradition law has a double criminality provision relative to extradition to Guinea, sec. 15(b).

propounding a strict interpretation of double criminality so that extradition could be had only if the offense of receiving money fraudulently obtained was specifically recognized under the law of Illinois where the accused had conveniently found asylum.[37] The Supreme Court in a somewhat strained opinion offered a broad interpretation of double criminality, which accorded with the British contention in the case, taking it to mean that extradition will be granted where "an identified offense is generally recognized as criminal in both countries . . . ," which view the court considered to be consonant with the procedural provisions of Article X of the Webster-Ashburton Treaty which was in force with the United Kingdom at the time of this litigation, and also consistent with United States practice.[38] The qualification of certain offenses in the 1889 treaty by the specific phrase, "made criminal by the laws of both countries," in the opinion of the court further supported this conclusion, the implication being that this phrase had a limiting effect only where used. It may be noted, however, that the phrase is often found in United States extradition treaties as a qualification of certain kinds of offenses, for example, bribery, desertion, embezzlement, fraud, perjury, or receiving property obtained illegally. The use of the phrase is probably predicated on a concern to distinguish the situation in which the same offense may be a misdemeanor in one country and a felony in the other.

The Supreme Court's view of the situation propounded in Factor is at variance with some Canadian cases in which the law of the asylum state has been taken literally as the law of a component part of the United States.[39] The concern of Canadian courts for a strict interpretation of double criminality proved particularly disappointing to the United States in the first case which

---

37. *Factor v. Laubenheimer*, 61 F. 2d 626 (7th Cir. 1932), aff'd. 290 U.S. 276 (1933), but see *In re Factor's Extradition*, 75 F. 2d 10 (7th Cir. 1934).

38. 290 U.S. 276, 298. The court's position is supported by John Bassett Moore in an opinion to the Department of State on the case. U.S. State Dept. MS. File 211.41, Factor, J./207 (1933). See *Wright v. Henkel*, 190 U.S. 40 (1903); *Kelly v. Griffin*, 241 U.S. 6 (1916); *Collins v. Loisel*, 262 U.S. 426 (1923).

39. *Re Collins* (No. 3), 10 *Can. Crim. Cas.* 80 (S. Ct. B.C. 1905); *State of Utah v. Peters*, 2 W.W.R. 9 (D.C. Alta. 1936); *Re Lamar*, 73 *Can. Crim. Cas.* 194 (S. Ct. Alta. 1940); *United States of America v. Link and Green*, 111 *Can. Crim. Cas.* 225, 231 (Sup. Ct. Que. 1954). See La Forest, *Extradition to and from Canada*, p. 124.

arose out of the 1951 supplementary treaty for the control of securities frauds. A Quebec judge, treating the indictments against the accused as a whole, denied extradition on the ground that in the proposed proceedings in the United States, the charges of violations of the Securities Act of 1933 and of mail fraud would be heard together with other charges including "fraudulent telephone calls constituting false pretenses and fraud committed in Canada without using the mails . . . ," which would violate the principle of double criminality.[40] This decision probably reflected the controversy in Canada over the ratification of the 1942 extradition treaty with the United States which included in the provision on sufficiency of evidence the statement that "it shall not be essential to establish that the crime or offense would be a crime or offense under the laws of the requested country."[41] Nonetheless, the 1951 treaty quashed any lingering concern about the sanctity of double criminality by the preambular provision that this treaty covers "any and all frauds which are punishable criminally by the laws of both contracting states, particularly those which occur in connection with transactions in securities. . . ."[42] Several years later, the same judge in Quebec granted extradition on a mail fraud charge, separating this from others comprised in the total indictment.[43] Shearer notes an anomaly which obtains as to double criminality in Australia. It arises from the fact that certain categories of offenses are defined by reference to certain British statutes, which statutes, however, have not been extended to Australia; consequently, the United States, for example, might request extradition for an offense recognized in American law and in the 1931 treaty but not recognized in Australian law.[44]

The main hazard of the system of listing offenses in extradition

40. *United States of America* v. *Link and Green,* 111 Can. Crim. Cas. 225, 233 (Sup. Ct. Que. 1954). The opinion has been criticized as a "gratuitous slur on the federal judiciary" (Loss, *Securities Regulation,* III, 2001–2002). See Timbers and Pollack, "Extradition from Canada," p. 321. Cf. *Bingham* v. *Bradley,* 241 U.S. 511 (1916).
41. Art. IX, U.S. State Dept. MS. File No. 211.42/204.
42. Preamble, 1951 supplementary treaty.
43. *United States of America* v. *Novick,* 128 Can. Crim. Cas. 319 (Sup. Ct. Que. 1960).
44. Shearer, "Extradition," pp. 572, 573.

treaties lies in the difficulty of exact identification of the offense charged by the requesting state with that listed in the treaty, and with that known to the laws of the asylum state. American courts do not tend to look for overly precise definitions. As the Supreme Court pointed out in 1922: "The law does not require that the name by which the crime is described in the countries shall be the same; nor that the scope of the liability shall be coentensive, or, in other respects, the same in the two countries. It is enough if the particular act charged is criminal in both jurisdictions."[45] In *New York State* v. *Kaslov* a Canadian court held that "grand larceny" was a "species" of theft which was comprehended in Canadian law and in the relevant treaty.[46] The objective of the law invoked may be questioned, however, as happened in several Canadian cases involving charges under the Harrison Narcotics Act which the United States Supreme Court had held to be a revenue measure for reasons of constitutional interpretation. Where it was argued that extradition could not be sought for narcotics offenses arising under a statute which was a revenue measure because the treaty did not list the offense of violating revenue laws, the extradition judge held that the act and the Supreme Court's interpretation of it must be considered "as a whole."[47] A year later an attempt to revert to the earlier contention was denied on grounds that American constitutional interpretation of the statute was not a matter of concern to a Canadian court.[48] In the Eisler case the Bow Street Police Court distinguished perjury committed in judicial proceedings from perjury committed in administrative proceedings, holding that the latter offense was not comprehended in the 1931 treaty.[49] As mentioned above, conspiracy to commit an offense against the narcotics laws has been subsumed by Canadian courts to the treaty provisions for offenses against the laws for the suppression of such traffic.[50]

45. *Collins* v. *Loisel*, 259 U.S. 309, 312 (1922).
46. 97 *Can. Crim. Cas.* 146 (Co. Ct. B.C. 1950). Cf. *Re Rosen*, 56 *Can. Crim. Cas.* 162 (S. Ct. B.C. 1931).
47. *Re Gifford* (No. 2), 52 *Can. Crim. Cas.* 293, 295 (K.B. Manitoba 1929).
48. *Re Sieman*, 1 W.W.R. 970; 2 W.W.R. 111, 412 (B.C. 1930).
49. *R.* v. *Eisler*, *Times* (London), May 28, 1949, p. 2a. Art. II(14) of the treaty provides for "perjury, or subornation of perjury."
50. *Re Brisbois*, 133 *Can. Crim. Cas.* 188 (High Ct. Ont. 1962). See also, *Re Devlin* (1964) 3 *Can. Crim. Cas.* 228, 233 (Co. Ct. Ont.).

The principle of specialty is found in the United States treaties with Canada, New Zealand, and the United Kingdom.[51] There is a presumption that the requesting state will not violate the rule; however, the 1870 Extradition Act of the United Kingdom is the prototype for the provision in the extradition statutes of Canada, Ghana, India, New Zealand, and Sierra Leone that extradition will not be granted unless specialty is provided for in the law of the requesting state or in the treaties with the asylum state.[52] In the Novick case denial of extradition was sought on grounds that the accused would be liable to double jeopardy in the United States, for if he were acquitted on the federal charge he would still be triable in New York on a state charge. The court held that the specialty clause in the 1951 treaty answered this argument.[53] *Re Arton* is the British authority for the proposition that an extradition court may not inquire into the judicial proceedings of a requesting state.[54] In an Australian case, it was held that the burden of proof of violation of the specialty rule rested upon the accused.[55] Specialty has been considered to be violated in an American case in which the fugitive was tried for a lesser offense than that for which he had been extradited.[56] The rule does not extend to offenses committed after extradition nor during the course of trial on extradition charges.[57] The possibility of internment as an enemy alien in the United Kingdom to which a German national was to be extradited during World War II led

51. Art. III, 1889 treaty; Art. 7, 1931 treaty. *United States v. Rauscher*, 119 U.S. 407, 422–423 (1886) assumes that specialty will be observed, although the Webster-Ashburton Treaty does not refer to it.

52. Extradition acts: Canada, sec. 33; Ghana, secs. 2(b), 15; India, secs. 21, 31(c); New Zealand, sec. 5(2); Sierra Leone, sec. 18; United Kingdom, sec. 3(2). See *Bingham v. Bradley*, 241 U.S. 511 (1916). In the Tarasov case, an Indian extradition judge rejected the contention that extension of the Extradition Act of 1962 to the Soviet Union (Act No. 4, 1963, *Gazette of India*, Extraordinary Part II, sec. 3(i), constituted an "extradition agreement" within the terms of sec. 31(c) of the 1962 act, which provides that extradition shall be denied unless specialty can be shown to exist in the laws of the requesting state or in its treaties with India (*Ind. Jour. Int. Law*, III [1963], 3).

53. *United States of America v. Novick*, 128 Can. Crim. Cas. 319, 330 (Sup. Ct. Que. 1960).

54. [1896], 1 Q.B. 108, 115.

55. *R. v. Butler* (1897), 18 N.S.W.L.R. 146. It is not clear whether the offender was surrendered by extradition or by informal rendition.

56. *United States v. Rauscher*, 119 U.S. 407 (1886).

57. *Collins v. Johnston*, 237 U.S. 502 (1915); *R. v. Waddell*, 25 N.B.R. 93 (1885).

the Legal Adviser's Office of the Department of State to suggest
that the warrant for surrender draw attention to the provision for
specialty in the 1931 treaty.[58] Specialty cannot be invoked, however, where the accused waives extradition and returns voluntarily to the requesting state.[59]

With regard to extradition procedure, the generalization can be
made that the Canadian, New Zealand, and British agreements
are not dissimilar. Although provisional arrest and detention prior
to formal requisition is not included in them, it is usually provided for by law or by practice.[60] No reference is made in the
treaties to the matter of whether nationals of the asylum state
may be extradited. Following the common law rule of territoriality of crime, nationals are presumably extraditable, but in practice their extradition may be denied as a matter of administrative
discretion, as is customary in Australia, and a contingency which
under the New Zealand Extradition Law of 1965 must be recognized in all treaties concluded after the effective date of that
law.[61] The several treaties make no provision for supplying legal
assistance to the requesting state without charge by judicial
officers of the asylum state, a provision which appears in many
United States treaties with Civil Law states. American diplomatic
or consular officers initiating extradition proceedings under these
treaties must also provide for legal counsel to represent this country at the hearing before the extradition magistrate, a situation
which contributes to the problem of expense which is one of the
main deterrents to the use of extradition for the purpose of international rendition.[62]

58. U.S. State Dept. MS. File No. 211.41, Graham, Alexander/45/47 (1940).
59. *R.* v. *Flannery*, 40 *Can. Crim. Cas.* 263 (S. Ct. Alta. 1923); *R.* v. *Liberty*, 52 *Can. Crim. Cas.* 370 (S. Ct. Alta. 1929); *R.* v. *Gagnon*, 117 *Can. Crim. Cas.* 61 (Que. 1956).
60. United Kingdom, Extradition Act, 1870, sec. 8. See La Forest, *Extradition to and from Canada*, p. 92; Shearer, "Extradition," p. 569.
61. *Re Galwey* [1896], 1 Q.B. 230. New Zealand, Extradition Act, 1965, sec. 5(7). See Shearer, pp. 580–581. See also Ivan A. Shearer, "Non-Extradition of Nationals," *Adelaide Law Rev.*, II (1966), 273–309, at 280.
62. This situation would have been remedied by the terms of the unperfected treaty of 1942 with Canada (State Dept. MS. File No. 211.42/204). In the Rivard case, an attempt to bribe counsel for the United States to agree to the release on bail of a notorious fugitive wanted in the United States for narcotics offenses led to an investigation by a Royal Commission which resulted in the resignation of the

With regard to standards of evidence, the treaties provide that evidence shall be sufficient to justify the arrest and detention for trial of the accused in the asylum state, or where the accused is a convicted person, to prove identity.[63] Sufficiency of the evidence adduced is a matter for the decision of the extradition magistrate. Extradition proceedings are commonly regarded in these countries as constituting a preliminary hearing in which the evidence should warrant committal of the accused for trial in the asylum state. This standard is not the same as sufficiency for conviction.[64] The order for committal may be attacked on a writ of habeas corpus. In habeas corpus proceedings the court can only determine whether the magistrate has jurisdiction of the extradition proceeding and whether any evidence has been adduced by the requesting state which would warrant committal for surrender; habeas corpus cannot be used to review on error.[65] In a recent American case, the accused, who was wanted in Canada for violations of the securities laws, twice sought unsuccessfully to bar extradition by resort to habeas corpus proceedings. His third effort, taking the form of a declaratory judgment action, may have been a pyrrhic victory. The Court of Appeals for the Fifth Circuit holding that a proceeding before an extradition magistrate could be collaterally reviewed by a district court under the Declaratory Judgment Act, noted that the district court was under no obligation to hold another evidentiary hearing if that court were satisfied that there had been full and fair hearings of the issues raised by the petitioner in the two previous habeas corpus proceedings.[66]

Canadian Minister of Justice. Special Public Inquiry 1964. *Report* of the Commissioner the Honorable Frederic Dorion, Chief Justice of the Superior Court for the Province of Quebec (1965).

63. Art. X, 1842 treaty; Art. VII, 1889 treaty; Art. 9, 1931 treaty. Shearer, "Extradition," p. 571. *Re Reddiar* (1962)(2), *Cri. Law Jour.* 697 (High Ct. Madras 1961).

64. *State of New York v. Wilby* (1944), 3 D.L.R. 693 (Ct. App. B.C.); *Re Deakins*, 133 *Can. Crim. Cas.* 275 (High Ct. Ont. 1962).

65. *R. v. Keeper of Cornwall Jail, ex parte Pendergast* [1964], 2 *Can. Crim. Cas.* 264 (High Ct. Ont. 1963); *Novick v. Gearney and Attorney-General of Quebec*, 128 *Can. Crim. Cas.* 333, 338 (Sup. Ct. Que. 1960); *Bryant v. United States*, 167 U.S. 104 (1897); *Collins v. Loisel*, 262 U.S. 426 (1923). See also *R. v. Godfrey* [1923], 1 K.B. 24, 26–27.

66. *Wacker v. Bisson*, 348 F. 2d 602 (5th Cir. 1965).

Informal Rendition

The use of expulsion for what the Indian Supreme Court has characterized as the more "cumbrous procedure" of extradition is one of the commonest types of informal rendition.[67] Both exclusion and expulsion rest upon the right of the state under international law to control the admission of aliens into its territory as well as the duration of their residence therein. Where immigration laws proscribe the admission of the alien sentenced abroad for extradition offenses included among those listed in the British Extradition Acts, 1870–1935, as does the Aliens Order, 1953, or "convicted of a crime involving moral turpitude," as in the United States Immigration and Nationality Act of 1952, he has only limited standing to challenge his exclusion, which, in fact, may deliver him to the authorities of the state of previous residence for prosecution on criminal charges or for the completion of a prison sentence. The element of public policy in any decision on exclusion is reinforced by considerations of international politics. In 1962 the United States, for example, is reported to have asked the United Kingdom, being a port of call for the airline on which Dr. Soblen was returning to the United States from Israel, to bar his entry there.[68] The United Kingdom was willing to oblige an ally; and so began the train of events leading to the order for his deportation, which he frustrated by committing suicide.

Under the expulsion process, the alien usually enjoys more procedural protection than under exclusion. In the United States the alien who is liable to deportation may offer to leave the country voluntarily; he has a limited choice of destination; he may offer the plea of fear of "persecution on account of race, religion, or political opinion" as a bar to expulsion; and he has access to the courts to challenge administrative proceedings held

67. *Muller v. Superintendent, Presidency Jail, Calcutta,* 22 *Int. Law Rep.* 497, 500 (S. Ct. India 1955).

68. New York *Times,* July 2, 1962, p. 1, col. 4 (late city ed.) For American practice regarding informal methods of rendition, see Alona E. Evans, "Acquisition of Custody over the International Fugitive Offender—Alternatives to Extradition: A Survey of United States Practice," *Brit. Year Book Int. Law, 1964,* XL (London, 1966), pp. 77–104.

before immigration authorities.[69] But again, the fact that the alien may be put in jeopardy of criminal process in the destination is no bar to expulsion. This is equally true of British practice as was evident in the Soblen case in which the "public good" was the overriding consideration in the issuance of the deportation order.[70] There are occasional instances in which a British court has recommended that administrative authorities deny expulsion because the alien might be subject to hardship in the destination; however, acceptance of such a recommendation is at the discretion of the home secretary.[71]

The proscription of rendition on political charges is a salient feature of extradition. But the political offender is particularly vulnerable to informal rendition. The British Aliens Order, 1953, and the Canadian Immigration Act of 1952 make no provision for the political offender; however, the United States Immigration and Nationality Act of 1952, as amended, takes some cognizance of the political offender in both exclusion and expulsion.[72] In expulsion proceedings the "Attorney General is authorized to withhold deportation of any alien within the United States to any country in which in his opinion the alien would be subject to persecution on account of race, religion, or political opinion and

69. Immigration and Nationality Act, 1952, secs. 242, 244(e), 243(h), 66 *Stat.* 208, 217, 212; 8 U.S.C. secs. 1252, 1254(e), 1253(h); as amended 79 *Stat.* 918.

70. *R.* v. *Secretary of State for Home Affairs, ex parte Soblen* [1962], 3 All E.R. 373; *R.* v. *Brixton Prison (Governor), ex parte Soblen* [1962], 3 All E.R. 641; Aliens Order, 1953, S.I. 1953 No. 1671 as amended by S.I. 1957 No. 597, sec. 20(2)(b); 664 Hansard, No. 158 (August 2, 1962), cols. 804–807. See Cedric H. R. Thornberry, "Dr. Soblen and the Alien Law of the United Kingdom," *Int. & Comp. Law Quar.*, XII (1963), 414; Paul O'Higgins, "Disguised Extradition: The Soblen Case," *Modern Law Rev.*, XXVII (1964), 521.

71. E.g. *R.* v. *Zausmer* (1911), 7 *Crim. App. R.* 41; *R.* v. *Friedman* (1914), 10 *Crim. App. R.* 72; *R.* v. *Irving* (1920), 15 *Crim. App. R.* 61. *United States, ex rel. Giletti* v. *Commissioner of Immigration*, 35 F. 2d 687 (2d Cir. 1929); *Moraitis* v. *Delaney*, 46 F. Supp. 425 (D. Md. 1942); *Matter of S—C—*, 3 I. and N. Dec. 350 (1949); *Matter of Banjeglav*, Interim Dec. No. 1298, I. and N. Dec. (1963).

72. Aliens Order, 1953, S.I. 1953 No. 1671; Immigration Act, R.S.C. 1952, c. 325. The Aliens Act of 1905, had an exception for persons who could show that they had emigrated in order to avoid religious or political persecution. 5 Edw. 7, c. 13, sec. 1(3). The Immigration and Nationality Act, 1952, exempts the person convicted of a "purely political offense" from the category of the excludable alien. 8 U.S.C. sec. 1182(a)(9)(10). The act was amended in 1965 to provide in terms for "conditional entry" of refugees not to exceed 10,200 per year, including those who have left a communist or communist-dominated country or a country in the Middle East "because of persecution or fear of persecution on account of race, religion, or political opinion," sec. 203(a)(7), 79 *Stat.* 911, 913.

for such period of time as he deems to be necessary for such reason."[73] This provision has several limitations. The burden of proof is on the complainant and is not easy to carry. The attorney general may accept the plea at his discretion. In administrative practice, the phrase "persecuted on account of race, religion, or political opinion" which Congress substituted for "physical persecution" in this section of the law in 1965, is as likely to be as rigorously interpreted as was the latter expression before its deletion. In some non-Commonwealth cases, the Board of Immigration Appeals rejected the plea as a bar to expulsion where it was made by a person who maintained that his long criminal record in the United States would subject him in the state of destination to severe restrictions upon his freedom; where the alien would be subject to prosecution for an offense against the laws of the state of destination; or where the alien feared potential persecution because of his opposition to the political organization in power in the state of destination.[74]

The long border between Canada and the United States and the long history of friendly relations between these two countries have contributed to the development of "close liaison" between their respective immigration officials for the purpose of controlling the use of their territories as havens by criminal elements. The annual report of the Immigration and Naturalization Service for 1965, for example, illustrates this relationship by listing seven cases of deportation to Canada of fugitives charged with offenses ranging from armed robbery to attempted murder.[75] In more than one instance Canadian authorities have notified American officials that a prisoner, known to be a fugitive from justice in the United States, would be deported upon completion of his

73. *79 Stat.* 918.
74. *Matter of Bufalino,* Interim Dec. No. 1517, I. and N. Dec. (1965); *Matter of Perez,* Interim Dec. No. 1351, I. and N. Dec. (1964); *Dunat v. Hurney,* 297 F. 2d 744 (3d Cir. 1961), and cases cited therein.
75. *Immigration and Naturalization Service Ann. Rep.,* 1965, pp. 9–10. Canada is currently reported to be a haven for "draft dodgers" from the United States, which is an unextraditable offense. New York *Times,* September 15, 1966, p. 8, col. 1 (city ed.). See also, the LeClerc case, in which four robbery suspects fled from jail in Winnipeg and flew to the United States in a stolen airplane. They were captured in Indiana and held for Canadian police. New York *Times,* September 5, 1966, p. 6, col. 1 (city ed.).

sentence and have forwarded to the United States information on the time and place of his departure from Canada.[76] Expulsion can be justified as a relatively inexpensive and practical alternative to extradition which has the further advantage of being available where extradition is not possible, as where the offense charged is not a treaty offense.[77] While the United States does not appear to consider expulsion a policy alternative to extradition today, nevertheless as between the United States and Canada, it has developed into a form of rendition not dissimilar to intra-Commonwealth rendition.

The Ker rule that a court's jurisdiction over the accused may not be ousted on the ground that the accused was brought under that jurisdiction irregularly is generally recognized in American and Commonwealth practice.[78] The main recourse for the fugitive is a suit for false arrest against the kidnappers, which in the circumstances is an unlikely move. The asylum state, if it feels aggrieved by the incident, has a choice among alternatives: it may protest through the diplomatic channel, seek the extradition of the kidnappers, or demand the return of the victim, as was reported to have occurred in the Higgs incident between Northern Rhodesia and the Union of South Africa in 1964.[79] There have been occasional instances of kidnapping across the Canadian–United States border. In the Unverzagt case, following Ker, the method was not admitted as ground for discharge of the petitioner on a writ of habeas corpus.[80] In the Mertz-Vaccaro incident, Canada's request for extradition of Vaccaro on the

76. U.S. State Dept. MS. File No. 242.11, Finkelstein, Sam (1937); U.S. State Dept. MS. File No. 242.11, Rosenthal, Jerome (1940); U.S. State Dept. MS. File No. 242.11, McNaughton, Edwin (1935).

77. U.S. State Dept., MS. File No. 242.11, Ryan, Emmet V. (Canada 1938); U.S. State Dept., MS. File No. 248.11, Long, John M. (Union of South Africa 1932); U.S. State Dept. MS. File No. 211.44 h Sm 6 (Jamaica 1917). See cases mentioned in *Immigration and Naturalization Service Ann. Rep.* 1954, 45; 1962, 9. See also U.S. State Dept., MS. File No. 341A.113, Drake Estate (United Kingdom 1932).

78. *Ker v. Illinois*, 119 U.S. 436 (1886). See also *Ex parte Scott*, 9 B. & C. 446 (1829). Shearer notes with O'Higgins that no British court, or Australian court, is bound by precedent to follow this rule. Shearer, "Extradition," p. 567.

79. New York *Times*, September 3, 1964, p. 3, col. 1 (int. ed.).

80. *United States v. Unverzagt*, 299 F. 1015 (W.D. Wash. 1924), aff'd. *sub nom. Unverzagt v. Benn*, 5 F. 2d 492 (9th Cir. 1925), *cert. den.*, 269 U.S. 566 (1925).

charge of forcibly abducting a Canadian national across the border in order to subject him to prosecution under United States narcotics laws was sustained judicially but denied administratively because of uncertainty as to the *locus* of the offense.[81] Although the validity of jurisdiction *in personam* effected through kidnapping may be sustained under the Ker rule, some modification of this rule should emerge as part of the overall concern for protection of the rights of the accused.

Conclusion

We have covered considerable ground geographically and in terms of subject matter while staying within the bounds of international rendition of fugitive offenders as seen in the relations of the United States with some of the independent members of the Commonwealth. Inevitably, the qualified statement has been sacrificed to generalization. A few more generalizations may be offered in conclusion.

Despite their individual differences, the states in the common-law tradition show considerable similarity in their practice of extradition. New departures may be expected of the new states, but in regard to extradition, one may hazard a guess that they will not depart far from the established practice. In the use of informal methods of rendition by the United States and the independent Commonwealth states, whether these have evolved through amicable relations as between the United States and Canada or been established in law as in intra-Commonwealth rendition or in the relation between Sierra Leone and Guinea, there can be discerned an uneasy awareness that the fugitive offender is something more than a pawn between states. The fact that the Commonwealth Law Ministers' Scheme borrows much from international extradition law may presage a general trend toward increasing use of extradition, and certainly, it reflects a widespread contemporary concern for the protection of the individual in this aspect of the criminal law.

81. *Vaccaro v. Collier*, 38 F. 2d 862 (D. Md. 1930), aff'd. in part and rev'd. in part 51 F. 2d 17 (4th Cir. 1931); see Hackworth, *Digest*, IV, 161–163.

7

Extraterritorial Application of Antitrust Legislation as Viewed from the Standpoint of Commonwealth States

Ivan R. Feltham*

Antitrust legislation is now an important part of the legal systems of most of the major trading nations.[1] The increasing bulk of legislation evidences widespread agreement on at least broad principles, although methods of enforcement and details vary.[2] The economies of the nations with antitrust legislation, all being major trading nations, are interrelated and interdependent, and the area of economic activity of each country overlaps those of the others. Conflict of jurisdiction to regulate economic activity is therefore inevitable. Actual or potential conflict, or extraterritorial application of antitrust legislation, is, however, but one aspect of complex legislation designed primarily to maintain a desirable level of competition within a national economy. This essay deals

* Baker and McKenzie, Chicago; formerly of the faculty of Osgoode Hall Law School, Toronto. The assistance of Mr. Peter J. H. Bentley, solicitor (England and Wales) and attorney (Illinois), Mr. Peter B. Powles, barrister (England), attorney and solicitor (New South Wales), barrister and solicitor (Victoria) and attorney (Illinois), and Mr. Premjit Singh, advocate (India), all of Baker & McKenzie, Chicago, is gratefully acknowledged.

1. The term "antitrust" will be used as a convenient reference to the full range of legislation on restrictive trade practices and monopolies.

2. See Corwin D. Edwards, *Trade Regulation Overseas, The National Laws* (Dobbs Ferry, N.Y., 1966), and *Control of Cartels and Monopolies, An International Comparison* (Dobbs Ferry, N.Y., 1967); U.S. Senate Committee on the Judiciary, Subcommittee on Antitrust and Monopoly, "Antitrust Development and Regulation of Foreign Countries," 1965 (Part 2 of "Foreign Trade and the Antitrust Laws," Senate Hearings pursuant to S. Res. 40, 89th Congress); *ibid.*, Hearings pursuant to S. Res. 191, 89th Congress, "International Aspects of Antitrust"; O.E.C.D., *Restrictive Trade Practices Legislation in Europe and North America*, looseleaf, current.

only with questions of extraterritoriality or conflict, but the broader context of the discussion should be borne in mind.

Experience to date in connection with conflict of legislative jurisdiction in antitrust matters has involved largely the enforcement of United States law and reaction to its enforcement in the United Kingdom and Canada, among Commonwealth countries, and in certain European countries, most recently in connection with attempts by the Federal Maritime Commission to inquire fully into international shipping practices. Because of the increasing importance of legislation against restrictive trade practices, and because of increasing concern about the reach of United States legislative power, the pressing need is for a definition of the proper limits of the exercise of national power. In this connection, reference should be made to the continuing work of the Committee of the International Law Association on the Extraterritorial Application of Restrictive Trade Legislation. The subject was discussed extensively at the meeting of the committee at the Helsinki Conference of the International Law Association in August, 1966, and at the Tokyo Conference in 1964.[3] As a result of such work, principles are emerging but as yet have not received formal recognition by international agreement or in national laws.

This article is a survey of the law and practice, the possibilities and prospects for extraterritorial extension of the laws, of four principal trading nations of the British Commonwealth, namely, Australia, Canada, India, and the United Kingdom. It is hoped that from this survey will emerge at least some indication of the type of action to be expected from those countries in the application of their laws, which laws are operative in the case of Canada and the United Kingdom, imminent in the case of Australia, and perhaps some distance in the future in the case of India. The laws and practices so identified, we can probably assume that they

3. International Law Association, *Report of the Fifty-First Conference* (Tokyo, 1964), p. 304. The printed report of the Tokyo Conference contains no less than 289 pages of invaluable material on the subject. It was also discussed at the Mexico City Conference of the International Bar Association in 1964 and at the Lausanne Conference of the IBA in July of 1966. It is to be hoped that participation of Commonwealth countries, in addition to the United Kingdom whose members have been active, in the important work of the ILA committee will increase.

give an important indication of the position which may be taken by those countries to the extent that they are active in the formulation of principles of international law. My purpose is thus to make a contribution to the international perspective which has to date focused heavily on reactions to United States power.[4]

The common legal heritage of the countries to be discussed allows us to summarize at the outset certain general principles of law which have application in those countries. Their precise formulation would undoubtedly be a matter for at least discussion and perhaps dispute among constitutional lawyers of the states involved. However, some formulation may provide a useful guideline and I offer the following:

1. Subject to constitutional division of legislative authority within the nation and certain other constitutional matters, Parliament is unfettered in its legislative power. When Parliament has enacted a rule, the courts are bound to give effect to it, the only limitation being the application of rules of interpretation when Parliament's intent is not clearly expressed.

2. In the absence of a clear expression of intent by Parliament, the courts have applied a general principle of interpretation that Parliament will be presumed to have intended to confine legislation to acts within the territory of the state and to its citizens with respect to their acts outside the state. The scope of the latter is unclear.

There is some reactive legislation, passed to curtail the reach of the United States law, specifically, the Business Records Protection Act of Ontario[5] and the Shipping Contracts and Commercial Documents Act, 1964 (United Kingdom).[6] These statutes do not set out general principles but confine themselves to the "protection" of what are thought to be local interests. There is also some reactive jurisprudence, again responsive to the reach of United States law—*British Nylon Spinners Ltd.* v. *Imperial Chemical Industries Ltd.*[7] There is no parallel to the principles developed

---

4. I am informed that the discussions at the Helsinki Conference of the ILA were characterized by a more general international approach.
5. Revised Statutes of Ontario, 1960, chap. 44.
6. United Kingdom Statutes, 1964, chap. 87.
7. [1953], chap. 19; [1955], chap. 37.

in United States cases which stop the application of United States law short of requiring contravention of the positive law of a foreign nation with regard to acts within that nation.[8] This state of Commonwealth law results from the fact that the statutes of the Commonwealth nations, either because of restraint on the part of administrative authorities or by accident of history, have not collided with the laws of foreign states. Apart from Canada, active enforcement of antitrust legislation is a relatively new experience for Commonwealth states, and this undoubtedly accounts for the fact that there is little jurisprudence. Enforcement of the Canadian law has been confined to purely domestic activities. However, the recent report of the Restrictive Trade Practices Commission on shipping conference arrangements and practices would apply the provisions of the Canadian Combines Investigation Act to the activities of the North Atlantic Conferences insofar as they touch shipping *both to and from* Canada and may presage a broadening of Canadian jurisdiction.[9]

Of the countries to be surveyed here, Canada has the oldest comprehensive antitrust legislation and Canadian law will therefore be considered first. The United Kingdom legislation has developed more recently and will be considered second. Australia will shortly bring new legislation into force and consideration of its law will follow that of the United Kingdom, to be followed in turn by a review of the legislation proposed by the Monopolies Inquiry Commission in India, where there is as yet no antitrust statute.

Canada

General Principles of Jurisdiction over Subject Matter. The Extraterritorial Act of Canada provides that

8. *U.S.* v. *Imperial Chemical Industries Ltd.*, 100 F. Supp. 504 (S.D.N.Y. 1951); 105 F. Supp. 215 (1952), and the Swiss Watchmakers case, final judgment January 22, 1964, 1963 Trade Cases, par. 70,600; modified February 7, 1965, 1965 Trade Cases, par. 71,352. In the final analysis, the latter became a matter of bilateral international agreement.

9. Canada, Restrictive Trade Practices Commission, "Shipping Conference Arrangements and Practices," 1965.

every Act of the Parliament of Canada now in force enacted prior to the 11th day of December, 1931 [the date of the Statute of Westminster], that in terms or by necessary or reasonable implication was intended, as to the whole or any part thereof to have extraterritorial operation, shall be construed as if at the date of its enactment the Parliament of Canada then had full power to make laws having extraterritorial operation as provided by the Statute of Westminster, 1931.[10]

In the *Cooperative Committee on Japanese-Canadians* v. *Attorney General for Canada*, the Judicial Committee of the Privy Council declared that "any lingering doubts as to the validity in law of an Act which for its effectiveness requires extraterritorial application were, it may be added, set at rest by the Canadian statute, the Extraterritorial Act, 1933."[11]

The historical difficulty resulted from the fact that the power of the colonial legislatures was limited insofar as extraterritoriality of legislation was concerned. However, any such limitation on the Canadian Parliament was removed by the Statute of Westminster, and this legal effect was made retroactive by the Canadian Act which followed shortly after, and was confirmed by judicial interpretation as set out in the decision of the board in the Japanese-Canadians case quoted above and, at about the same time, in *British Columbia Electric Railway Company Ltd.* v. *The King*,[12] in which Viscount Simon, speaking for the board, said

A legislature which passes a law having extraterritorial operation may find that what it has enacted is not invalid on that account and the courts of the country must enforce the law with the machinery available to them . . . the effect of the Statute of Westminster upon § 91 of the B.N.A. Act head 3, is to make the head read: "The raising of money by any mode or system of taxation, even though such laws have an extraterritorial effect."[13]

In the Exchequer Court, Thorson J. stated:

There is a presumption that Parliament does not assert or assume jurisdiction which goes beyond the limits established by the common consent of nations. And it is a rule that statutes are to be interpreted,

10. Revised Statutes of Canada, 1952, chap. 107, sec. 2. The Extra-Territorial Act was first enacted in 1932/33, chap. 38, sec. 3.
11. [1946], A.C. 87, 104.   12. [1946], A.C. 527.
13. *Ibid.*, p. 543.

provided that their language admits, so as not to be inconsistent with the comity of Nations.[14]

In summary, Canadian law adopts the general rule that Parliament has unlimited power but that acts will be interpreted to have extraterritorial application unless the appropriate intention is evident in the terms of the statute.

There is a substantial volume of jurisprudence, including decisions of the Judicial Committee of the Privy Council, dealing with the relation between "international law" and Canadian "municipal law," but I have discovered no cases dealing with economic relations or specifically with the extent of jurisdiction over subject matter under antitrust law. The bulk of the material relates to territorial waters, customs, and collisions at sea.[15] It falls within or is analogous to the areas of experience covered by the statement of Lord MacMillan in *Croft* v. *Dunphy*[16] that "it has long been recognized that for certain purposes, notably those of police, revenue, public health and fisheries, a state may enact laws affecting the seas surrounding its coast to a distance seaward which exceeds the ordinary limits of its territory."[17]

The decision of the Canada Labour Relations Board in the case of the Seafarers International Union of North America (applicant) and Iron and Ore Transport Co. (respondent) and National Union of Seamen (intervener) *et al.*,[18] affords an instructive illustration of judicial or quasi-judicial treatment of Canadian legislation. The case involved application by the unions for certification as the bargaining agent for units of employees of the

14. 2 Dominion Tax Cases 692, 698 (1945).
15. See Jean Gabriel Castel, *International Law, Chiefly as Interpreted and Applied in Canada* (Toronto, 1965), pp. 554 ff.
16. [1933], A.C. 156.
17. His Lordship went on to deal with the legislative power of the Parliament of Canada. He referred to sec. 3 of the Statute of Westminster, 1931, in the following observation:

> Their Lordships' attention was drawn to s. 3 of the Statute of Westminster, 1931, by which it is "declared and enacted that the Parliament of a Dominion has full power to make laws having extra-territorial operation," and it was suggested that this section had retrospective effect. In the view which their Lordships have taken of the present case it is not necessary to say anything on this point beyond observing that the question of the validity of extra-territorial legislation by the Dominion cannot at least arise in the future.

18. CCH Canadian Labour Law Reporter, 1955–59, No. 16,075.

respondents. The two companies named in the application as owners of the vessels were incorporated under the Companies Act of Canada. The vessels were registered in the United Kingdom and operated under management agreements with an English company under which the latter supplied the masters and crews for the vessels. The owner companies controlled the destination of the vessels and the nature of the work.

During a period in 1956, the vessels were engaged continuously in Canadian waters carrying iron ore from Sept Iles to Contrecoeur in the Province of Quebec. Although this was a regular run, the vessels occasionally delivered ore to ports outside Canada when the hoppers at Contrecoeur were full. From about the end of the navigation season in the St. Lawrence River in the late fall of 1956, the vessels were engaged in other waters entirely outside Canada.

The evidence indicated that of the crews of the vessels there was only one man who was a Canadian and practically all the rest from the masters down were British. All were engaged in England to serve on the vessels and were signed on under the Merchant Shipping Act of 1894 (United Kingdom).

The board stated its reasons for refusing the application, as follows:

In the Board's opinion the terms of the Industrial Relations and Disputes Investigation Act are wide enough to enable the Board to exercise jurisdiction in respect of the crews of these vessels, but two vital questions remain. Is the Board required to exercise jurisdiction, and if not, do the circumstances of this case disclose a situation in which the Board should exercise jurisdiction?

The rules of International Law have a bearing on these questions and require consideration. In the first place, Canadian law recognizes the rule of International Maritime Law that the nationality of a ship is determined not by the nationality of its owner but by the state in which it is registered and whose flag it flies. Under this rule these ships, therefore, are to be regarded as British ships not Canadian ships. By Canadian as well as International Law Canadian courts have no jurisdiction over the ships and crews of other states except when they are within Canadian territorial waters. Again under International Law, recognized by Canada, one state through its courts or otherwise, for reasons of comity, may and usually does refuse to exercise jurisdiction over the ships and crews of another state while in the territorial waters of the first, in respect of many matters and particularly in respect of matters of internal management or discipline or relations between the master and crew. Labour relations are included within the terms "internal management" and "relations between the master and crew."

This being the position in International Law, the further question arises: Does the Industrial Relations and Disputes Investigation Act require the Board to exercise jurisdiction under the circumstances of this case? Unless the wording used by Parliament clearly indicates a contrary intention, the courts of Canada interpret legislation in accordance with the rules of International Law. The Board has found nothing in the Industrial Relations and Disputes Investigation Act which requires the Board to exercise jurisdiction where International Law for reasons of comity would justify refusal to do so. The board has therefore come to the conclusion that while it possesses jurisdiction to deal with applications affecting the crews of these vessels, it may in its discretion refuse to exercise jurisdiction. . . .

The Board has come to the conclusion that the case is one in which for reasons of comity, it should decline to exercise jurisdiction. The applications are therefore refused.

Although the regulation of labor relations in the circumstances clearly involves many peculiarities of those circumstances, the case does afford an interesting example of possible collision of jurisdiction and avoidance of it in a manner which at least does no damage to the development of rational principles of international law, whatever may have been the practical result regarding the regulation of labor relations on the Great Lakes.

A similar decision was reached by the Supreme Court of the United States in *McCulloch* v. *Sociedad de Marineros de Honduras*.[19] In that case, Justice Clarke concluded:

The presence of such highly charged international circumstances brings to mind the admonition of Mr. Chief Justice Marshall in The Charming Betsy, (U.S.) 2 Cranch 64, 118, 2 L. Ed. 208 226 (1804), that "an act of Congress ought never to be construed to violate the law of nations if any possible construction remains. . . ." We therefore conclude, as we did in Benz, that for us to sanction the exercise of local sovereignty under such conditions in this "delicate field of international relations there must be present the affirmative intention of the

19. 83 S. Ct. 671; 372 U.S. 10 (1963).

Congress clearly expressed." 353 U.S., at 147, 77 S. Ct., at 704, 1 L. Ed. 2d 709. Since neither we nor the parties are able to find any such clear expression we hold that the Board was without jurisdiction to order the election.[20]

On the question of the proper scope of inquiry to discover possible non-compliance with Canadian law, a decision in the tax field is instructive. In *Canadian Bank of Commerce* v. *Attorney General of Canada*[21] the Assistant Deputy Minister of National Revenue for Taxation, acting on behalf of the Minister of National Revenue and relying on Section 126(2) of the Income Tax Act, addressed a requirement to the bank to produce information and documents relating to the accounts of the Union Bank of Switzerland, a customer of the bank. Section 126(2) provides that "the Minister may, for any purpose related to the administration or enforcement of this Act . . . require from *any person* any information . . . including a return of income or a supplementary return, or production . . . of any books, letters, accounts, invoices, statements (financial or otherwise) or other documents."[22]

The bank's tax liability was not under investigation and the result of compliance with the requirement would be to disclose much private information in respect of the business and affairs of many corporations and individuals both resident and non-resident, some of whom were not under investigation and might not be subject to tax. It was admitted that the requirement related to a genuine and serious inquiry into the tax liability of specific persons and that the minister had reason to believe that the persons were among those concerning whom information would be disclosed by compliance with the requirements. Various arguments were advanced by counsel for the bank which would result in limiting the power to require the disclosure of information under the Income Tax Act. However, the Supreme Court of Canada affirmed the lower courts in holding that the required information must be disclosed. The reasoning of the court appears to be confined to consideration of principles of domestic administrative law and the interpretation of the statute in ques-

20. 372 U.S. 10, 21–22. 21. 35 D.L.R. 2d 49 (1962).
22. Emphasis added.

tion and to show no concern at all for the possible extraterritorial application of the Income Tax Act. Of course, in the circumstances, the Department of National Revenue was seeking only records of a Canadian company maintained in Canada.[23] However, by virtue of the fact that the head office of the bank was notified by its branches of all accounts in the name of its customer at any of its branches whether domestic or foreign, transactions having no connection with Canada other than the fact of their being recorded there at the head office of a Canadian banking corporation were brought within the purview of the order.

In the field of antitrust law, as in some other fields, the dicussion in Canada has been reactive in nature. This is reflected in at least one piece of legislation, namely, the Business Records Protection Act of Ontario,[24] which prohibits the removal from Ontario of business records "pursuant to or under or in a manner that would be consistent with compliance with any requirement, order, direction or subpoena of any legislative, administrative or judicial authority in any jurisdiction outside Ontario." Exception is made, as one would expect, for the normal flow of records between parts of a corporate structure, provision of information in connection with public offerings of shares with the consent of the persons involved, and for cases specifically provided by any law of Ontario or of the Parliament of Canada. The statute was enacted in response to American investigations into certain aspects of the pulp and paper industry.[25]

Canadian Legislation: The Combines Investigation Act.[26] Section 32, dealing with horizontal agreements, contains no reference to the territorial or other limits of the jurisdiction. It is framed in the usual broad language which includes "every one" who does any of the prescribed things. Section 32(4) does refer to the terri-

23. Cf. *Application of Chase Manhattan Bank* 297 F. 2d 611 (C.C.A. 2d 1962).
24. R.S.O. 1960, chap. 44.
25. There are numerous instances of complaint about the extraterritorial reach of United States law. In the antitrust field, see Ivan R. Feltham, "The Canadian Radio Patents Case and the Peat Moss Case," *U.B.C. Law Rev.*, I (1960), 340. For a general discussion, see Kingman Brewster, *Law and United States Business in Canada* (Montreal, 1960), and John Lindeman and Donald Armstrong, *Policies and Practices of United States Subsidiaries in Canada* (Montreal, 1961).
26. Revised Statutes of Canada, 1952, chap. 314, as amended.

tory of Canada in that it exempts combinations relating only to the export of articles from Canada. Section 32(5), which limits the export exemption, likewise refers to "exports" and "export business," which by necessary implication must refer to the geographical territory of Canada and to the "exporting of articles from Canada."

Section 33—which prohibits mergers and monopolies as defined in Section 2(e) and (f), respectively—and these definitions themselves are general in wording and contain no indication of territorial limitation. Section 33A, dealing with discriminatory prices, does in Subsection 1(b) restrict the offense to discrimination in prices between one area of Canada and another with certain effects and for certain purposes, but contains no indication of territorial limitation with respect to the seller's place of business. Section 33B, dealing with discriminatory allowances, contains no territorial reference. Similarly Section 33C, which deals with misleading advertising, and Section 34, which prohibits resale price maintenance, subject to certain defenses such as cutting off supplies to a dealer who uses articles as loss leaders, contain no territorial restriction. The miscellaneous offenses set out in Part VI of the act (failing to comply with orders of the commission, impeding an inquiry under the act, etc.) are framed in general terms capable of application to the world.

There being nothing in the act, with the minor exceptions noted, to limit its application in terms of jurisdiction over subject matter, we are left with such general principles of Canadian law as exist to determine the scope of the act. These have been discussed above and leave us very little in the way of established principle.

Mr. D. H. W. Henry, Q.C., the director of investigation and research under the Combines Investigation Act, dealt with the application of the act to international trade in his address to the Section of Antitrust Law of the American Bar Association at its meeting in Montreal in August, 1966.[27] He emphasized that "companies carrying on activities in Canada are subject to the Combines Investigation Act regardless of nationality of corporate

27. Mimeo. text, pp. 25–32. See American Bar Association.

ownership." He went on to mention several factors which he said should be borne in mind and emphasized the fact that

in a small market the size of Canada, the impact of the large international firm can be relatively great and is likely to be more significant in any given industry than would be the case in the United States with its considerably larger markets and industrial structure. A decision made by the large international firm to change its competitive policy in the Canadian market, or to refuse its Canadian subsidiary the right to penetrate export markets in which the parent is interested, can have a significant effect upon the state of competition in the Canadian economy. The same may be said of a decision abroad by such a firm to withhold supplies from the Canadian market to protect a related company in Canada, or pursuant to an international cartel agreement. The point I emphasize is that because of the relatively small size of the Canadian market, decisions by large international firms can have a much greater relative impact on competition in Canada than would be the case in the context of the much larger United States market.

He did not elaborate fully on the extent of Canadian jurisdiction to protect Canadian interest in free competition in the Canadian economy.[28] He did say however that

it must also be remembered that when the decision-making power is shifted abroad, as would be the case where a foreign company acquires a Canadian company and retains active control of policy, questions of jurisdiction arise and the problem may become insoluble if decisions or activities complained of in fact take place in the foreign country and are executed by a foreign company over which Canadian courts do not have jurisdiction. A very simple example is the *Surgical Supplies Case*[29] which involved resale price maintenance in Canada by an American company selling the product in Canada through a manufacturer's agent. There being no plant or office of the manufacturer in Canada, it was not possible to charge the company with the offence and it became necessary to charge the manufacturer's agent who was within the territorial jurisdiction of Canada, and he was duly convicted and sentenced.[30] Somewhat analogous problems may arise, al-

28. He was, of course, explaining the act and not exploring the limits of legislative jurisdiction which Parliament might have exercised.

29. *R. v. Campbell* [1964], 2 O.R. 487 (appeal to Supreme Court of Canada dismissed).

30. The desired effect of protecting the Canadian market was presumably achieved, and the prosecution limited to the person who acted within Canadian territory.

though they do not necessarily arise, in connection with the shifting abroad of decision-making pursuant to a merger or joint venture.

A brief look at several hypothetical situations may serve to clarify the issues. Let us consider mergers involving the following circumstances.

(a) Two American companies who are competitors each have a Canadian subsidiary. The American parents merge, one acquiring control over the other. The two Canadian subsidiaries immediately come under common control and by direction of the parent harmonize their policies. The net effect would *prima facie* be the elimination or serious impairment of the former competition between them. Unless a monopoly is thus created in the Canadian market this situation would not appear to be capable of enforcement or correction under the Combines Act.[31] The Canadian companies are not parties to a merger, nor do they necessarily act in collusion with each other, and in any event it is doubtful whether either of the subsidiaries could, in law, successfully be convicted of a conspiracy either with the parent or with each other.

(b) An American company physically located in the United States acquires a Canadian company physically located in Canada. Here the merger may well be said to be consummated in Canada, although control is shifted to the United States. The effect on competition in the Canadian market will depend upon the facts of the particular case. The result of the merger may merely be to substitute one competitor for another and competition may be unaffected; alternatively, competition may be sharpened by reason of control of the Canadian company shifting to a more imaginative and aggressive competitor who will inject new vigour into the market. Indeed, this may very well occur. However, if the acquiring company was formerly exporting into the Canadian market in competition with the Canadian company, the merger may have the effect of eliminating a competitor since it is unlikely that the American parent would both produce goods through its Canadian subsidiary and export goods to Canada as before. If the acquired Canadian company is not a competitor but a supplier or an outlet, a detrimental effect on competition in the Canadian market may result by the foreclosure of the source of supply or the outlet to competing firms. In either case, competition could be lessened to the detriment of the public within the meaning of the merger provision. This situation, which has not as yet given rise to an inquiry in Canada, poses legal problems in effective enforcement. In such a case, consideration would be given to accomplishing a *de facto* divestiture indi-

31. That is, as the act now stands. That is not to say that principles of jurisdiction would prevent its extension to the situation the Director is discussing.

rectly by obtaining an injunctive order directed to the Canadian subsidiary. Proceedings could not, of course, be taken directly against the parent which is outside the territorial jurisdiction of Canada.[32]

(c) A Canadian company located in Canada acquires an American company located in the United States. Here the merger presumably takes place in the United States and primarily affects competition in the United States market. This would not be of concern to the Combines Branch unless the effect of the merger were to lessen competition in the Canadian market, as for example, by significant limitation of previously existing import competition from the American company which by reason of the merger and the policy of the new Canadian parent is eliminated or seriously impaired. If that should occur and the impairment of competition was of the degree sufficient to constitute a breach of the merger provision, in my view the Canadian authorities could proceed against the Canadian parent with the object of seeking a divestiture.

Turning now to joint ventures, we find some corresponding situations.

(a) Two American companies in the United States, competing with each other, form a joint venture in the Canadian market. They jointly form a new company in Canada. Any competition that existed previously between the two companies in the Canadian market now has disappeared. If this is significant, it may be detrimental to the public. However, as I see it, the Combines Act may not be capable of effective enforcement, particularly if proceedings would have to be initiated against the parties to the joint venture which are abroad, outside the territorial jurisdiction of Canada. Whether proceedings could succeed against the jointly formed Canadian company for conspiring with its parent organizations, would have to be tested in Canadian courts. The joint venture might, of course, operate through Canadian subsidiaries of the two parties to the joint venture. They may clearly be guilty of conspiracy; it is also possible that although an express agreement is avoided, there may arise between the two Canadian subsidiaries an unlawful understanding or tacit agreement sufficient to attract an inquiry and subsequent legal proceedings. Should the effect of the joint venture be to produce in Canada a company falling within the definition of monopoly in the Combines Act, proceedings might then be taken against the monopoly if it is operated to the detriment of the public. The decision-makers controlling the joint venture in these circumstances (monopoly) have it within their power so to conduct the enterprise that it does not give rise to such a challenge.

32. There would undoubtedly be individuals in Canada who participate in causing detrimental effects in the Canadian market and they could be reached by appropriately framed legislation.

Perhaps I should add that to the extent that the joint venture is viewed as a conspiracy or agreement in restraint of trade, any overt act in furtherance of the conspiracy that takes place in Canada would give Canadian courts jurisdiction over the persons doing the act as a party to the conspiracy. Let me again remind you that, to be unlawful, the agreement must have the object or effect of limiting competition unduly and that according to the tests laid down by the Canadian jurisprudence under section 32 of the Act, the parties to the agreement must account for a substantial segment of the market before the agreement is tainted with illegality.

(b) A joint venture takes place between an American company and a Canadian company. If the effect of the joint venture is to limit competition unduly, within the meaning of section 32 of the Combines Act, in relation to the Canadian market, then this would give rise to an inquiry and subsequent legal proceedings under the Combines Act. The Canadian company being within the territorial jurisdiction of Canadian courts, it can be brought before those courts as a party to the offence, notwithstanding that its American partner in the joint venture could not unless it also is physically present within Canadian territory.

The foregoing is necessarily somewhat theoretical and speculative in view of the fact that, as I have previously indicated, such a small number of merger cases have reached the Canadian courts, and no cases of joint ventures have been dealt with by Canadian courts. *The principles that I have outlined, however, would be those that would guide me, as Director under the Combines Investigation Act, in determining whether or not a formal inquiry should be undertaken into any such merger or joint venture.*[33]

It should be emphasized that the Director was discussing the Combines Investigation Act as it now exists. The act may not fully exploit Canadian jurisdiction. The Canadian Parliament could probably go some distance toward control over the illustrative cases without offending international law notions of the proper extent of jurisdiction.

I venture the suggestion that the difficulty described by the Director in merger illustration (a) is not a question of jurisdiction, because he supposes a situation in which the Canadian subsidiaries harmonize their policies. Whether the Canadian subsidiaries act through Canadian resident officers or directors or are

33. Emphasis added.

directed in all respects from abroad, there is at least a tacit agreement between the separate legal entities. If the subsidiaries could not be convicted of conspiracy in the circumstances, as concluded by the Director, it is not a question of the proper reach of Canadian antitrust law but simply a question of the substance of it even in its purely domestic operation. Again, in his merger illustration (b) the defects seem to be in domestic Canadian law rather than a result of international jurisdictional notions. All the illustrations involve some sort of activity within Canada, and therefore it seems that there can hardly be any objection to the assertion of jurisdiction over the actors to carry out the agreement in Canada.

Further, the form of the organization should not be a bar to effective implementation of the law—the difficulty presented by withdrawal of the two competing companies in illustration (a) about joint ventures and the substitution of a single new Canadian company could be overcome by a change in the statute without any offense to principles of international jurisdiction.

A significant development in connection with the possible extraterritorial application of the Canadian Act is the Report of the Restrictive Trade Practices Commission on "Shipping Conference Arrangements and Practices."[34] The inquiry arose out of the "Helga Dan" incident. The motor vessel "Helga Dan" was specifically fitted for winter navigation in the Baltic and other northern waters and was owned and operated by the Lauritzen Line of Copenhagen. The Lauritzen Line, not a member of any of the shipping conferences, was invited by the Industrial and Trade Bureau of Greater Quebec to sail to the port of Quebec in February, 1959, to pick up cargoes for shipment to Europe at a time when conference vessels could not navigate in the river. Conference lines refused to release shippers from their exclusive contracts with the conference lines although the lines did not have service from the port of Quebec in February. The conference lines took steps to bring pressure on the shippers to adhere to

34. "A Report in the Matter of an Inquiry under the Combines Investigation Act in Connection with the Transportation of Commodities by Water from and to Ports in Eastern Canada" (Ottawa, June 17, 1965).

their agreement with the conference lines. The refusal of the conferences to permit shippers to use the non-conference service of the Lauritzen Lines led to an investigation under the Combines Investigation Act.

Having completed his investigation, the Director submitted allegations to the Restrictive Trade Practices Commission that the Combines Investigation Act had been breached by the shipping conferences with respect to both eastbound and westbound traffic. Named in the allegation were ten companies, none of which are incorporated in Canada. Many, if not all of them, maintain offices or agents in Canada and all, of course, carry freight to and from Canadian ports.

The commission discussed at length the history and operation of the conference arrangements as they affect Canada, concluded that the named lines had lessened competition unduly (the key word of Section 32, the charging provision with respect to horizontal agreements) and then went on very briefly to record that counsel representing several of the conference lines had argued at the hearings before the commission that the Combines Investigation Act has no application to the agreement of member lines of the *westbound* Canada–United Kingdom conference.[35] The Director stated that

this agreement was a lawful agreement in Great Britain, where it was made, and is not subject to the terms of the Combines Investigation Act.[36] Nothing in Canadian combines legislation, Mr. O'Brien asserted, would permit an interpretation that would make the legislation applicable extraterritorially.

The Commission considers that where any overt act which takes place in Canada flows from an agreement which is contrary to the public policy, public interest or public order of Canada, such agreement comes within Canadian jurisdiction even if it was not made in Canada. In such circumstances, even if the agreement does not violate the law of the country where it was made it is within the purview of the Canadian courts. In the present instance, the agreements *were acted upon in Canada and had clear effects in Canada.*[37] Since the

---

35. Apparently counsel distinguished the westbound conference from the eastbound conference.

36. Cf. Meyer Heine decision of the High Court of Australia, below.

37. Emphasis added.

Combines Investigation Act of Canada is a law pursuant to which the public interest is protected and under which remedies are provided for detriment to the public, it is a law of public order to which these agreements are subject. Nevertheless, such parts or terms of the agreements as remain legal pursuant to the Combines Investigation Act are enforceable in Canada against Canadian importers and exporters. The Commission also considers that Canada may insist upon compliance with Canadian laws by owners of vessels trading into Canadian ports and by carriers or shippers who seek to enforce such portions of the agreements between them as are valid under Canadian law.[38]

The commission thus summarily dismissed the issue about the extraterritorial limits of the act and would apparently apply it even to agreements which have no connection with Canada other than that the shipper and the carrier, both being unconnected with Canada except to the extent that the carrier transports goods to Canada and perhaps maintains an office there for that purpose, make an agreement in a foreign country for the carriage of goods to Canada. Of course, shipping arrangements are not that simple and the carriers involved carried freight both to and from Canada. Further, the importer may well be the shipper in some cases, having become the owner of the goods in question f.o.b. the foreign port or at some earlier point in the process of shipment.

The commission concluded that the "basic agreements of *both the eastbound and westbound* Canada–United Kingdom conferences and their contract arrangements with Canadian shippers or consignees and their other practices affecting trade in Canadian ports fall within the scope of the Combines Investigation Act."[39] However, the commission recognized the desirability of stable arrangements for ocean transportation to and from Canada and concluded that "the lines in the Canada–U.K. trades should be allowed to continue such arrangements as are necessary for the efficient handling of Canada's exports and imports, subject to appropriate safeguards for the public interests."[40] Specific recommendations were made, and it is clear from the tenor of the report that the commission would not expect prosecution to follow even though there had been a breach of the act.

38. Combines Investigation Act, p. 98.   39. *Ibid.,* p. 99, emphasis added.
40. *Ibid.,* p. 100.

It seems that there should be one law for the shipping conferences and another for other industries, and if this is to be the case (as in the United States and under the new Australian Act), it is certainly desirable that the discrimination be provided for by special legislation. There has been no public announcement of any action having been taken with regard to the report on the shipping conference arrangements and practices. No doubt this report is being considered as part of the general study of the Canadian law which has been under way for some time.

Although my survey has not been exhaustive, I believe that no attempt has been made in the history of the enforcement of Canadian legislation to apply it to activities outside Canada.[41] All the cases have clearly involved facts and acts which occurred in Canada. However, the tenor of the statement by the Restrictive Trade Practices Commission in the shipping conference report indicates a willingness to apply the act to any agreements and activities having economic consequences in Canada so long as the parties themselves or some of them can be brought within the effective power of Canadian tribunals by reason of residence or other factors which give "personal" jurisdiction. By contrast, the Director's statements are conservative, and Canadian governments, having had to contend with overreaching United States law, may well be careful not to give offense themselves.

United Kingdom[42]

General Principles of Jurisdiction over Subject Matter. The well-established English principles are authoritatively summa-

41. The McGregor Report on International Cartels (1945, p. 43) stated the conclusion of the commissioner that Canadian laws are not applicable to "private international law agreements."

42. The jurisdictional aspects of United Kingdom law have recently been very well canvassed by Alfred Drucker in the report of the International Law Association Committee on the Extraterritorial Application of Restrictive Trade Legislation, prepared for the Helsinki Conference in August of 1966 (pp. 20–26); in the report for the 1964 Tokyo Conference of the ILA (prepared by Lord Wilberforce and Alfred Drucker); by Jeremy Lever, "The Extra-territorial Jurisdiction of the Restrictive Practices Court," *Int. & Comp. Law Quar.*, supplementary publication No. 6, *Comparative Aspects of Antitrust Law in the United States, the United Kingdom and the European Economic Community* (1963), pp. 117–130; and in

rized by Wade and Phillips in their leading work on constitutional law, as follows:

The supremacy of Parliament is not limited so far as British courts are concerned by the rule of international law. The courts have nothing to do with the question whether the legislature has or has not done what foreign States consider a usurpation. Neither are they concerned whether an Act of Parliament is *ultra vires* on the ground that it contravenes generally accepted principles of international law. No statute will, however, be held to apply to aliens with respect to transactions outside British jurisdiction unless the words are perfectly clear. In practice Parliament only enacts legislation which can be enforced and, in accord with international law, attempts to exercize authority only within its own territories, or over its own citizens when abroad. Indeed our territorial conception of law is stronger than that of most other countries and the extent to which citizens of the United Kingdom and Colonies are affected by English law while in foreign countries is small.[43]

The principles were approved recently in *Collco Dealings, Ltd. v. Inland Revenue Commissioners.*[44] The appellant was incorporated in Ireland and sought to avoid the application of United Kingdom tax legislation by reference to principles of international law limiting the extraterritorial effect of the legislation. The court unanimously rejected the argument and approved the statement in Peter B. Maxwell on *Interpretation of Statutes:*[45] "if the statute

---

the principal work on the United Kingdom legislation, Lord Wilberforce, Alan Campbell, and Neil Elles, *The Law of Restrictive Trade Practices and Monopolies* (2d ed.; London, 1966). An early reaction by G. W. Haight to the 1956 Act is recorded in "Antitrust Laws and the Territorial Principle," *Vanderbilt Law Rev.*, XI (1957), 27.

43. E. C. S. Wade and G. Godfrey Phillips, *Constitutional Law* (5th ed.; London, 1957), pp. 41–42 (footnotes omitted). The limited extension of United Kingdom law is illustrated in the text which goes on as follows:

A few crimes committed in a foreign State by citizens of the United Kingdom and Colonies are justiciable in this country, such as treason, murder, manslaughter, bigamy, piracy. Any one British subject employed by the Government of the United Kingdom in the service of the Crown who commits in a foreign country, when acting in the course of his employment, any offence which, if committed in England, would be punishable on indictment, can be proceeded against in England for that offence: Criminal Justice Act, 1948, Section 31(1). The National Service (Foreign Countries) Act, 1942, which was repealed after the end of hostilities, empowered the Crown to impose military service on British subjects in foreign countries. (p. 42)

44. [1961], 1 All E.R. 762; [1962], A.C. 1; 39 T.C. 526.

45. (10th ed.; London, 1953), p. 149.

is unambiguous, its provisions must be followed, even if they are contrary to international law." At the same time, their Lordships all approved, expressly or by clear implication, the general principle that statutes will, in the absence of clear legislative intent, be construed so as not to conflict with established principles of international law. In the case, the appellant's claim was regarded as being entirely without merit (a surplus stripping device had been attempted) and the court did not examine the principles.

In the antitrust field, some indication of both parliamentary and judicial definition of the appropriate legislative jurisdiction of states may be gathered from reaction to attempts to extend United States power, namely, in the Shipping Contracts and Commercial Documents Act[46] and in the British Nylon Spinners case.[47]

Briefly stated, the act was passed in reaction to attempts by the Federal Maritime Commission of the United States to obtain documents which it thought might contain information pertaining to possible breaches of United States antitrust laws.[48] The policy of the act is indicated by the long title in which it is stated that it is intended "to secure Her Majesty's jurisdiction against encroachment by certain foreign requirements. . . ." The act gives to the government the power to determine whether certain requests of foreign courts, tribunals, or administrative authorities addressed to persons in the United Kingdom to produce or furnish any commercial document not within the territorial jurisdiction of the foreign country constitute "an infringement of the jurisdiction which, under international law, belongs to the United Kingdom."[49] Further, the act authorizes the minister of transport to determine what acts of foreign countries "regulating or controlling the terms or conditions upon which goods or passengers may be carried by sea or the terms or conditions of contracts or arrangements relating to such carriage constitute an infringement

---

46. N. 6 above.   47. N. 7 above.
48. See Nial Osborough, "The Extra-Jurisdictional Impact of Antitrust Enforcement," *Northern Ireland Legal Quar.*, XVI (1965), 239–261; F. A. Mann, "Anglo-American Conflict of International Jurisdiction," *Int. & Comp. Law Quar.*, XIII (1964), 1460–1465; ILA Tokyo Conference Report, pp. 577–592.
49. Sec. 2(i).

of a jurisdiction which, under international law, belongs to the United Kingdom."[50] When the minister of transport has made such an order, every person in the United Kingdom carrying on business of the carriage of goods by sea has the duty to give the minister notice of any requirement imposed on him by the courts or authorities of the foreign country, and the minister may give to any such person in the United Kingdom directions for prohibiting compliance with any such requirement *"as he considers proper for maintaining the jurisdiction of the United Kingdom."*[51]

Anticipating the breadth of the final decree of the American court in *U.S. v. Imperial Chemical Industries Ltd.*,[52] British Nylon Spinners Limited instituted proceedings in England seeking specific performance of a contract under which ICI had agreed to transfer to BNS nylon patents originally acquired by ICI from Du Pont.[53] On the appeal from an interlocutory order enjoining ICI from complying with the American order to reassign the patents to Du Pont, the master of the rolls, Sir Raymond Evershed, quoted Judge Ryan's statement that "it is not an intrusion on the authority of a foreign sovereign for this court to direct steps to be taken to remove the harmful effects on the trade of the United States"[54] and declared:

If by that passage the judge intended to say (as it seems to me he did) that it was not an intrusion on the authority of a foreign sovereign to make directions addressed to that foreign sovereign or its courts or to nationals of that foreign power effective to remove (as he said) "harmful effects on the trade of the United States," I am bound to say that, as at present advised, I find myself unable to agree with it.[55]

Thereafter, Danckwerts J., in the Chancery Division, declared that ICI was bound by English law to carry out its agreement and granted specific performance to the plaintiff.[56]

---

50. Sec. 1(1). The principles are not defined.
51. See 1966 ILA committee report, p. 21; emphasis added.
52. 100 F. Supp. 504 (S.D.N.Y. 1951); 105 F. Supp. 215 (1952).
53. *British Nylon Spinners Limited* v. *Imperial Chemical Industries Ltd.* [1953], chap. 19; [1955], chap. 37.
54. 105 F. Supp. 215, at 229.
55. [1953], chaps. 19, 25; [1953], 2 All E.R. 780, 782.
56. [1955], chap. 37.

Interesting as they may be in the context of relations between the United States and countries thought to be affected by United States antitrust enforcement, the decisions in British Nylon Spinners are negative in substance and do not add much to the body of English law indicating the proper scope of jurisdiction. They do, of course, indicate that any attempted extraterritorial application of English law to the extent of the orders complained of in the cases would not be tolerated by the English courts unless specifically directed by a statute in that behalf.

To the extent that the United Kingdom's principles are principles of the English common law, they may generally speaking be taken as the law of the other Commonwealth countries that follow English law. Of course, to the extent that the principles are statutory, they may be peculiar to the United Kingdom— similarity with other laws would be only coincidental, although perhaps resulting from a conscious desire to follow the United Kingdom law.

United Kingdom Legislation: The Restrictive Trade Practices Act, 1956.[57] Part I of the 1956 act provides for the registration of certain types of agreements and gives power to the Restrictive Practices Court to declare agreements contrary to the public interest.[58] The application of Part I of the act is limited to "any agreement between two or more persons carrying on business within the United Kingdom in the production or supply of goods, or in the application to goods of any process of manufacture, whether with or without other parties, being an agreement under which restrictions are accepted by two or more parties in respect of the following matters. . . ."[59] The parties who accept the restrictions need not be the same as those who carry on business in the United Kingdom and consequently may be persons who do not carry on business in the United Kingdom.[60]

Specific exemptions are enumerated in Subsection 8 of Section 8, as follows:

57. United Kingdom Statutes, 1956, chap. 68.
58. Sec. 20.   59. Sec. 6(1).
60. ILA 1964, p. 432; Wilberforce, Campbell, and Elles, *Law of Restrictive Trade*, sec. 555.

This part of this Act does not apply to an agreement in the case of which *all such restrictions* as are described in subsection (1) of section six of this Act relate *exclusively*—

(a) to the supply of goods by *export* from the United Kingdom;

(b) to the production of goods, or the application of any process of manufacture to goods, *outside the United Kingdom;*

(c) to the acquisition of goods to be delivered outside the United Kingdom and not imported into the United Kingdom for entry for home use; or

(d) to the supply of goods to be delivered outside the United Kingdom otherwise than by export from the United Kingdom;

and subsection (7) of section six of this Act shall not apply in relation to recommendations relating exclusively to such matters as aforesaid.[61]

Section 14 gives to the registrar certain powers to obtain information, but his power to give the relevant notice requiring the filing of information is limited to "a *person carrying on within the United Kingdom* any such business as is described in subsection (1) of section 6 and a trade association the members of which consist of or include persons *carrying on business* in the United Kingdom *or representatives of such persons.*"[62] The apparent intention is to confine the jurisdiction to companies and persons who have penetrated the United Kingdom economy to the extent of carrying on business there. However, the subject matter of the inquiry is not so limited.

Section 15, which confers on the High Court the power to order examination, is expressly limited to persons to whom notice has been given under Section 14. The power conferred on the High Court by Section 18 to require any party to an agreement to furnish particulars is not expressly so limited. Wilberforce, Campbell, and Elles, presumably on a view of the part as a whole, suggest that it is by implication limited to the same jurisdiction as that of the registrar conferred by Section 14.[63]

Section 20 is the principal provision governing the jurisdiction and powers of the Restrictive Practices Court and contains important limitations. Restrictions in respect of matters described in paragraphs (b) to (d) of Subsection 8 of Section 8 (set out

61. All emphasis added.   62. All emphasis added.
63. *Law of Restrictive Trade,* p. 216.

above) are exempted by Subsection (1) from the general jurisdiction of the court to declare agreements contrary to the public
interest. Further, Subsection (3) provides that where registrable
agreements are found by the court to be contrary to the public
interest "the agreement shall be void in respect of those restrictions" but the restraining order which the court may make is
limited to "all or any of the persons party to the agreement who
carry on business in the United Kingdom."

The question of what constitutes carrying on business in the
United Kingdom is of fundamental importance. The statute provides a negative restriction in Section 36(3) to the following
effect: ". . . a person shall not be deemed to carry on a business
within the United Kingdom by reason only of the fact that he is
represented for the purposes of that business by an agent within
the United Kingdom."[64] Neither the statute nor other sources
provide a definition of the term "carrying on business." Resort
may be had to the body of case law on (*a*) the service of civil
proceedings, (*b*) liability to income tax, and (*c*) questions of
jurisdiction of English courts of limited territorial jurisdiction
such as the county courts. It may also be relevant to refer to the
requirements of the Companies Act, 1948, regarding the registration of foreign companies which establish a place of business in
Great Britain. However, it has been held that when the legislature selected the phrase "establishes a place of business in Great
Britain," it meant something other than carrying on business in
Great Britain,[65] and I agree with the conclusion expressed in
Wilberforce that the questions involved in the application of the
Companies Act are not relevant to the Restrictive Trade Practices
Act.[66] A full discussion of the concept of "carrying on business"
would require analysis of the service-of-process, tax, and venue
cases, which is beyond the scope of this paper.

It appears to be agreed by the commentators that it is not
intended that a foreign company be deemed to carry on business

64. Wilberforce, Campbell, and Elles leave open (p. 212) the definition of
"agent" for the purposes of the act.
65. *Re Tovarishestvo Manufactur Lindvig-Rabenek* [1944], chap. 404; *Deverall*
v. *Grant Advertising* [1955], chap. 111.
66. Wilberforce, Campbell, and Elles, *Law of Restrictive Trade*, pp. 210–211.

in the United Kingdom through a subsidiary, unless, of course, the subsidiary acts in the capacity of an agent so as to bring the parent company within the jurisdiction. English case law distinguishes the corporate personality of a subsidiary from that of a parent.[67] However, Lever concludes that

there are quite strong reasons to support a contention that the existence within the United Kingdom of an associate company (i.e., a parent or a subsidiary or a fellow subsidiary company), results in a foreign company being treated as carrying on business within the United Kingdom, regardless of the fact that it has no other contacts with this country. It is unlikely that this result was intended.[68]

He then goes on to examine the contention which is based on the provisions of Sections 6, 7, and 8 of the act dealing with agreements made between interconnected bodies corporate.[69] By contrast, he notes that

there is no provision in the Act that, for the purposes of section 20, interconnected bodies corporate are to be treated as a single person and it therefore follows that there can be no question of the mere existence within the United Kingdom of an associate company making a foreign corporation liable to an injunction preventing it from giving effect to the agreement before the Court or making any other agreement to the like effect.[70]

Generally speaking, the United Kingdom legislation appears to justify Haight's early conclusion that "the greatest care has been exercised in the provisions of the new law and by the Monopolies Commission in its own proceedings to observe the limitations of territoriality"[71] and that "the greatest care has been exercised to confine the operation of this law, notwithstanding its non-criminal character, to the territory of the United Kingdom and, by the limitations imposed on the jurisdictional competence of the new court, to avoid conflicts with foreign jurisdictions."[72] Wilberforce,

---

67. *Gramophone & Typewriter Limited* v. *Stanley* [1908], 2 K.B. 89, 106, and *English Sewing Cotton Ltd.* v. *IRC* [1947], 1 All E.R. 679. See Wilberforce, Campbell, and Elles, *Law of Restrictive Trade*, pp. 212–213, and Lever, pp. 121 ff.
68. Lever, "Extra-territorial Jurisdiction," p. 122.
69. Canvassed by Wilberforce, Wilberforce, Campbell, and Elles, *Law of Restrictive Trade*, sec. 641, pp. 287 ff.
70. Lever, "Extra-territorial Jurisdiction," p. 129.
71. Haight, "Antitrust Laws," p. 38.   72. *Ibid.*, p. 39.

Campbell, and Elles reach the same conclusion: "By reason of these explicit statutory limitations upon the jurisdiction of the Restrictive Practices Court, it does not appear likely that any conflict with the courts or administrative authorities of foreign states will arise."[73]

United Kingdom Legislation: The Monopolies and Restrictive Practices (Inquiry and Control) Act, 1948; The Monopolies and Restrictive Practices Commission Act, 1953; The Monopolies and Mergers Act, 1965.[74]

Activities coming within the purview of the Monopolies Commission are dealt with at some length in the 1964 and 1966 International Law Association committee reports. After a summary of the statutory provisions, Dr. Drucker concludes that

it is obvious that these provisions may well extend to and cover restrictive agreements or arrangements made outside the United Kingdom, by foreign individuals or companies. They must, however, have effect on the supply of goods or services *in the United Kingdom,* the processing of goods *in the United Kingdom* or the export of goods *from the United Kingdom.*[75]

Section 10(4) of the 1948 act, dealing with the powers of the Board of Trade (and other government authorities) to make orders, bears setting out in full:

Nothing in any order of a competent authority under this section shall have effect so as to apply to any person in relation to his conduct outside the United Kingdom *unless* he is a British subject, a body corporate incorporated under the law of the United Kingdom or some part thereof, *or a person carrying on business in the United Kingdom* either alone or in partnership with any other person, but, save as aforesaid, any such order may be so made as to *extend to acts or omissions outside the United Kingdom;* and any such order may also extend so as to prohibit the carrying out of agreements already in existence at the date of the making of the order.[76]

---

73. *Law of Restrictive Trade,* p. 73.
74. Respectively, United Kingdom Statutes, 1948, chap. 66; 1953, chap. 51; and 1965, chap. 50.
75. At p. 23 of the 1966 committee report, which amends the conclusion on p. 430 of the 1961 ILA conference report. (Emphasis added.)
76. Emphasis added.

Wilberforce and Drucker conclude in the 1964 ILA report that "this provision is in accordance with principles normally applied by the Courts."[77]

Australia

General Principles of Jurisdiction over Subject Matter. The recent decision of the High Court of Australia in *Meyer Heine Pty. Ltd.* v. *The China Navigation Co., Ltd. and another*[78] is undoubtedly the touchstone for general principles. A fairly full statement of the facts of the case will be necessary to set out the context of the principles enunciated by the court.

The plaintiff sued for treble damages under Section 11 of the Australian Industries Preservation Act, 1906–1950, a Commonwealth statute, of which the pertinent provisions are as follows:

4.—(1.) Any person, who, either as principal or as agent, makes or enters into any contract, or is or continues to be a member of or engaged in any combination, in relation to trade or commerce with other countries or among the States—

(a) in restraint of or with intent to restrain trade or commerce; or

(b) to the destruction or injury of or with the intent to destroy or injure by means of unfair competition any Australian industry the preservation of which is advantageous to the Commonwealth, having due regard to the interests of producers, workers and consumers,

is guilty of an offence.

11.—(1.) Any person who is injured in his person or property by any other person, by reason of any act or thing done by that other person in contravention of this Part of this Act, or by reason of any act or thing done in contravention of any injunction granted under this Part of this act, may, in the High Court, before a Justice without a jury, sue for and recover treble damages for the inquiry.

The plaintiff alleged that until July, 1964, it carried on the business of a shipping line, carrying goods from Australia to other countries including Japan, and from other countries including

77. ILA 1964, p. 431.
78. *Australian Law Jour. Rep.*, XXXIX (1966), 448.

Japan and Hong Kong to Australia. The defendants carried on business in competition with the plaintiff but unlike the plaintiff were members of a group of companies known at one time as the Australian-Eastern Shipping Conference and more recently as the Australian and New Zealand–Eastern Shipping Conference. Members of the conference carried substantially all the wool shipped from Australia to Japan and substantially all the general cargo from Japan and Hong Kong to Australia.

The conference was governed at all material times by an agreement made in Sydney in May of 1961. The plaintiff alleged that within the framework of the conference agreement three classes of special agreements were made between members of the conference, including the defendants, and individual shippers. The first class consisted of agreements with the shippers of all or practically all the goods shipped at the relevant times by sea from Japan to Australia; the second consisted of agreements with the shippers of all or practically all the goods shipped at relevant times by sea from Hong Kong to Australia; and the third consisted of agreements with the importers and/or spinners in Japan of all or practically all the wool shipped at relevant times by sea from Australia to Japan. The agreements provided, generally speaking, for discounts for exclusive patronage. The plaintiff alleged that the agreements of the first and third class were entered into in Japan and of the second class in Hong Kong.

The defendants were incorporated in the United Kingdom and registered as foreign companies under the law of New South Wales.

In summary, the reported facts disclose the following points of contact with Australia: (*a*) The conference agreement was made in Australia. (*b*) Exclusive patronage agreements covered the carriage of goods both to and from Australia. (*c*) The defendants were registered under the law of New South Wales and presumably maintained some form of establishment there.

The matter came before the Full Court on a series of demurrers by the defendants to parts of the statement of claim and a series of demurrers by the plaintiff to parts of the defense. The point of concern in this discussion is the allegation of the defendants that

Section 4(1) of the act did not apply to the making or entering into of a contract outside Australia, at least by a company which like each of the defendants owed its incorporation to the laws of another country.

Kitto J. treated this question as one of "pure construction."[79] Having concluded that the proper construction of the act itself limited its operations in the relevant circumstances to agreements made in Australia, his Lordship dealt only briefly with the general principles which would apply were the statute open to the construction that it applied extraterritorially. He did remark as follows:

There being no express geographical restriction upon the generality of any of the expressions "any person," "makes or enters into," and "any contract," the question is whether such a restriction is implied. I take it to be clear that no basis for a conclusion on this question is to be found by consideration of any limit upon constitutional power. If implication there be, it must arise either from other provisions of the statute or from the general rule that "if any construction otherwise be possible, an Act will not be construed as applying to foreigners in respect to acts done by them outside the dominions of the sovereign power enacting": per Lord Russell of Killowen, *Reg.* v. *Jamieson,* [1896] 2 Q.B. 425, at p. 430.

If I thought that the Act itself gave no relevant indication of intention I should find it necessary to discuss more fully than I do the arguments for and against the application of the general rule; but as it is I need say but little about them. Questions of the same general description arising under the *Sherman Act* in the United States have arisen in a series of important cases, from *American Banana Co.* v. *United States* (1909), 213 U.S. 347 (in which the judgment of Mr. Justice Holmes gives full effect to the rule abovementioned) to the much-debated *Alcoa Case; United States* v. *Aluminium* [*sic.*] *Co. of America* (1945), 148 Fed. 2nd. 416, and *Steele* v. *Bulova Watch Co.* (1952), 344 U.S. 280. A case of a combination of shipping lines is *Thomsen* v. *Cayser* (1916), 243 U.S. 66. These and the later case of *United States* v. *Watch-makers of Switzerland Information Center Inc.* (1964) are the subject of valuable discussions, to which we have been referred, in papers presented to the 1964 conference at Tokyo of the International Law Association. Such discussions have relevance to questions of statutory construction because, as Lord Russell of Kil-

79. *Ibid.*, p. 450.

lowen said in the *Jamieson Case* after stating the general rule in the terms I have quoted: "That is a rule based on international law by which one sovereign power is bound to respect the subjects and rights of all other sovereign powers outside its own territory." In the present proceeding, however, it is not necessary to decide what view should be recognized by Australian courts upon the question, about which unanimity among nations is lacking, of the legislative jurisdiction of a country in regard to acts done outside its territory but intended to have and actually having adverse effects upon the international or external trade of that country. No doubt much may be said for the view that the state of international opinion in 1906 was such that an enactment passed in that year in the general terms of s. 4(1) should be taken to apply only to the making and entering into of contracts within Australia; and that an enactment passed in 1910, when s. 4(1) took its present form, that is to say after Mr. Justice Holmes had delivered the judgment of the Supreme Court in the *Banana Case* (1909), 213 U.S. 347, should with all the greater assurance be taken to apply only to such contracts.[80]

His Lordship went on to consider the sections of the act which in his opinion compelled the conclusion "that in creating offenses the Act intends to speak territorially."[81]

Dealing with the question of jurisdiction, Taylor J. stated:

The words of the section are general but, *prima facie*, "the persons, property, and events in respect of which Parliament has legislated are presumed to be limited to those in the territory over which it has jurisdiction" (per Isaacs J. in *Morgan* v. *White* (1912), 15 C.L.R. 1, at p. 13) and "it is always to be understood and implied that the legislature of a country is not intending to deal with persons or matters over which, according to the comity of nations, the jurisdiction properly belongs to some other sovereign or State" (per Dixon J. (as he then was) in *Barcelo* v. *Electrolytic Zinc Co. of A/asia Ltd.* (1932), 48 C.L.R. 391, at p. 424, quoting from the judgment of James L.J. in *Niboyet* v. *Niboyet* (1878), 4 P.D. 1, at p. 7—see also *Jumbunna Coal Mine, No Liability* v. *Victorian Coal Miners' Association* (1908), 6 C.L.R. 309, at p. 363, and *Reg.* v. *Foster; Ex parte Eastern and Australian Steamship Co. Ltd.* (1959), 103 C.L.R. 256, at p. 275). It was with these shortly stated principles in mind that we were referred by the defendant to the attention which has been given in recent years by distinguished lawyers to problems associated with the extraterritorial operation of the restrictive trade legislation of various

80. *Ibid.*   81. *Ibid.*

countries. In particular we were referred in some detail to the proceedings of the Committee on The Extra-Territorial Application of Restrictive Trade Legislation at the Tokyo Conference of the International Law Association. But the rule, as I have stated it, is one of interpretation only and, if by a local statute otherwise within power, provision is made "in contravention of generally acknowledged principles of international law" it is binding upon and must be enforced by the courts of this country (*Polites* v. *The Commonwealth* (1945), 70 C.L.R. 60, per Latham C.J., at p. 69: Starke J., at p. 75: Dixon J., at p. 77: and McTiernan J., at p. 79).

For the plaintiff it is asserted that the very subject matter with which the Act deals makes it manifest that the legislative intention was that the section should extend to acts done beyond the Commonwealth. It was intended for the protection of the trade and commerce of this country with other countries and among the States and both categories of trade, and particularly the former, can just as well be affected adversely by contracts and combinations made and entered into in other countries as by contracts and combinations made or entered into in Australia. But I do not find in these very general considerations any clear indication that s. 4(1) was intended to apply to acts done or performed outside Australia. Indeed, there is, I think, manifest in the provisions of s. 9 a recognition that the other provisions of Pt II do not so apply.[82]

Taylor J. appears to rely somewhat more than Kitto J. on the territoriality principle which he enunciated primarily by reference to the decision of Isaacs J. in *Morgan* v. *White*. However, his conclusion is identical with that of Kitto J., namely, that the act by its terms is confined to "acts" done in Australia. Although not expressed, it appears that the act to which he directed his exclusive attention was the making of the agreements and not the operation of them.[83]

On the general principle, Windeyer J. states categorically that "the *prima facie* presumption of English law is that a statute is to be construed as limited in its operation to the territory *or* the nationals of the state which enacts it. . . . The broad question in the case remains whether the *prima facie* presumption that the Act does not extend to penalize acts done outside of Australia by foreigners has been displaced."[84] In short, he takes the traditional

82. *Ibid.*, p. 453.
83. *Ibid.*, p. 454.
84. *Ibid.*, p. 458.

view, as he expresses it himself, that "if it had been intended that it was to be so widely construed one would expect some clear and express indication of this in its words."[85] He goes on to concur expressly in the reasons of Kitto J. McTiernan J. also concurred expressly in the judgment of Kitto J.[86]

Menzies J. dissented on the proper interpretation of the act. However, he does not differ from the other members of the court on the general principle and indeed states that the issue

raises no question of power, for a law which is with respect to trade and commerce with other countries can validly control conduct outside Australia. . . . The question is simply one of the construction of a section expressed in language amply wide enough to cover acts done outside Australia. The defendants, however, to limit the section relied upon the well accepted general principle of statutory construction that, *prima facie,* penal laws of one country are not intended to reach into the territory of another country to make punishable in the courts of the former acts done in the territory of the latter. Having given full weight, however, to this principle, I am not satisfied that the operation of s. 4 should be limited to acts done within Australian territory.[87]

He then goes on to construe the act to apply to the acts alleged to have been done outside Australia. "On this aspect of the matter I find myself in full agreement with the decision of the Circuit Court of Appeals reported in *United States* v. *Aluminium* [*sic.*] *Co. of America,* 148 F. 2nd 416 . . . upon which the legislation here under consideration was largely based."[88] He then quotes substantially from Judge Learned Hand.

The plaintiffs demurred to paragraphs of the statement of defense which set up distinct grounds of defense to be relied upon if it should be held that the fact of a contract having been entered into in Japan or Hong Kong afforded by itself no answer to a charge that by entering into it the defendants contravened the act. To the allegations that the contracts were entered into if at all at those places, the paragraphs in question added certain further allegations such as that the other parties were domiciled

85. *Ibid.*
87. *Ibid.,* p. 456.
86. *Ibid.,* p. 449.
88. *Ibid.*

in those places, or domiciled and possessed nationality there; and some of them added also that the conduct complained of was justifiable by the local law.

Kitto J. held that the views he had expressed as to the implied territorial restriction upon the sections of the act made it unnecessary to deal with the plaintiff's demurrers.[89] Taylor J. dealt with the point as follows:

In substance, the answer to these demurrers is provided by what has already been said concerning the operation of the statute but the defendants' contention that the contracts which were entered into and the conduct complained of on the part of the defendants were lawful according to the laws of Japan or Hong Kong respectively represents an attempt to introduce into this field the principles upon which an action may be brought in this country for a tort committed in a foreign country. The circumstances in which they may be done are discussed in *Phillips* v. *Eyre* (1870), L.R. 6 Q.B. 1, and *Koop* v. *Bebb* (1951), 84 C.L.R. 629, but the principles therein enunciated have no application to the circumstances of the present case. If it were to be held that the statute disclosed an intention that it was to have an extraterritorial operation the fact that an act in contravention of the statute was lawful according to the place where it was done would be of no relevance whatever.[90]

Menzies J. expressed the same view.[91] It is submitted that their Lordships' statements on this point should be confined to the context of the rule that so far as the courts are concerned, they are bound to apply the law laid down by the legislature within its proper constitutional power. There being no question about the constitutional power of the Australian Parliament to enact the law, and to give it extraterritorial effect, the question of justifiability by a foreign law does, of course, become irrelevant for the court. However, the question is still very relevant in assessing the jurisdiction of any national legislature by reference to principles of "international law."

Section 3 of the Statute of Westminster, 1931, which conferred on Australia and Canada, *inter alia*, the "power to make laws

89. *Ibid.*, p. 452.   90. *Ibid.*, p. 456.
91. *Ibid.*, p. 458.

having extra-territorial operation" is noted in the discussion of Canadian law. The same considerations apply with respect to Australia.

Australian Legislation: The Trade Practices Act, 1965. The Trade Practices Act was assented to December 18, 1965,[92] but aside from certain administrative provisions and parts relating to the constitution of the Trade Practices Tribunal and the appointment of various officers, is yet to be proclaimed in force.[93]

The basic scheme of the act involves the registration of examinable agreements. Such agreements are to be examined by the Tribunal with a view to ascertaining whether they ought to be struck down or curtailed as being against the public interest.

Section 7 of the act provides:

Operation of Act with reference to the Constitution.

7.—(1.) The restrictions referred to in section 35 of this Act, and the practices referred to in section 36 of Part IX. of this Act, include restrictions and practices that are (whether exclusively or not) applicable to, or engaged in in relation to, or that tend to prevent or hinder, transactions, acts or operations—

    (a) in the course of trade or commerce with other countries or among the States;

    (b) in or for the production, supply or acquisition of goods or services for, or goods or services required for, the purposes of any such trade or commerce;

. . .

7.—(2.) The restrictions referred to in section 35 of this Act include restrictions, coming within the terms of that section, accepted under an agreement by a party to the agreement who is a foreign corporation, or a trading or financial corporation formed within the limits of the Commonwealth.

7.—(3.) The practices referred to in section 36 and Part IX. of this Act include practices on the part of a person who is a foreign corporation, or a trading or financial corporation formed within the limits of the Commonwealth.

---

92. No. 111 of 1965. The 1966 act is discussed below.
93. At the time of writing, June 5, 1967, I understand that staffing is largely completed and that proclamation is expected this year.

The marginal note to Section 7 indicates that it is to delimit the operation of the act with reference to the operation of the Constitution of the Commonwealth. However, in attempting to confine the statute to the constitutional powers of the Commonwealth Parliament, vis-à-vis the states, the foreign commerce aspect is thrown more sharply into focus because it is one of the subjects which is clearly within the constitutional power of the Commonwealth Parliament.

Section 35 of the act, which defines examinable agreements, and Section 36, which defines examinable practices, are drawn in broad terms which could apply equally to acts and agreements done or made outside Australia as well as to those done or made within Australia. Moreover, Section 91(3) provides that a reference to an agreement shall be read as including a reference to an agreement made outside Australia. Section 7(2) of the act states that Section 35 includes restrictions accepted under an agreement by a party to the agreement who is a foreign corporation but makes no reference to the territorial location of any activity. Section 7(3) is in the same terms with respect to the examinable practices defined in Section 36. It follows therefore that the Alcoa rule could be applied in the application of the act.[94] However, it is more likely that the restrictive principle described above will operate in the absence of express indication in the statute that it is intended to apply to activities which occur outside the Commonwealth.

Section 37, which deals with monopolization, confines itself as follows: "For the purposes of this Act, a person engages in monopolization if, being in a dominant position in the trade in goods of a particular description or in the supply of goods of a particular description, in Australia or in a part of Australia. . . ." Dominant position is defined in Section 37(4)(b) by reference to the proportion supplied of the market for goods or services, and the supplier could presumably be a foreign exporter with no place of business in Australia.

Section 38, which exempts certain arrangements or agreements

---

94. *United States* v. *Aluminum Co. of America* (1945), 148 F. 2d. 416.

from the category of examinable agreements, contains nothing pertaining to international territorial limitations of jurisdiction. Section 39, which exempts certain practices, is similarly not relevant to notions of international territorial jurisdiction over subject matter.[95]

Section 67 of the act under Part VII relating to the enforcement of orders of the Tribunal is similar to Section 9 of the Australian Industries Preservation Act[96] in that it provides that

a person who . . . (b) aids, abets, counsels or procures, or is in any way directly or indirectly knowingly concerned in, or party to—
(ii) the doing of an act outside Australia that would, if done within Australia, be such a contravention . . . is guilty of a contempt of the Tribunal.

Following the reasoning of the majority of the court in the Meyer Heine case, this incidental provision of the act might be taken as an indication that the substantive provisions of the act are to be confined to acts done within Australia. However, following the reasoning of Menzies J. who dissented in the Meyer Heine case, it seems to be giving too much weight to a merely incidental provision of the act to construe other sections of the act by reference to it. In any event, the section deals only with contempt of the Tribunal and not with other offenses.

Section 85 of the act which deals with collusive tendering contains express reference to tendering for the supply of goods to a person carrying on business outside Australia where the successful tenderer is required to export the goods or where it is apparent from the terms or circumstances of the invitation to tender that the goods are to be exported for the purpose of that business or the services are to be supplied outside Australia. A collusive tender in such cases is not an offense. Section 86 dealing with collusive bidding at auctions is confined to "an auction in Australia."[97]

Section 103 of the act gives broad powers to the commissioner

95. Sec. 39(3) of the 1965 act did exempt acts done in relation to the carriage of goods by sea. This subsection will not be effective after the commencement of Part XA, added by the 1966 amending act, discussed below.
96. Discussed in the Meyer Heine case, above.
97. Sec. 86(1).

to require the production of documents and information relating to matters that constitute, or may constitute, an examinable agreement or an examinable practice. No restriction is placed on territorial scope of such an order. Presumably such an order would not be made if it contravenes a statute such as the Shipping Contracts and Commercial Documents Act of 1964 of the United Kingdom. However, the Australian statutory scheme does not in its terms recognize such restriction on the jurisdiction.

Australian Legislation: The Trade Practices Act, 1966. The Trade Practices Act, 1965, provided that references in the charging sections of the Australian Industries Preservation Act, 1906–1950, to trade and commerce were to be construed as if they referred only to trade and commerce by way of carriage of goods by sea between Australia and places outside Australia. Section 38(i) provided that in determining whether an agreement was to be an examinable agreement, regard should not be had to any provision to the extent that it gave rise to a restriction in relation to the carriage of goods by sea between Australia and places outside Australia, and Section 39(3) contained the same limitation with regard to examinable practices.

The Trade Practices Act, 1966,[98] added Part XA to the Trade Practices Act, 1965,[99] to deal with "Overseas Cargo Shipping." The Australian Industries Preservation Acts will be wholly repealed on the commencement of Part XA, which will come into force by proclamation.[100] The act is confined to outward cargo shipping from Australia and applies to certain restrictive agreements in that connection.[101] Agreements are to be filed with the clerk of shipping agreements, and the minister for trade and industry may require shipowners and parties to an agreement to take part in negotiations with regard to arrangements for shipping cargo from Australia. Further, the government may disap-

---

98. No. 39 of 1966.
99. The statute is to be cited as the "Trade Practices Act 1965–1966."
100. Presumably the proclamation of Part XA may not coincide with the proclamation of the rest of the act, and secs. 3(3) and 3(4) of the 1966 act refer separately to the proclamation of Part XA and the other provisions of the act.
101. Sec. 90C.

prove conference agreements whereupon the agreement becomes unenforceable as regards outward cargo, but a transaction entered into under the conference agreement is not unenforceable by reason only of the order. Parties to a disapproved agreement are prohibited from acting in pursuance of it, and similar prohibitions may be placed on a shipowner. Certain injunctive powers are conferred on the court and civil remedies are given to persons injured by acts in contravention of prohibitions issued under the statute.

The rule applied in the Meyer Heine case would prima facie confine the operation of the shipping provisions, as well as other provisions of the statute, to acts done in Australia. Section 90 ZD(1)(b) is identical to Section 67(b)(ii), and both are very similar to Section 9(b) of the Australian Industries Preservation Act, which was construed by the court in Meyer Heine to indicate that the act is to be confined to offenses committed in Australia. However, it is hardly conceivable that Parliament could have intended so narrow an interpretation. Throughout the part, it is evident that the government is intended to have wide discretionary power to police restrictive agreements and practices regarding shipments from Australia. Such agreements have a direct and, presumably, intended effect on Australian commerce, and Australia is justified in seeking to control them.[102] Nevertheless, the 1966 act was passed after the decision of the High Court in Meyer Heine, and it might be assumed that Parliament would have used language calculated to curtail the effect of Meyer Heine had it desired to remove doubt about the extraterritorial extent of the jurisdiction intended over cargo shipping agreements and practices.

India

General Principles of Jurisdiction over Subject Matter. The Constitution of India expressly recognizes the power of Parlia-

---

102. Cf. the Report of the (Canadian) Restrictive Trade Practices Commission on shipping conferences and arrangements, p. 133, above.

ment to make laws with extraterritorial operation.[103] It is likely that Indian courts would follow the established English law principles and exercise restraint in interpreting Indian statutes which do not expressly provide for extraterritorial operation.[104]

Indian Legislation. There is no Indian legislation to regulate restrictive trade practices.[105] The government of India appointed a Monopolies Inquiry Commission in April, 1964, under the following terms of reference:[106]

(a) to inquire into the extent and effect of concentration of economic power in private hands and the prevalence of monopolistic and restrictive practices in important sectors of economic activity other than agriculture with special reference to—
   (i) the factors responsible for such concentration and monopolistic and restrictive practices;
   (ii) their social and economic consequences, and the extent to which they might work to the common detriment; and
(b) to suggest such legislative and other measures that might be considered necessary in the light of such enquiry, including, in particular, any new legislation to protect essential public interests and the procedure and agency for the enforcement of such legislation.

The committee was asked to submit its report by October 31, 1965, and did so by the report dated at New Delhi on October 28. The report covers causes of concentration, productwise concentration, countrywise concentration, monopolistic and restrictive practices, and the consequences of concentration. Certain nonlegislative recommendations are advanced, foreign legislation is canvassed and a bill recommended: "The Monopolies and Restrictive Trade Practices Bill, 1965." It is entitled, "A bill to provide that the operation of the economic system does not result in the concentration of economic power to the common detriment for the control of monopolies and the prohibition of monopolistic

103. Constitution of India, Art. 245(2).
104. See Narotam Bindra, *The Interpretation of Statutes and General Clauses Acts* (4th ed.; Allahabad, 1965), pp. 134 ff.
105. Apart from the provisions of the Indian Contracts Act making some restrictive agreements unenforceable.
106. *Report of the Monopolies Inquiry Commission, 1965,* Intro.

and restrictive trade practices when found contrary to the public interest and for matters connected therewith or incidental thereto." Briefly stated, the bill would provide for a compulsory registration of all restrictive practices. Registration of a practice would not mean either its approval or condemnation. The register would be open to public inspection "so that wide publicity is given to restrictive practices that prevail in different trades and industries. The light of publicity may itself be of some use in inducing many to stop practices that are likely to attract general public criticism and so to damage the reputation of the concern."[107] Provision would be made for investigation and judicial examination of the alleged restrictive practices and where a finding is made that one or more enterprises are guilty of pursuing a restrictive practice which is to the common detriment, a commission would be given power to order discontinuance of practice. Much that is found in the registration statutes of the United Kingdom and Australia has been adopted. However, at the time of writing, the government has taken no action on the report of the commission.

Although the commission report has not been acted on, it may be of interest to look briefly at possible extraterritorial effects of the draft bill.

Chapter 3 deals with concentration of economic power and the concept of a "dominant undertaking," which is defined to mean an undertaking or inter-connected undertakings which account for one-third of the market in India for any goods or services.[108] The definition of "monopolistic undertakings" includes a dominant undertaking and an undertaking which with others supplies one-half of the goods—including imported goods that are produced, supplied, or distributed in India—or provides not less than one-half of any service in India.[109] These provisions are broad enough to include activities outside India which have an effect in India as stipulated.

The provisions dealing with restrictive trade practices do not appear to have any territorial limitations.[110] Restrictive trade

---

107. *Ibid.*, p. 160.
109. Sec. 17.

108. Sec. 2(1)(iv).
110. Sec. 20 ff.

agreements are to be registered, and it appears to be the intention that registrable agreements and the obligation to register should not be limited. Explanation 1 in Section 23, which deals with the registration of agreements, provides:

Where any agreement subject to registration under this section relates to the production, supply or distribution of goods or the performance of any service in India and any party to the agreement carries on business in India, the agreement shall be deemed to be an agreement within the meaning of this section, notwithstanding that any other party to the agreement does not carry on business in India.

Section 25 deals with the power of the registrar to obtain information and provides in general terms that if the registrar has reasonable cause to believe that any person is party to an agreement subject to registration under Section 23 he may give notice to that person requiring him within such time as may be specified in the notice to notify the registrar whether he is a party to any such agreement and, if so, to furnish the registrar with such particulars as may be so specified of the agreement. There is no restriction on the power of the registrar which would limit his inquiry to persons who carry on business in India.

The provisions dealing with resale price maintenance are directed exclusively at control of r.p.m. as it might operate in India and would in terms prohibit a supplier whether within or without India from engaging in r.p.m. practices.[111] The reasoning of *R. v. Cooper Campbell* in Canada would appear to apply.[112]

Section 34 deals with the powers of the commission, and Subsection 4 of that section provides that "for the purpose of enforcing the attendance of witnesses, the local limits of the commission's jurisdiction shall be the limits of the territory of India." Territorial limitation is similarly recognized in Section 36, which provides:

Where a monopolistic or restrictive trade practice relating to the production, supply or distribution of goods (including imported goods) of any description or the provision of any service is substantially within one or more of the practices falling within this Act and any party to the practice does not carry on business in India, an order

111. Secs. 28, 29.   112. P. 141, above.

may be made under this Act with respect to that part of the practice which is carried on in India.

Although the Indian draft bill is not so carefully drawn as the English act of 1956 to restrict its territorial application, there is evidence as noted above that the framers of the act intended to limit its operation to business carried on in India. However, some provisions, particularly those dealing with obtaining information, are broader in their scope and might be applied unduly widely.

Although it is not possible within the scope of this note to discuss analogous jurisdictional questions in tax laws, it is instructive to note in regard to India that the "business connection" doctrine set out in the Indian Income Tax Act, 1961, as follows:

Section 9(1)

The following income shall be deemed to accrue or arise in India—
   (i) all income accruing or arising, whether directly or indirectly, through or from any business connection in India. . . .

is given wide scope. It is held to apply to any systematic and regular exploitation of business in India and the existence of an exclusive distributor or exclusive agent is held conclusive of business connection. Section 163 provides that for the purposes of the act, "agent, in relation to a non-resident, includes any person in India. . . . (b) who has any business connection with a non-resident; or (c) from or through whom the non-resident is in receipt of any income, whether directly or indirectly. . . ." Sections 160 and 161 make the agent liable for tax in respect of income of a non-resident specified in Section 9(1)(i), set out above. This extraordinarily wide claim to tax jurisdiction may presage a similarly broad claim to jurisdiction in antitrust matters if legislation is enacted.

Conclusion

The practice and jurisprudence of the Commonwealth nations do not evidence the existence of precise principles governing the proper extent of jurisdiction to enact antitrust laws. It is clear, however, that the English common law as it has developed in those countries tends to restrict jurisdiction and, in so doing, may well render legislation ineffective to deal with restraints which directly affect a national economy and which are not subject to regulation in any other jurisdiction, unless legislative intent is clearly stated. It seems unlikely that satisfactory rules can be developed unilaterally, and it is therefore to be hoped that multi-lateral arrangements can be concluded. The members of the Organization for Economic Cooperation and Development have made a start in this direction, but as yet there appears to have been little progress toward formulation of generally acceptable principles.

8

The Commonwealth and International Sanctions: Two Cases

*Rita F. Taubenfeld and Howard J. Taubenfeld**

This brief review of the action of the members of the Commonwealth of Nations is perhaps of more interest in a historical sense than as an exploration of some patterned phenomena. Of necessity, there is more to be said about Great Britain than about the other states-members.

As used in this paper, "sanctions" means only coercive action undertaken pursuant to a decision or recommendation of an international organization. Even with this limitation in mind, we deal only briefly here with a few of the pertinent events of the past half-century.

The British Commonwealth, Italy, and the League of Nations

In a broad sense, the League system of peacekeeping relied principally on the force of world public opinion marshaled against one who breached the Covenant of the League. Even the very bestowal of the label "aggressor" was considered a significant weapon for peace. While the horrors of 1914–18 and the force of world public opinion were looked upon as the great deterrents to new wars, Article 16 of the Covenant of the League also in fact described the action, economic and military, which members were obliged to take against a member which went to

* Professor, Law School, Southern Methodist University.

war in violation of the Covenant.[1] This action was from the first called "sanctions" by everyone, though the term itself does not appear in the Covenant. In French law "sanctions" means the penalties that can be imposed through legal proceedings, and the term found its way into the preliminary discussions of the Allies when plans for a League were under consideration.

The genesis of Article 16 of the Covenant, like that of the League more generally, is found in the response of the Allied Powers to President Wilson's note of December 18, 1916, raising the question of a League of Nations. The Allies replied with an enthusiastic welcome but pointed out that any arrangements "must provide the sanctions necessary to insure their execution, and so prevent a false security from serving simply to facilitate new aggressions." Every preliminary plan for a League—British, French, American, Italian, German, neutral nations—contained a provision for sanctions as an integral part of the system. Indeed, the ultimate form of Article 16 owes much to the report of March 20, 1918, of a British Foreign Office committee, presided over by

---

1. Article 16:

   (1) Should any Member of the League resort to war in disregard of its covenants under Articles 12, 13 or 15, it shall *ipso facto* be deemed to have committed an act of war against all other Members of the League, which hereby undertake immediately to subject it to the severance of all trade or financial relations, the prohibition of all intercourse between their nationals and the nationals of the covenant-breaking State, and the prevention of all financial, commercial, or personal intercourse between the nationals of the covenant-breaking State and the nationals of any other State, whether a Member of the League or not.
   (2) It shall be the duty of the Council in such case to recommend to the several Governments concerned what effective military, naval or air force the Members of the League shall severally contribute to the armed forces to be used to protect the covenants of the League.
   (3) The Members of the League agree, further, that they will mutually support one another in the financial and economic measures which are taken under this Article in order to minimize the loss and inconvenience resulting from the above measures, and that they will mutually support one another in resisting any special measures aimed at one of their number by the covenant-breaking State, and that they will take the necessary steps to afford passage through their territory to the forces of any of the Members of the League which are cooperating to protect the covenants of the League.

   Paragraph 4 went on to add expulsion from the League by action of the Council as another sanction for breach of the Covenant.

Lord Phillimore,[2] and, interestingly enough, to the views offered by General Smuts of South Africa in his highly influential *The League of Nations—A Practical Suggestion*[3] which captured President Wilson's interest.[4]

While ample documentation supports the view that the creators of the League intended Article 16 to mean what it clearly says, from the very first days of the League's existence the question of the political reinterpretation of the meaning of Article 16 engaged the attention of the members. This was inevitable in view of the failure of the United States to become a member but probably would have occurred in any event. A total ban on all normal relations with an aggressor state had been considered a sure, quick, and relatively costless technique for preventing or suppressing aggression. With the United States left free to trade with the violator, the effect of non-military sanctions was no longer so certain and the United States record of insistence on its right to trade and sail the seas gave a basis for an argument that the dangers of interfering with the United States would fall on a few sea powers, primarily Great Britain. Whether or not this argument was in fact realistic, it apparently proved a substantial factor in League discussions.[5]

In 1920, a League study group, the International Blockade Committee, studied the whole question of economic sanctions. As indicated by Lord Robert Cecil, many nations at that time regarded a blockade, "in view of the wording of Article XVI—'shall *ipso facto* be deemed to have committed an act of war'— . . .

2. On the "Phillimore Plan," see Document 1 in David H. Miller, *The Drafting of the Covenant* (New York, 1928), II, 3–4. Most of the proposals of the United States and the Allies are also printed in Department of State, *Foreign Relations of the United States,* 1919 (Paris Peace Conference), I, 319–324, 497–532. For other drafts, see also Miller, *The Drafting of the Covenant,* II, 7 (Col. House), 12 (Wilson's first draft), 106 (British draft).

3. The book appeared in December, 1918.

4. See, e.g., Wilson's third draft, January 20, 1919, Art. VI, Miller, *The Drafting of the Covenant,* II, 101. For suggestions of Miller and for draft proposals of other countries (France, Italy, Germany), see I, 177–178, 181; II, 239–243, 253, 629–630, 641–643, 761.

5. See F. P. Walters, *A History of the League of Nations* (Oxford, 1952), I, 148. Indeed, when a member of the League a few years later inquired as to the United States' position if the League acted against a member-aggressor, it was informed that the United States must be expected to insist on maintaining full rights of neutrality. See U.S. State Dept., *Foreign Relations of the United States,* 1925, I, 17–18.

[as] a war measure."[6] In answer to a League inquiry in that period, only Great Britain and Finland reported that they were constitutionally able to take action under the Covenant at once if needed.[7]

Other British positions affected later developments at the League. One of the stumbling blocks in Article 16 for those who preferred the *gradual* application of sanctions, for example, was the term "immediately." While Cecil, for England, was forthrightly prepared simply to eliminate the word,[8] others preferred to interpret it away. Also, in the late twenties an attempt was made to provide a means for preventing in advance the defeat of a weak state by one far more powerful. By 1930, the League Assembly by unanimous vote was able to approve a draft treaty under the terms of which a sum up to fifty million pounds, backed by the League's credit, could be made available to an attacked state by a vote of the Council. This Convention on Financial Assistance never came into force either, primarily because of British fears of having to bear much of the cost. Britain insisted that the convention come into force only simultaneously with the first general disarmament treaty, a condition which was never fulfilled.[9]

Aside from this, throughout the late twenties and early thirties formal discussions of Article 16 were studiously avoided. Suggestions for further analysis by the League of its meaning and the advance organization of sanctions measures were rejected by a majority of the members.

The British, Canadian, and South American delegates feared that it might end in fresh definitions or proposals which they could hardly refuse without seeming to fail in their duty as Members of the League, yet which might prove in practice to be an unwelcome limitation of their freedom. The French, Poles, Czechoslovaks and others, on the contrary, feared that it might lead to declarations by particular States

6. Proceedings of the First Assembly, chap. ii, p. 266.
7. The British government apparently relied on the Treaty of Peace Act, 1919, which authorized the Crown to make such Orders in Council as were necessary to carry out the Treaty of Versailles.
8. Proceedings of the Second Assembly, chap. 1, pp. 305–306.
9. Walters, *A History of the League of Nations*, I, 382.

which would diminish the theoretical and practical value of the sanctions system.[10]

League Sanctions Against Italy, 1935/36. Any collective sanctions action is meaningful only against a backdrop of the world politics of the time, and League action against Italy in 1935/36 is no exception.[11] Moreover, there was a special situation with respect to Ethiopia in which Italy, Britain, and France had expressed varying degrees of interest over the years. Agreements between Britain and Italy (1891), Britain-France-Italy (1906), Britain-Italy (1925), and Italy-Ethiopia (1889, 1928) contributed to Italy's feeling of special rights in Ethiopia.

As early as 1928, Italy began to consider the conquest of Ethiopia, and when an appropriate incident occurred in late 1934, a skirmish between Italian and Ethiopian forces at Wal Wal, the Italian government was ready to seize on it.[12] Italy demanded an apology, cash reparations, punishment of those responsible, and a salute to the Italian flag at Wal Wal which it now claimed as Italian. Italian aircraft flew over Ethiopian posts near Wal Wal and some bombs were dropped. An Ethiopian telegram on January 3 reported the massing of troops and attacks by Italian forces and asked that the League's Council take measures to safeguard the peace,[13] but here the realities of European politics overtook the hopes of those who placed their confidence in the League. Britain and France and even Russia looked to Mussolini as a bulwark against Hitler. Had he not in July, 1934, rallied to Austria's support and forced the Germans to hold back? Moreover, in the words of the League's able historian, F. P. Walters:

The British and French governments were not only concerned with Ethiopia as a fellow Member of the League. They were also her neighbours in Africa. They too, like Italy, had for many years cherished hopes of economic expansion in Ethiopia. By the Three-Power Treaty of December, 1906, they had joined her in delineating zones of influence within the frontiers of the Empire; and if they had been less

10. *Ibid.*, p. 380.
11. The authors have in progress a major study of this episode.
12. See Marshal Emilio de Bono, *La conquista dell' Impero la preparazione e le prime operazioni* (Rome, 1937), pp. 8 ff, and, on the secret plan of 1928, *Captured Italian Docs.*, Bag 10, Folder 224/R, Container 1134. On 1934/35, see also Walters, *A History of the League of Nations*, II, 622 ff.
13. See, e.g., *L.N.O.J.*, February, 1935, pp. 252, 258.

resentful than she when the vigilance of the Ethiopian government had brought their plans to nothing, it was only because they had, unlike her, far greater colonial interests elsewhere. Like Italy, they had suffered from frontier raids. With her, they had intervened in the administration of justice, and organized a control over the importation of arms. If now Italy was unwilling to allow the Council to discuss her relations with Ethiopia, if she felt it as an affront to have to deal in public, on equal terms, with the representative of Haile Selassie, this attitude was only too well understood in the Foreign and Colonial Offices of London and Paris. In common with Italy, Britain and France had for fifty years formed an effective zone of separation between Ethiopia and the rest of the world. It seemed to them only natural that the new trouble should also be dealt with among themselves, and that Ethiopia herself and the rest of the League should be expected to approve the result of their discussions. Accordingly, the proceedings of the Council were made to alternate with conversations between Britain, France, and Italy, in which the Covenant was often forgotten and the interests of the League were treated as of small account.[14]

Throughout the spring, negotiations continued to no avail. Moreover, Ethiopia was shunted aside in March when Hitler denounced the prohibition on German rearmament in the Versailles Treaty and reintroduced conscription, and the United Kingdom and France, in response to this developing threat, at once began talks with Italy which culminated in the Stresa Conference of April 11–14. At this meeting, the three powers repledged mutual co-operation in keeping Germany in line and reaffirmed their Locarno commitments, indicating to many the high value of keeping Mussolini friendly.[15]

It was reported that the Ethiopian question, due for League consideration the next day after the conference ended, was never discussed by the parties despite evidence on all sides of Mussolini's preparation for armed conflict. If these reports are true, it may well be, as Mussolini argued, that he was misled by what he considered a proof of Franco-British acquiescence in his colonial move, perhaps a *quid pro quo* for his stand against Germany in

14. *A History of the League of Nations*, II, 628.
15. For reports and comment, see *Times* (London), 1955, April 11, 12, 13, 15. The "Locarno Pact" of 1925 (Cmnd. 2525), to which France, the United Kingdom, Belgium, Germany, and Italy were parties, included guarantees of the Franco-German and Belgian-German frontiers.

what most Europeans probably felt was the more important arena.[16]

Later, in another attempt to avoid direct action, Eden was sent by the British government to Mussolini on May 23 with a compromise offer. Mussolini dismissed the offer out of hand. Eden reported to his government that Mussolini appeared shocked that Laval's "free hand" was not to be interpreted broadly and that he was apparently firmly fixed in his purpose.[17] Thereafter, in May, the League Council sought to insure a settlement through conciliation and arbitration within a three-month limit, but by early July it was obvious that Italy would not co-operate. During all of July, the British Cabinet remained unwilling to give clear answers to diplomatic inquiries as to how far Britain would go in support of the League. The League Council procrastinated again on July 31.

In August, three-power negotiations were conducted by the United Kingdom, France, and Italy, from which Ethiopia was excluded, in which Italy was offered limited territorial acquisitions and economic advantages. These collapsed on August 18 when Italy rejected all proposals.[18]

In this same period, Italy was relatively successful in another technique for crippling Ethiopia. When Ethiopia tried to procure arms, the Italian government let it be known to other governments that any sales would be regarded as "unfriendly" acts and "acts of deliberate hostility." During the summer of 1935, such countries as France, Czechoslovakia, Belgium, and Denmark banned sales of arms to Ethiopia while Britain embargoed sales to

16. See Winston Churchill, *The Gathering Storm* (Boston, 1948), pp. 133–134, and Gaetano Salvemini, *Prelude to World War II* (New York, 1954), pp. 191–199.

17. For an account of this mission, see Anthony Eden, *Facing the Dictators* (London, 1962), pp. 247–252. For comment, see Mario Toscano, "Eden's Mission to Rome on the Eve of the Italo-Ethiopian Conflict," in Arshag Sarkissian, *Studies in Diplomatic History and Historiography in Honor of G. P. Gooch* (London, 1961), and Henderson B. Braddick, "The Hoare-Laval Plan: A Study in International Politics," *Review of Politics*, XXIV (1962), 342–364, at 346–347.

18. See Walters, *The Drafting of the Covenant*, II, 640, and Eden, *Facing the Dictators*, pp. 279–284. For a statement of the Italian position in these various negotiations in the spring and summer of 1935 and an indication of how unreasonable the Italians felt other nations were in not agreeing to outright Italian annexation of parts of Ethiopia and domination over the rest, see *Secret Report on Political Conditions in France*, 1935, Italian Foreign Office, *Captured Italian Docs.*, Container 1291, pp. 16–20. On the three-power talks see L.M. Doc. C 411 (1) M 207 (1) 1935 VII and, for summary, see *Times* (London), August 19, 1935.

both Italy and Ethiopia, the latter having no manufacturing plants at all. Further, the French authorities at Jibuti, the only entry port for such arms as Ethiopia could buy, made transit almost impossible.[19]

By August, the fact of Italian intentions had penetrated public thinking in other countries, and a conflict in Africa, and perhaps in Europe as a result, was widely anticipated and widely feared. Sentiment in England and France was clearly divided but certain patterns had emerged.

In England, there was popular support for a firm stand in the League, even including such sanctions as the closing of the Suez Canal, if necessary, and this included the backing of the Trades Unions and the Labour party despite a generally felt hatred of war and recent widespread pacifist tendencies.[20] The famed "Peace Ballot," the results of which were reported in late June, 1935, showed some 11 million votes (97 per cent) favoring Britain's remaining in the League; 10 million (94 per cent) supporting economic sanctions if needed; and a surprising 6.8 million (74 per cent) approving the use of force against any aggressor.[21]

Many groups—business interests fearing Italian confiscations and loss of markets, elements of the labor movement concerned with getting into an "imperialist" war, and the unreconstructed among the pacifists who wanted no chance of war with Italy or any other nation—continued to urge against the possibility of

19. On claims as to difficulties caused Ethiopia by the embargo and these acts, see statements of the Empress of Ethiopia, *For. Rel.*, III (1936), 70–72, and Walters, *The Drafting of the Covenant*, II, 641.
20. On September 2, 1935, William Kean, president of the Trades Unions Congress, spoke in favor of sanctions, including "the further step of closing the Suez Canal to Italian ships [which would] bring her campaign to a standstill" even if it meant war (*Times* [London], September 3, 1935). A huge majority at the Labour party conference in late September also supported the sanctions policy. See *Times* (London), October 3, 1935. (For oppositions' views, see statement by New South Wales Labour Council, *ibid.*, September 27, 1835.) See also, the study of opinion in the United Kingdom made by P. Vaucher and P. H. Siriex, *L'Opinion Britannique* (*La S.D.N. et la Guerre Italo-Ethiopienne*) (1936), and of opinion in the United Kingdom and France in an unpublished thesis by P. H. Arnot, *Problems Connected with the Application of League of Nations' Sanctions against Italy* (University of Calif., Berkeley, 1955), *passim*. For news reports and comment on the opposition to sanctions, see also *Times* (London), September 23, 1935, and New York *Times*, September 22, 23, 1935.
21. On the "Peace Ballot," see Adelaide Livingstone and M. S. Johnston, *The Peace Ballot* (London, 1935), *passim*, and New York *Times*, July 2, 1935.

sanctions. Additionally, the "Maffey" Committee, an interdepart-
mental committee of the British government set up on March 17
to study United Kingdom interests in Ethiopia, reported secretly
in June that an Italian conquest would not necessarily interfere
with British interests in Africa.[22] Nevertheless, the Italian moves
in general offended both the British sense of justice and (in
rejecting all British efforts for a peaceful settlement) the sense of
national pride, and the government was, if anything, pushed on
by public opinion. The Italian threats were widely considered to
be a challenge to the existence of the League and to the United
Kingdom in the Mediterranean in particular as well. There was
also concern over the effect of an Italian victory on English colonies and on the loyalties of colored peoples generally and a fear
that Italy in Ethiopia might endanger British interests in the
upper Nile and also might raise a "black army" to attempt further
African expansion.[23]

On the other hand, the Admiralty insisted that Britain was very
weak in the Mediterranean and urged a cautious policy. Malta
was relatively defenseless, and even proposed slight increases in
that island's antiaircraft defenses had not been effected as late as
September.[24] The British Cabinet, meeting in emergency session
on August 22, was apparently still not sure enough of its ground
to take a firm decision with respect to League action and ad-
journed to await developments.

In France, unlike Britain, while there was some support for a
strong stand in the League, French newspapers, except for the
Left, strongly campaigned for lenient and considerate treatment
of Italy. Moreover, France was particularly angered by an Anglo-German Naval Treaty of June 15, 1935, which permitted German naval construction up to 35 per cent of British strength, in
direct contravention of the Versailles Treaty. Indeed, this treaty

22. See Arnold Toynbee and V. M. Boulter, *Survey of International Affairs*
(London, 1935), II, 42–44.
23. For a frank discussion of the threat to United Kingdom interests in the
Mediterranean and in Ethiopia, including the desire to protect Lake Tsana, the
source of the Blue Nile, see lead article, *Financial News*, September 23, 1935, and
on other factors mentioned in this paragraph as making for support of a firm
policy, see telegrams from Atherton, U.S. Chargé, August 20, 22, 1935, *For. Rel.*, I
(1935), 633, 636–637.
24. Eden, *Facing the Dictators*, pp. 279, 284.

appears to have frightened the Italians as well since England seemed quite willing to risk offending France in an effort to appease Hitler and, perhaps, send him east or south, rather than west.[25] The French in general appear to have echoed Laval's question of early September to England: "Italy now gives France security against German aggression. What is the British contribution?"

In September, Sir Samuel Hoare, speaking in the Assembly, indicated what seemed clearly to be a firm intent on the part of the British government to uphold the Covenant vigorously and to take a strong stand against any overt move by Italy. It may of course have been the contemplation of elections, in view of widespread popular British sympathy for support of the League, which impelled the government to take its stand. While it has also been suggested that the strong speeches on and after September 11 are "tainted" by a Franco-British understanding that, at most, mild sanctions would be applied, even mild sanctions were more than most observers were then predicting. And Hoare's words announcing Britain's willingness to resist "all acts of unprovoked aggression," were cheered at Geneva and by the press and most of the public in Great Britain.[26]

The French Premier continued through early September to stress that Italy was a "pillar of European security" and that French concern centered on Germany first, but in a speech on September 13, he shocked the Italians by stating that "our obligations are inscribed in the Covenant. France will not fail to discharge them." This development was attributed in Italy to British pressure on Laval.[27]

The Italian diplomatic and propaganda campaign against damaging sanctions was now brought to a high pitch. Italian-inspired

25. See *ibid.*, pp. 257–259; Churchill, *The Gathering Storm*, p. 139; D. C. Watt, "The Anglo-German Naval Agreement of 1935: An Interim Judgment," *Jour. of Modern History*, XXVIII (1956), 155–175.

26. See Eden, *Facing the Dictators*, Book I, chap. 14 and pp. 292–294, and *Times* (London), September 12, 1935, September 16, 1935, editorial, "A Plain Issue," New York *Times*, September 12, 1935.

27. *Secret Report on Political Conditions in France*, 1935, Italian Foreign Office, *Captured Italian Docs.*, Container 1291, p. 25. Cf. V. Gayda, editorial in *Giornale d'Italia*, September 11, 1935, on "methods" by which England is attempting to sever the bonds between France and Italy.

reports were circulated early in August that most types of sanctions would be regarded as "unfriendly" and that some, for example, the closing of the Suez Canal, meant war. Mussolini declared in interviews that *military* sanctions, at least, meant "war" with the consequence that millions would die and the map of Europe might be revised.[28] By September, the British Ambassador reported that "in their present mood, both Signor Mussolini and the Italian people are capable of committing suicide if this seems the only alternative to climbing down. Rome today is full of rumors of an impending declaration of war on Great Britain. . . ."[29] Laval too insisted that general war was extremely likely and that a "mad dog" attack on the British fleet in the Mediterranean or on Malta was certain.[30] This was all nonsense but it had its effect.[31]

As late as September 24, the British Foreign Secretary was insisting to the Cabinet on a cautious approach to sanctions and in fact Mussolini apparently was advised by Britain that military sanctions would not be considered.[32] Finally, on October 3, at the end of the African rainy season, Italy invaded Ethiopia.

The Sanctions Measures. There is little point here in detailing the sanctions measures. The first five adopted undertook to cut off sale of many products to Italy, to limit her exports, to cut off credit, to cut off arms, and to provide mutual assistance for affected League members. To avoid the possibility of a veto, sanctions action was co-ordinated by a co-ordination committee of the whole, excluding Italy and Ethiopia. Its guiding body, the Committee of Eighteen, included Britain, Canada, and South Africa.[33] All action was in fact taken with certain limited assur-

28. *Le Matin*, September 17, 1935, and *Daily Mail*, September 26, 1935.
29. Eden, *Facing the Dictators*, p. 294.
30. *Ibid.*, p. 296.
31. See, e.g., telegram from U.S. Consul, Geneva, September 19, 1935, U.S. State Dept., File 765.84, No. 1361; *Times* (London), September 18, 19, 1935; Eden, *Facing the Dictators*, pp. 297–298.
32. *Ibid.*, pp. 300, 302.
33. On proceedings in the Council and Assembly, see John Fischer Williams, "Sanctions under the Covenant," *Brit. Year Book Int. Law, 1936* (London, 1936), 130–149. For analysis see Julius Stone, *Legal Controls of International Conflict* (rev. ed.; New York, 1959), pp. 176–184.
Descriptions of the setup and functioning of the Coordination Committee and its lesser organs are found in Phillips Bradley, "Some Legislative and Administrative

ances in mind, for despite numerous bellicose pronouncements, Italy reportedly gave private assurances to France that economic sanctions would *not* mean war.[34]

Indeed, while many proposals for sanctions were discussed in the Committee of Eighteen, "military" measures, including a naval blockade and/or the closing of the Suez Canal, were promptly and publicly ruled out for France and the League by Laval.[35] While his statement remains unconfirmed in its full sweep, Laval later told the French Chamber of Deputies on December 28, 1935, that he had met with Hoare, Eden, and Lord Vansittart on September 10 and that there had been agreement "upon ruling out military sanctions, not adopting any measure of naval blockade, never contemplating the closure of the Suez Canal . . . in brief, we agreed to rule out everything that might lead to war."[36]

While Italy's neighbors—Austria, Hungary, and Albania—refused to comply with the League's measures and while neutrals did somewhat increase trade with her, the general compliance with the sanctions, certainly by Britain and the Commonwealth members, was reasonably good. It is nevertheless true that even after international agreement on the measures had been reached, substantial segments of British and especially French internal public opinion continued to oppose sanctions for what were basically Europe-oriented political reasons. As we have seen, the continuing political grounds for opposition included, in England, a desire for non-participation in "European" affairs and basic pacifism.[37]

Aspects of the Application of Sanctions," *Trans. Grot. Soc.*, XXII (1937), 113; R. A. Levitch, *La collaboration dans l'application des sanctions* (Paris, 1938), pp. 55–75; Stone, *Legal Controls*, pp. 176–184, *passim*.

34. For report of private assurances to France, see New York *Times*, October 3, 1935.

35. For Laval's statement of October 13, 1935, disclaiming armed sanctions, see New York *Times*, October 14, 1935, *Times* (London), October 14, 1935. On armed sanctions, see Stephen Heald, ed., *Documents on Int. Affairs*, 1935 (London, 1937), II, 316, 343, 368, 403–404.

36. See Toynbee and Boulter, *Survey of International Affairs*, II, 185. Cf. A. C. Johnson, *Anthony Eden* (London, 1938), p. 293.

37. On England, see *Report of a Franco-British Conference on Collective Security* (non-governmental), December 27–31, 1935 (Int. Student Serv.), pp. 43–44, 46; C. A. W. Manning, "Sanctions—1935," *Politica*, II (1936), 44–55. On differing French views, see Conference Report, cited above, pp. 50–53; telegram

In addition there were many economic problems which were implicit in the implementation of sanctions, including fear of repercussions on participants, the "legal" difficulties in "breaking" contracts, losses in special industries, *sudden* loss of markets, alternative supply sources, and the job of controlling re-exports.[38] In short, economic factors, the potential loss of business at a time of unemployment and depression during the sanctions period, and the further fear of permanent loss of the Italian market also entered into the molding of public opinion and made it more difficult for governments to apply sanctions wholeheartedly, particularly since no punishment was meted out by the international community to non-co-operating members.

In spite of all difficulties, some states, like Great Britain and the Commonwealth countries, after some early confusion on enforcement problems, seem to have been able to make the restrictive policy of sanctions function quite well. Other states, either deliberately or through inherent inertia and malfunction, never solved the administrative problems of sanctions or set up sufficiently comprehensive control organizations.[39]

Italian forces in Ethiopia made certain early gains but soon lost impetus, and on November 16, Marshal Bagdolio replaced Marshal de Bono as commander in chief, and the late fall and winter months were spent in consolidating positions captured. During this time, League members debated the advisability of adding other strategic materials to the effective embargo, while France and Britain, with reluctant League approval, went on with the attempt to conciliate and, in effect, appease Mussolini. In December, the "Hoare-Laval Proposals" were developed, which would have given Italy a large portion of Ethiopia outright and would have assured privileges to Italy in the southern half of the coun-

---

from the U.S. Chargé, France, October 14, 1935, U.S. State Dept. File 765.84, No. 1804 (on the French press); and, for the statement on the "communist" menace, made by Laval to U.S. Ambassador Straus, see *For. Rel.*, I (1935), 675 (Oct. 29, 1935).

38. See telegram from Gilbert, U.S. Consul, Geneva, October 19, 1935, U.S. State Dept., File 765.84, No. 1938. For summary of reported French fears, see New York *Times*, October 9, 1935.

39. For a description of the national systems employed and the difficulties encountered in 1935/36, see Elton Atwater, *The Administration of Export and Import Embargoes 1935-36* (Geneva, 1938).

try.[40] The terms were so favorable that Italy was expected to agree promptly; the plan had in fact been conditioned on Italy's immediate acceptance. The British Cabinet accepted it on this express basis, for example, on December 9. The proposals were to be kept secret as well but were leaked. The plan was of course formulated *after* the British fall elections which saw a Conservative sweep, based at least in part on support for the League.

In any event, public opinion in England and even in France was dismayed by the actions of the governments concerned.[41] Ethiopia received the plan with "hostility," and it was reported to have contributed to a "profound pessimism . . . and loss of will to resist."[42] As a result, Hoare resigned and Laval spoke of the need to bring Italy back into the European balance through a "fair" settlement in Africa. Privately, he spoke of his doubts of being able to get the French to fight if war broke out elsewhere because of a continuation of the crisis, and many French and foreign diplomats agreed with both his views.[43] The plan died with its exposure to light.

In February, Italian troops achieved some sizable victories. Now, by hinting at withdrawal from the League and a rapprochement with Hitler if new sanctions were imposed, Italy obtained an indication from the French Ambassador, Chambrun, on February 27, that France would do all in its power to avoid further sanctions.[44] Then, on March 7, any real threat of increased sanc-

40. For details of the plan, see L.N., *Off. Jour.*, January 1936, p. 39, and British White Paper, Cmnd. 5044, Ethiopia No. 1 (1935). In general, see Salvemini, *Prelude to World War II*, pp. 389–408.

41. For background, see report by the U.S. Ambassador, France, January 29, 1936, *For. Rel.*, III (1936), 100–102. For adverse comment in England, France, Canada, Geneva, etc., see *Times* (London), December 11, 13, 19, 1935; New York *Times*, December 10, 11, 13, 14, 15, 1935, sec. 4 (Survey at Geneva). To the same effect as to England, see reports by the U.S. Ambassador, England, December 11, 1935, *For. Rel.*, I (1935), 700–701, 703–705 (noting the reaction despite strong pressure from "industrial and financial interests" to avoid war).

42. See dispatch from Engert, U.S. Minister Resident in Ethiopia, May 5, 1936, *For. Rel.*, III (1936), 68–70.

43. On Hoare's resignation and reasons therefor, see *Times* (London), December 19, 1935, and sources cited, n. 49 below. On Laval, see telegram from U.S. Minister, Switzerland, December 12, 1935; U.S. Ambassador, U.K., December 16, 1935; and U.S. Ambassador, France, December 17, 1935, reporting on Laval's speech in the Chamber on December 17, *For. Rel.*, 1 (1935), 708, 712–713, 714–715.

44. See report, U.S. Ambassador, Italy, March 2, 1936, *For. Rel.*, III (1936), 113.

tions vanished as German troops marched into the Rhineland. The Italian government asserted that sanctions had ended any Italian obligation to take a stand against a German move, and though Italy agreed with England, France, and Belgium that a clear violation of Locarno had occurred, no action was taken. The French government reportedly pressed for action against Germany at this time, but the British government, unwilling to take the chance of armed conflict, refused to take any firm steps.[45] On March 20, French Foreign Minister Flandin told the Chamber of Deputies that he was seeking to end rapidly both the war in Africa and sanctions as well.[46]

In April, Eden stated that Britain was willing to consider further sanctions, and Denmark, Rumania, and Turkey spoke in a similar vein, but no proposals to this end were made and most of the nations were obviously resigned to an Italian victory. Still, the Council voted to maintain the sanctions then in force, and Italy's use of poison gas came in for much criticism. The British press and public continued to urge a strong League stand, but the French press now made it clear that France would support Italy, not Britain or the League.[47]

In June, the Italians consolidated their conquest of a large part of Ethiopia, and pressure increased within the League from many countries which desired to bring Italy back into the fold as a counterweight to Germany, while Mussolini renewed his threats to leave the League and mobilize fully if sanctions were not dropped.[48] Rumors were also current of an Italo-German agreement, and on June 10 Neville Chamberlain, then chancellor of the

45. Churchill, *The Gathering Storm,* pp. 193–202. For the view of the Soviet government that the German move had ended the possibility of further sanctions, see report of the U.S. Ambassador, U.S.S.R., March 7, 1936, U.S. State Dept., File 765.84, No. 3900.
46. See New York *Times,* March 21, 1936.
47. On the French outlook at this time, see reports of the U.S. Consul, Geneva, April 11, 1936, and the U.S. Minister, Switzerland, April 20, 1936, *For. Rel.,* III (1936), 119, 127–128. For press reports, see New York *Times,* 1936, April 17, 19, sec. 1. See also e.g., *Le Temps* and *Liberté,* April 11, 1936. On Britain, see editorial, *Times* (London), April 8, 1936, New York *Times,* May 8, 9, 1936.
48. See, e.g., report of threat made to the U.K. Ambassador, Sir Eric Drummond, New York *Times,* June 13, 1936, and speech by Mussolini on June 22, New York *Times,* June 22, 1936. For reports of Czech and Soviet desires to get Italy back into the fold, fearing Germany as the only enemy, see New York *Times,* June 13, 14, 1936, sec. 4, June 21, 1936, sec. 4.

exchequer, termed the continuation of sanctions "the very midsummer of madness." The Cabinet agreed to end sanctions on June 17, and on June 18 Eden announced in the House of Commons that sanctions no longer served a useful purpose.[49] All this was done without consultation with the French or other League members. Sanctions were ended by the League on July 4, effective July 5.

Measures Not Adopted by the League: The Suez Canal and a Petroleum Embargo. There were two measures which might have seriously interfered with and perhaps totally prevented aggression in Ethiopia: the closing of the Suez Canal to Italian shipping and the addition of petroleum and its by-products (and certain other items as well) to the embargo list. The Suez closure would have been a more stringent measure than the economic sanctions actually employed, but it was recognized by all concerned in 1935 that such a sanction, undertaken in time, would have substantially prevented Italy's sending men and supplies to the war front and would have made the conquest almost impossible. Indeed, Toynbee remarked at the time on

the inexplicable ineptitude of His Majesty's Government in deliberately releasing [Mussolini] from the strategic trap into which he had wantonly walked when he had placed a huge Italian army—as a pawn commanded by British naval pieces—on the further side of the Suez Canal, with the British Fleet concentrated in the Levant, while the Italian Army . . . was at Great Britain's mercy even for obtaining its supplies of drinking water.[50]

Through the canal, by April, 1936, passed 450,000 Italian soldiers and workers. The important League powers were aware of the importance of the Suez link. In speaking to this point after the failure of sanctions, Foreign Minister Eden summarized for the House of Commons the significance of the Suez move and the reasons why it was not taken:

49. See Hansard, June 18, 1936, pp. 1199 ff. (House of Commons, Parl. Debs., Vol. 313, 5th ser., 1204). The Debates in Commons on June 18 and 23, 1936, are conveniently reprinted in *Int. Conciliation*, No. 322 (September, 1936), pp. 329–431. For comment, see *Times* (London), June 19, 1936, and New York *Times*, June 19, 20, 1936.
50. Toynbee and Boulter, *Survey of International Affairs*, II, 451.

There was only one sanction that could be immediately effective and that sanction was to deny to Italy the use of the Suez Canal. That sanction must inevitably have entailed military action; you could not get out of it. That military action must, in my judgment, inevitably have led to war. . . .

[y]ou cannot close the Canal with paper boats. . . . It is perfectly clear from [Article 1 of the Suez Canal Convention] . . . that the Canal could not have been closed except by League action. . . .

In view of the attitude of many Governments and even of [the *Daily Herald*, the Labour party spokesman] towards sanctions, . . . [could] a unanimous League Resolution . . . have been passed to close the Canal? I am absolutely convinced that there was never the least hope for it.[51]

Nevertheless, though full details are still lacking, there are indications that in June, 1935, Eden had in a measure threatened Mussolini with a closure of the canal. "When questioned by Mussolini during a meeting of June 24–5, 1935, as to what the British Government's reaction would be to a comprehensive military campaign by Italy, [Eden] is reported to have said that in that case the Suez Canal would no longer be available for Italian troopships."[52] There were also then-current reports that Eden and Laval, in informal talks, discussed the closing of the canal during the summer of 1935 while the Italian preinvasion buildup was in progress. A violent campaign by Italian officials and press including repeated threats that such a closure was the equivalent of a "declaration of war" was the Italian reaction to all such suggestions.[53]

In general, the nations of the world, for various reasons, were not willing to face up to even a hint of war. While it appears that the British government, supported by the British people, may

51. Report of the debate, *Times* (London), May 7, 1936, p. 8, col. 2.
52. Johnson, *Anthony Eden*, pp. 280–281.
53. For hints at talks in the summer of 1935, see New York *Times*, August 11, 1935, sec. 1, p. 25, col. 3. The authoritative *Times* (London) discussed the possibility of closing the canal on August 21, 1935, and took the position that, though the United Kingdom would not take this step unilaterally, it could do so on a League of Nations "mandate" (p. 10, col. 1). For the Italian threats, see e.g., V. Gayda, editorial, *Giornale d'Italia*, August 22, 1935 (closing Suez violates the Convention of 1888 and is illegal—"sanctions signify war").

have renewed overtures to the French government in early October, 1935, as to the closing of the canal and the Strait of Gibraltar as well, the French flatly refused to support any such steps, and military and naval measures, or a Suez blockade in support of the League, do not seem to have come up for serious consideration after this early display of interest.[54] Indeed, by October 22, 1935, Hoare referred, in the House of Commons, to rumors of a closing of the canal as "provocative" and "without foundation," and Laval, it may be recalled, had already insisted on October 13 and thereafter that there was no question of armed sanctions or a blockade.[55]

If discussion of closing the Suez Canal was thus largely kept out of the League's council chambers, the possibility of adding petroleum and its derivatives, pig iron, iron, and steel in various forms, coal, and coke to the embargo lists received extensive airing, though no effective action was taken in this direction either. Of this list, petroleum was the most important to Italy and was most widely discussed in the League. When the petroleum embargo was not effectuated, the other items dropped from consideration as well.

The dependence of Italy on imported oil was well understood at the time and she appeared extremely vulnerable to an embargo on oil, a key product in modern warfare as, of course, in modern industry. Indeed, Britain and the Scandinavian countries controlled most of the world's oil tankers and could see to it that they were unavailable to Italy.

54. On British willingness at various times, on British-French talks, and on the French refusal to consider these steps, see telegram, Gilbert, U.S. Consul, Geneva, October 6, 1935, U.S. State Dept., File 765.84, No. 1681; *Times* (London), August 21, 1935, p. 10, col. 1; Memorandum, January 29, 1936, U.S. State Dept., Office of Arms and Ammunition Control, File 765.84 (1936), No. 3602 (information from a "Tory M.P."), and report of an interview of Eden by Felix Morlay, editor of the Washington Post, cited *For. Rel.,* III (1936), 151. Note again that there was continuing *public* support for a Suez closure. Thus, on September 2, 1935, William Kean, president of the Trades Union Congress, called for sanctions, including the closing of the canal, even if it meant war (*Times* [London], September 3, 1935, p. 12, col. 7).

55. On the British debate, see *Times* (London), October 23, 1935, pp. 8–9 (esp. p. 8, cols. 3–7). For Laval's statement of October 13, see New York *Times,* October 14, 1935, p. 8, col. 1. In general, see Heald, *Documents on International Affairs, 1935,* II, 316, 343, 368, 403–404.

For these reasons, a petroleum embargo was recommended on November 6, to be effective "as soon as the conditions necessary to render this extension effective have been realized." The measure never came into force, despite British efforts, because the French, Russians, Rumanians, and others were in fact very reluctant, through fear of political and economic losses, to consider the extension, particularly to oil.[56]

The Italian government was very much aware of the potential dangers of an oil embargo and engaged in vigorous measures of stockpiling, limiting home use, and using alternative fuels. Indeed, our own estimate, aided by hindsight knowledge of actual Italian war needs, is that even if the League had adopted the sanction at the start, no gross interference with the war would have occurred. Nevertheless, it was an essential part of a program of economic pressure against the Italian economy. Even without American participation, as the League's experts pointed out (and as Italy's fears, preparations, and threats testify), such an embargo would have made purchases by Italy "more difficult and more expensive" and hence would have further drained Italy's economic reserves. It would certainly have caused additional strains on Italian war industry. Furthermore, it would have vastly inconvenienced the populace to whom Mussolini sought to bring an easy victory. Most important, it would have added to the loss of Italian foreign exchange for needed purchases. Since all of these factors were clear and were clearly recognized by most observers, and since an oil embargo was obviously the type of economic pressure which belonged in any effectively designed program of economic sanctions against Italy, the political reasons for its omission reveal the genuine motives, fears, intentions, and delusions of the League sanctionists.

If we lay aside as not decisive the campaigns conducted in England, France, and other countries by those who sympathized

---

56. See in general, report of U.S. Consul, Geneva, September 9, 1935, *For. Rel.*, I (1935), 862–863. On the credence given in many European nations to Italian threats of war and vaunted Italian air, sea, and land power and on the contribution of these beliefs, however erroneous, to the failure to push through additional measures, see Salvemini, *Prelude to World War II*, pp. 265–268.

with Mussolini's aim and sought to speed an Italian victory, we find one recurrent theme on all sides compelling inaction, particularly with respect to closing Suez, but also in connection with an oil embargo. As Eden put it, in the comment cited earlier: "That military action [the closing of Suez] must, in my judgment, inevitably have led to war. . . ." If we accept this judgment at face value, and if the use of armed forces was an intolerable possibility even for those who rallied to the standard of collective security, then Mussolini's course was plain. Any sanction which was serious enough to cause certain immediate interference with his plans must be denounced as "a cause for war."[57]

Were these threats believed? Laval told United States Ambassador Strauss that war was certain if petroleum was embargoed, that Italy would be strangled and Mussolini would fight rather than face civil war. He continued to assert his belief as late as 1945 that an oil sanction would have meant war.[58] Certain British leaders proclaimed the same view. Sir Samuel Hoare, defending his plan in the House of Commons on December 19, 1935, stated that from all sides he had reports that Italy would consider an "oil embargo as a military sanction or act involving war against them." He added that the United Kingdom was not "afraid" of Italy but that it would have led to the dissolution of the League if the United Kingdom stood alone.[59] In any event, no one could guarantee that Mussolini would not take a rash step rather than be forced out of power in the event he was forced to bring the

57. See statements by Mussolini to Laval, reported by U.S. Ambassador, Italy, November 26, 1935, U.S. State Dept., File 765.84, No. 2750. A correspondent of the *Times* (London) also reported that Italians seemed to feel that an oil sanction would justify a military reaction in substantially interfering with the campaign: "Let us bring down others with us in our fall if fall we must" (*Times* [London], November 28, 1935, p. 14, col. 4). See also New York *Times*, November 24, 1935, p. 1, col. 8, and Herbert Feis, *Seen from E.A.* (New York, 1947), p. 250. In the Chamber on December 7, 1935, Mussolini stated that the threat of an oil sanction raises "considered anger" and the Foreign Office again termed it "military" in January. See report of U.S. Ambassador, Italy, *For. Rel.*, III (1936), 88, and *Times* (London), December 9, 1935, p. 13, col. 1.

58. U.S. State Dept., File 765.84, No. 2966; see also France, Haute Courde Justice, *Procès du Maréchal Pétain* (Paris, 1945), p. 185.

59. The debate in Commons is set out in full in *Times* (London), December 20, 1935, pp. 6 ff. Cf. telegram from Wilson, U.S. Minister in Switzerland, December 6, 1935, reported talk with Motta, U.S. State Dept., File 765.84, No. 2939.

troops home or failed to overcome a blockade of Suez.[60] As one American diplomatic observer has summarized the situation:

I believe that some members of the British Cabinet were impressed with the continued reports from Italy that Mussolini and the Italian people were in a frame of mind to assault Great Britain if the League adopted the petroleum embargo which was then under discussion. Even those members of the Cabinet who did not so believe were unable to guarantee that this was not the fact. The British had found that in spite of the assurances given by the French Government, the French people could not be relied on to take a stand against Italy.[61]

Since for some it was enough that there could be no absolute certainty that war would not ensue and, for others it was enough that any success against Italy could alienate and weaken Mussolini, the "needed ally" against Germany, it was easy to feel morally justified in not calling the Duce's bluff.[62]

Mussolini in fact appears to have been quite aware of Italy's military shortcomings, as explicitly pointed out to him in reports from the Italian General Staff, and dreaded war with England as

60. On the "edginess" of the Italian population over Suez in September, and on the possibility that Mussolini might go wild if threatened with defeat, see report of U.S. Ambassador Long, September 24, 1935, U.S. State Dept., File 765.84, No. 1342. "Cairo opinion was reportedly to the effect that the UK was loathe to close the Canal due to fear of war" (report of the U.S. Chargé, Cairo, October 28, 1935, U.S. State Dept., File 765.84, No. 2709). In addition to making threats, the Italians frequently pointed out to *Egypt* that a UK threat to close the canal would be an "implicit denial of Egyptian independence." (Senator Forges-Davanzoti, "The Power that Threatens Egypt," *Tribuna* (Rome), April 29, 1936. Cf. Report, U.S. Chargé, Rome, May 1, 1936, U.S. State Dept., File 765.83. No. 23.

61. Hugh R. Wilson (former U.S. Minister to Switzerland), *Diplomat between Wars* (New York, 1941), p. 319.

62. The British General Staff and Admiralty were reported to believe that they could handle Italy alone and that, if France helped, they could overwhelm Mussolini.

In early October, the British asked the French government if it would support the United Kingdom in the event of an Italian attack on the British fleet. After some hesitation, the French agreed. By the end of December, France, Greece, Turkey, and Yugoslavia agreed to support the United Kingdom but *only in the event* of an Italian attack on the British fleet in the Mediterranean, and the League was so informed on January 22, 1936. See report of U.S. Ambassador, London, December 28, 1935, U.S. State Dept., File 765.84, No. 3270. For texts, etc., of the mutual aid arrangements, see Cmnd. 5072, Ethiopia No. 2 (1936); *Dispute Between Ethiopia and Italy* (correspondence, January, 1936). See also *Times* (London), October 5, 1935, p. 12, col. 3, and October 11, 1935, p. 11, col. 4. No action was ever taken under the arrangements. On their termination, see New York *Times,* July 26, 1936, p. 25, col. 1, and July 28, 1936, p. 1, col. 6.

an evil to be avoided even at great cost.[63] Thus, in a secret letter to De Bono, commander of the Italian forces in Africa, Mussolini wrote that if, after the attack was made on Ethiopia, "we get into trouble with the English we would naturally renounce our offensive and confine ourselves to the defensive in order to preserve the entity of the colony."[64] In addition, on September 28, 1935, it was unanimously agreed that all efforts should be made to avoid extending the conflict, and shortly thereafter, a "secret" order (which became general diplomatic knowledge) was sent to all Italian merchant ships to submit peaceably to search immediately if stopped by a British war vessel.[65]

While the closing of the Suez Canal seems to have been opposed within most member states largely because of the fear of war of any kind together with the fear of loss of Italy as a worthy ally, the oil sanction was met by an additional somewhat contradictory and perhaps equally compromising objection made by several members and supported in part by the League's Committee of Experts, namely, that it was pointless for members to apply a petroleum embargo since the United States could supply all of Italy's requirements. Even in the United Kingdom, which supported an oil sanction, the government noted the fears of its own producers as to the current and *possibly permanent* loss of the Italian market.[66] The Scandinavian countries were concerned as well in that some 275,000 tons of Norwegian and Swedish shipping had been engaged in carrying oil to Italy and the Italian colonies principally from the Gulf of Mexico in the second half of

63. The reports demonstrated Italian weakness as compared with the British in naval and air forces. See documents published in the *Corriere d' Informazione* (Milan), January 14–17, 1946.

64. De Bono, *La conquista*, p. 137.

65. Telegrams from U.S. Ambassador, Italy, September 28 and November 13, 1935, U.S. State Dept., File 765.84, Nos. 1452, 2518. See also *Times* (London), October 16–18, 1935 (*passim*), October 25, p. 14, col. 3 (on the Italian withdrawal).

On Italian fears as late as the spring of 1936 that the United Kingdom might take serious action, see letter from Amadeo Landini, Italian Consul, Paris, to Ciano, April 18, 1936, *Captured Italian Docs.*, Containers 416–418, Frame 008641.

66. Oral communication to the U.S. government, December 5, 1935, *For. Rel.*, I (1935), 871–872. On fears in other countries on these grounds, see New York *Times*, December 8, 1935, sec. 3, p. 1, cols. 1, 6.

1935—a lucrative business, particularly since freight rates had been advanced 50 to 100 per cent in the period.[67]

The argument that the United States could supply all Italian needs is contradictory of the "threat of war" objection to a petroleum embargo in that the former suggests that such a measure would be ineffective because of other potential sources of supply while the latter suggests that the restriction would be so effective as to make Mussolini consider it cause for war. It was technically correct that the United States was the chief producer of petroleum in the world, but this same statement could have been made about many other products.[68] It, of course, totally ignored the point that Italy was not in a position financially to purchase extensively from the United States since cash payment was required. Such purchases, if possible, would have constituted a severe drain on Italy's gold and foreign asset reserves, a result which was one of the principal aims of sanctions in any case. In any event, no formal approach was made by the League to the United States on the question of co-operation in an oil embargo, on the one hand because of the desire of the United States government to steer an "independent" course and, on the other, because of the awkwardness of the position of League members who did not want such an embargo if the United States had agreed to co-operate.[69] Unlike the proposal for closing the Suez Canal then, which was so "deadly" that it could barely be mentioned in Geneva's halls, the petroleum embargo was discussed and discussed until Italy's victory made it superfluous to kill it formally.

Thus, in part because of the plea of fear of war by League members, and in part because of fear of economic loss, the scope

67. Rates increased some 30 per cent from August to December on oil cargoes to Italy and some 70 per cent to Eritrea in that period—Greek and Danish vessels also participated in the traffic and profits. See *Times* (London), December 27, 1935, p. 9, col. 3, and New York *Times*, January 28, 1936, p. 10, col. 5.
Other European countries were reported as resisting the embargo through fear that a precedent might be established which might some day be used against them in turn! (*ibid.*)

68. On United States petroleum production, see U.S. Dept. of Interior, *Minerals Yearbook* (Washington, D.C., 1938), pp. 815–854. On United States exports, see U.S. Dept. of Commerce, *Commerce Reports*, XXXIX (February 15, 1936), 121.

69. See Debates in the House of Commons, June 18 and 23, 1936; Cordell Hull, *Memoirs* (New York, 1948), I, 415, 426–434, *et passim*; and M. J. Bonn, "How Sanctions Failed," *Foreign Affairs*, XV (January, 1937), 350–361, at p. 359.

of international sanctions was permitted to be dictated by the convenience of the country being subjected to them. In the context of the times, and with the German menace the overwhelming concern of France, these fears were not incomprehensible. Nevertheless, Winston Churchill's assessment, at a later date, of the actual military potentials of Italy and England is applicable to the League in general in 1935/36:

> Apart from a limited advantage in modern light cruisers, her navy was but a fourth the size of the British. Her numerous conscript army, which was vaunted in millions, could not come into action. Her air power was in quantity and quality far below even our modest establishments. She would instantly have been blockaded. The Italian armies in Abyssinia would have famished for supplies and ammunition. Germany could as yet give no effective help. If ever there was an opportunity of striking a decisive blow in a generous cause with a minimum of risk, it was here and now.[70]

Yet the "decisive blow" was never delivered. Perhaps it is appropriate to cite here too an allusion to the period made by Anthony Eden in Commons on November 1, 1956, while defending his role as Prime Minister in sending troops into Egypt:

> Now may I go back to the personal accusation made yesterday, that I myself was too much obsessed by the events of the "thirties and, in consequence, old fashioned?" However that may be, is there not one lesson of that period which cannot be ignored? It is that we best avoid great wars by taking even physical action to stop small ones. Everybody knows that the United Nations is not in a position to do that. We and the French have the forces available. We must face the fact that the United Nations is not yet the international equivalent of our own legal system and the rule of law.[71]

It is true that, being in part the victim of the internal dynamics of its own propaganda and its own committed course of action, the Italian government might, if pushed to the wall by such a measure as the Suez closing, have "felt it more honorable to be defeated by the United Kingdom than by the League. . . ."[72] In

---

70. *The Gathering Storm*, p. 177.
71. Brit. Info. Serv., Doc. T.60, November 1, 1956.
72. Compare telegrams from Wilson, U.S. Minister, Switzerland, December 12, 1935, and from Atherton, U.S. Chargé, U.K., U.S. State Dept., File 765.84, Nos. 3038, 3055. At the time, the British certainly did not discount the Italian threats completely.

the political setting of the times, this possibility proved sufficient to cool both the British ardor for any non-League-supported closing and other members' support for any such League-approved action as well. The closing of the Suez and any effective positive support for Ethiopia had no real chance, and the petroleum embargo was foredoomed by the same factors, combined with an out-and-out desire not to lose potential profits to an "outsider." All of this sounds familiar today.

The Effects of the Sanctions on Britain. In the status of British-Italian trade relations at that time, participation in the sanctions does not appear to have been very costly to Britain. The potentially adverse effects of the employment of sanctions on economic conditions within such major powers as England and France seem to have been played up in advance in those countries by groups which sought to prevent the adoption of the measures, and they were kept before the public by those who desired to bring sanctions to a speedy end, including the official representatives of Italy in the United Kingdom. Of perhaps greater importance was the position of certain business interests which not only disliked the loss of possible trading gains during the sanctions period but also feared the possible permanent loss of the Italian market, in accordance with threats made by the Italian government, and the redirection of that market to competitors such as Germany and the United States.

The United Kingdom and the Commonwealth in general adopted all of the League measures promptly. Trade with Italy for the period of sanctions quickly reached a very low point. For the entire sanctions period, exports to Italy fell off to $3.9 million from about $35.4 million for the equivalent 1934/35 period. Nevertheless, the general improvement in world trade during this period, from which England was one of the chief beneficiaries, permitted the United Kingdom as a nation to offset this loss successfully by increased trade to other countries, thus immediately correcting the dire forecasts of some of the most outspoken early critics of sanctions that any United Kingdom participation in economic measures would automatically mean economic ruin.

Britain's trading prosperity clearly facilitated the support of sanctions by the government. If there had been no such general expansion of trade it might have been more difficult to rally sustained public sentiment in favor of sanctions which in fact reduced United Kingdom exports to Italy to 5 per cent of their previous value by January, 1936. This loss, of course, was partly balanced in a sense through the receipt by certain domestic industries of orders formerly given to Italy, as was the case with Lancashire cotton mills and other textile producers.[73]

Overall trade between the two countries had in any event been on the decline for several years, and banks in the United Kingdom had cut down on commercial credits to Italy in August, 1935, well in advance of the League action, primarily for business reasons, since it had proven impossible to collect commercial debts from Italy promptly and Italy's balance of payments position was steadily growing worse.[74] In October, 1935, before sanctions became effective, Italy was a clearing debtor to Great Britain under the then-current clearing agreement to the extent of some $8–10 million. British imports of silk cocoons, raw silk, silk yarns, and silk manufactures, rayon manufactures, hemp, and hides, in particular, all fell off before November, 1935, as Italian wholesale prices rose under the impact of Italian stockpiling. In related fashion, English firms as early as June began to demand immediate payment for bunker coal. In July, export to Italy of pig iron was cut off since producers had not yet been paid for February deliveries. British coal, wool, cotton, and oil producers voiced similar complaints.[75]

On the other hand, Britain did lose her position as a major source of coal to Italy at about the time of sanctions and experienced a drop of about 10 per cent in total coal exports for 1936. Coal was not a prohibited product, but Italy, being short of

73. See, e.g., New York *Times*, October 28, 1935, p. 23, col. 6.
74. The reluctance of British importers to sell except for payment in gold because of fears of indefinite postponement of payments was explained in an aide-mémoire from the United Kingdom to the United States, dated August 17, 1935 (*For. Rel.*, I [1935], 628, 630). See also *Financial News* (London), August 23, 1935; New York *Times*, September 21, 1935; and "Sanctions and Italian Trade," *Bull. of Int. News*, XII (May 23, 1936), 872 ff.
75. For press reports, see New York *Times*, July 24, August 1, and October 1, 1935.

sterling and gold, found it preferable to satisfy most of her needs in Germany and Poland where barter agreements were available. This switch in suppliers, however, merely accentuated a probably inevitable condition which had become a definite trend before the sanctions period.[76] Clearly, the coal miners and operators of England were experiencing difficulties in the mid-thirties which had nothing to do with sanctions, but these problems were intensified even before sanctions by the shift in Italian purchases, equal to about 10 per cent of expected exports of coal, or more than 1 per cent of production.

In general, comparing overall Italo-British trade for the years before and after sanctions leads to the conclusion that, although participation in sanctions produced no significant permanent alteration in the general trend of United Kingdom–Italian trade, trade between the two countries had, in fact, been declining all during the thirties as part of the general breakdown of the world trading and international currency systems, as well as the probable gradual obsolescence of some British industry. The autarchical measures of the Italian government, together with the difficulties experienced by the British in obtaining payment for goods sold, had begun to have an effect by 1935 quite apart from the sanctions which came into force toward the end of the year. As Walter Runciman, president of the Board of Trade, reaffirmed to the House of Commons in July, 1936, the precise economic effects of participating in sanctions could never be estimated with accuracy since, even in the field of trade where United Kingdom exports (including re-exports) declined to $2.4 million for the period December, 1935–June, 1936, from about $31 million for the same period in 1934/35, "it is not possible to attribute the whole of this decline to sanctions."[77] Owing to payment difficulties and Italian import restrictions, United Kingdom exports to Italy were declining before sanctions were imposed. Since Italy accounted for only 2–3 per cent of British trade in normal years, and, as we have seen, British overall trade *increased* during the sanctions period, it is not easy to discern any general, serious short-range

76. See Lord Templemore, Hansard, May 6, 1936, col. 833.
77. New York *Times*, July 21, 1936.

effect on the general economy of the United Kingdom. Without sanctions, of course, it is logical to suppose that overall British trade would probably have been even greater.

On the other hand, regional British difficulties may have been aggravated by sanctions for a period, as with the coal industry, and some business firms certainly suffered losses. Others may well have profited by supplying goods which could no longer be imported from Italy. Again, an exact balance for the economy as a whole is impossible to calculate.

In general, then, and despite the near-impossibility of separating the economic effects of sanctions from all the other factors bearing on an economy, it seems probable that the British economy suffered neither permanent nor serious overall effects from strong participation in sanctions. Moreover, while pressure from business interests may have contributed to the British government's willingness to sponsor such appeasing measures as the Hoare-Laval proposals and to terminate sanctions by the summer of 1936, even the Italian Foreign Service recognized that the British public in general was unimpressed by trade considerations and remained steadfast behind the sanctions measures.[78] The effects on other members of the Commonwealth appear to have been even less noticeable.

Of course no one experience can indicate the total range of potentials. Italy of 1935 is not Africa of 1966, in which Britain has perhaps $6 billion in overall investment.[79] It is to southern Africa that we now turn briefly.

South Africa, Southern Rhodesia, and South-West Africa

The United Nations Charter, unlike the Covenant, provides, in Chapter VII, for a set of circumstances in which the organization's members can legally be required to participate in measures

78. See *Secret Report on Political Situation in the U.K.*, 1936, Italian Foreign Office, *Captured Italian Docs.*, Container 1289.

79. See G. V. Doxey, "The South African Problem: A Conflict of Nationalism," *Int. Journal*, XVIII (1962/63), 501–512.

up to and including the use of armed force. In practice, with very few exceptions, the United Nations too has only *recommended* "sanctions." There have been a number of such instances. The most dramatic perhaps was Korea where members of the "old" Commonwealth, especially Britain, Australia, and New Zealand, actively supported the United States in its role as the United Nations Command and where others, and even India, aided the international activities. Southern Africa is especially instructive both in the light of Commonwealth development and the attempts of the United Nations to exert influence through sanctions measures. A brief review will separate three questions for analysis—South Africa, South-West Africa, and Rhodesia—though all are closely linked.[80]

The Republic of South Africa. South Africa, the most prosperous and technologically advanced nation on the African continent, is an unquestionably independent state whose internal policies differ so markedly from those professed by other nations that most of the United Nations members have voted to call for a change in her domestic constitutional arrangements and her prevailing domestic ideology and ethical system.[81] Indeed, some states, at least, advocate the use of international force if needed to impose the demanded internal political changes.

South Africa is a country of mild climate and rich treasures whose major products include diamonds and much of the world's new monetary gold. The Dutch traders who established a village

80. The studies which follow draw heavily on the paper prepared by the authors for the December, 1966, Hammarskjold Forum of the Association of the Bar of the City of New York entitled *Race, Peace, Law, and Southern Africa.*

81. For detailed studies, see, among many, Colin Legum and Margaret Legum, *South Africa: Crisis for the West* (New York, 1964); Amelia Leiss, ed., *Apartheid and United Nations Collective Measures: An Analysis* (New York, 1965); E. A. Walker, *A History of Southern Africa* (3d ed.; London, 1957); Ronald Segal, ed., *Sanctions Against South Africa* (Baltimore, 1964); D. Hobart Houghton, *The South African Economy* (Capetown, 1964); Leopold Marquard, *The Peoples and Policies of South Africa* (3d ed.; Capetown, 1962); Julius Lewin, *Politics and Law in South Africa; Essays on Race Relations* (New York, 1963); Richard Dale, "South Africa and the International Community," *World Politics,* XVIII (1966), 299, an excellent review article; Waldemar Nielsen, *African Battleline: American Policy Choices in Southern Africa* (New York, 1965); Amelia C. Leiss, "American Policy and the Future of Southern Africa," *World Politics,* XIX (1966), 151–165, a review article. For a brief account, especially of apartheid, see *Wall Street Journal,* July 13, 1966.

at the Cape of Good Hope in 1652 were the first white men to settle in the empty area in the southern extreme of the continent. There are now some 3.4 million whites who rule some 12 million Bantu (blacks), 1.5 million Coloureds (mulattoes), and a half million Asians.

During the Napoleonic Wars, England seized Capetown from the Dutch. Gold and diamonds were discovered in the 1870's and 1880's, and as the British moved in the South, the Boer (farmer) descendants of the Dutch moved farther inland, fighting and pressing back the Bantu who made their appearance along the frontier. The Boers established the Republic of Transvaal and the Orange Free State in the north while the British formed Natal and the Cape Colony in the south. In a war from 1899 to 1902, the British defeated the Boers and unified the country.

In conformity with the Commonwealth concept, then primarily for European-stock self-governing members, South Africa became largely autonomous by the end of World War I. After World War II, the Afrikaner-dominated Nationalist party obtained parliamentary control, and the policy of apartheid (official separate development) became the rule of the land, formalizing and further elaborating in law the already existing white discriminations and control and intensifying and sanctioning in law all types of racial segregation. In 1961 the Republic of South Africa was born as the country left the Commonwealth after being denounced on the apartheid issue.

South Africa's policies and way of life came to the attention of the United Nations in its first sessions.[82] In 1946 India brought to the General Assembly a complaint about the treatment of people of Indian origin in South Africa. Discriminatory measures against the Indians had led to passive resistance movements directed by Ghandi in 1907 and 1913, followed by agreements between India and South Africa in 1927 and 1932; but additional discriminatory legislation in 1943 and 1946 led to Indian protests, the withdrawal of the Indian high commissioner to South Africa and a trade embargo by India. India's boycott, incidentally, led to a

---

82. See sources cited in n. 81.

shift by South Africa to use of Pakistan as a major supplier of jute, much to India's annoyance. At the United Nations, India urged that this was both an international dispute and a violation of the United Nations Charter provisions barring racial discrimination. South Africa argued that Article 2(7) prevented even discussion of the matter, and that the Charter did not define human rights, so that either the issue should die for lack of legal certainty of the rights to be protected or the question of the General Assembly's competence should go to the International Court of Justice.[83] India urged that "fundamental violations of the principles of the Charter" and human rights could not be matters of domestic jurisdiction.[84] The Assembly adopted resolutions on these issues at almost every session through the sixteenth, at which time the question was merged into that of apartheid. Positions have not subsequently changed.[85] South Africa was urged to negotiate with India and to ameliorate the economic, legal, and social condition of those of Indian descent in her population, but South Africa has not yielded at all on this issue.

In general on these issues, the older Commonwealth members—the United Kingdom, New Zealand, Australia, Canada—for many years favored limited steps at most. They supported procedures before the ICJ in 1947. They favored discussion and conciliation between the parties. They doubted the right of the United Nations to act vigorously. They opposed or abstained on most of the General Assembly resolutions urging relief for those of Indian origin. Only Pakistan joined India in most cases through 1954. In 1956, Ceylon joined India's side and on occasion so did Ireland and Canada. In 1957, Malaya was added. In 1958, Ghana arrived. By 1962, several more votes for India's position were added.

83. See, e.g., *U.N. Journal*, No. 54, Supp. A-A/:.V/50, p. 349. The United States, the United Kingdom, Sweden, and some other states supported the suggestion of an ICJ opinion (*ibid.*, pp. 350–353).
84. *Ibid.*, p. 356; Panama, p. 370; China, p. 363.
85. For a summary of the resolutions, see Carnegie Endowment, *Synopses of United Nations Cases* (New York, 1966), p. 5, and I *Repertory of UN Practice*, Arts. 1–22 of the Charter (1955), 67–75, Art. 1054 of the Charter, Supp. No. 1 (1958), 29–32; I *ibid.* Arts. 1–8, Supp. No. 2 (1964), 126–129. See also Marjorie M. Whiteman, *Digest of International Law* (Washington, D.C., 1965), V, 336–343.

In 1961, however, when a draft resolution proposed sanctions against South Africa, including expulsion, the United Kingdom, Australia, and New Zealand opposed it and the draft was not adopted. Then, in September, 1962, the Indian issue was combined with the general issue of apartheid.

Apartheid as a separate issue has been before the United Nations since 1952, when India, Pakistan, and other African and Asian countries, thirteen in all, placed it on the agenda as a threat to international peace as well as a violation of basic principles of human rights.[86] Initially, of the Commonwealth, the United Kingdom, Australia, and New Zealand joined South Africa in urging that the United Nations lacked competence to discuss this "internal" matter and that, in any event, peace was not endangered. Canada was less sure.[87] Other countries rejected South Africa's position completely.[88] In the end, a three-member commission was appointed to study the racial situation in South Africa.[89] That commission, on October 3, 1953, concluded that action of the Assembly with respect to human rights was not "intervention" within the meaning of Article 2(7) and that South Africa's racial policies violated the Charter and the Universal Declaration of Human Rights which were said to ban discrimination on racial lines and also impaired friendly relations among states.[90]

The General Assembly discussed and adopted resolutions on South Africa's racial policies at every session thereafter, and the Security Council has, less frequently, acted as well.[91] On April 1, 1960, after the Sharpeville massacre, the Council recognized that the situation in South Africa had led to international friction, and

---

86. For summary of action to date, see Carnegie Endowment, *Synopses of United Nations Cases*, pp. 27–28; "Issues Before the 21st General Assembly," *Int. Conciliation*, No. 559 (September, 1966), pp. 113–119. See also Whiteman, *Digest*, V, 364–377.

87. For survey of South Africa's responses to UN demands, see A/AC.115/L.103 (Index of December 21, 1964).

88. Discussion took place in the Ad Hoc Political Committee and in Plenary Meetings (GAOR, 7th Sess., *passim*).

89. Res. 616A (VII), and see Res. 615 (VII).

90. See GAOR, 8th Sess., Suppl. No. 16.

91. See, e.g., Moses Moskowitz, *Human Rights and World Order* (London, 1959), pp. 37–43. For a list of various ineffectual measures adopted over the years by the United Nations and the Organization for African Unity and Conference of Non-Aligned Countries, see UN Doc. S/6210, Annex VI.

if continued, might endanger international peace and security, and it called for measures to bring about equality and racial harmony.[92] In 1961, the Assembly also resolved that South Africa's policies had led to international friction and that they endangered international peace.[93] As we noted above, a proposal at this time to recommend economic sanctions failed to obtain the needed two-thirds vote.

Again, on these earlier votes concerning apartheid, the "white" Commonwealth tended, in 1952–59, to oppose United Nations condemnations, using negative votes or abstentions. By 1956, the newer members began to arrive—Ceylon, Ghana, Malaya, Cyprus, Nigeria, Sierra Leone. By 1960, even the older members were voting for some of the broader condemnations, and even earlier, on some occasions, Canada or New Zealand had voted with India.

Then, in November, 1962, the Assembly was able to muster the votes to adopt a resolution condemning South Africa's "determined aggravation" of racial issues. Members were asked to end diplomatic relations with South Africa, to close their ports and airspace to her ships and aircraft, and to impose an embargo on imports from and exports to her, especially arms.[94] A Special Committee on Policies of Apartheid was established to keep South Africa's racial policies under review and report regularly to the United Nations. The Security Council was asked to take appropriate measures, including sanctions, to secure South Africa's compliance with United Nations resolutions. Among the sixteen states voting against the resolution, however, were South Africa's chief trading partners—Britain, the United States, France, Canada, Australia, Japan, and Belgium.[95] All the recommended economic and diplomatic sanctions to date have had little perceptible effect on South Africa's economy or her policies.

In August, 1963, the Security Council called on states to cease

---

92. Sec. Council Res. 134 (April 1, 1960).
93. Res. 1598 (XV). See also G.A. Res. 1663 (XVI).
94. Res. 1761 (XVII).
95. Of the Commonwealth countries, New Zealand also opposed the resolution, while Ceylon, Cyprus, Malaya, Ghana, India, Jamaica, Nigeria, Pakistan, Sierra Leone, Tanganyika, Trinidad and Tobago, and Uganda supported it.

the sale of arms, munitions, and military vehicles to South Africa;[96] in October the Assembly called for the release of South African political prisoners; and in December the Council asked for the establishment of a group of experts to examine the whole problem.[97] In April, 1964, that group called for the convening of a truly representative national assembly, on the basis of one man, one vote, to alter South Africa's constitutional structure to provide an integrated non-racial society. The commission recommended the use of mandatory economic sanctions if South Africa failed to agree. The General Assembly accepted this report and its suggestions for the internal political reorganization of South Africa.[98] Needless to say, the South African government has not complied and no mandatory sanctions have been ordered by the Council.

In March, 1965, a study of economic sanctions prepared by a committee of experts at the request of the Security Council was presented to the United Nations.[99] Here, the nature of the South African economy was explored at length, and its peculiar strength as a well-industrialized, if small, country and as an exporter of gold and diamonds, both light in weight and greatly sought after, were noted. It was also suggested that for an economic break to have any substantial effect, it would have to be sharp and total both in goods and countries involved, that it probably needed at least a naval blockade to make it effective, and that in addition to the costs of such a naval campaign, which are high, it would doubtless be costly to many of the participating states in loss of trade and potential South African countermeasures with respect to foreign investments and property.[100] South Africa has heeded all

96. Sec. Council Res. 181 (August 7, 1963).
97. See S/5471 (December 4, 1963). For other resolutions in 1963, see G.A. Res. 1978A (XVIII) and 1978B (XVIII), 1881 (XVIII), and Sec. Council Res. in S/5386.
98. The report is in S/5658 (April 20, 1964). It has been separately printed as *A New Course in South Africa*, U.N. Sales No. 64. I. 13. The experts were Alva Myrdal, Edward Asafu-Adjaye, Hugh Foot, Dey Ould Sidi Baba, and Josip Djerja (resigned in March, 1964).
99. S/6210 (March 2, 1965). The committee was established by Sec. Council Res. S/5773 (June 18, 1964).
100. The Security Council adopted the report but with only six votes in favor (including the United Kingdom).
For other studies of the potential efficacy of economic measures against South

the warnings in these studies and United Nations actions by stockpiling, intensifying the search for reliable access to resources—especially oil—at home, in Angola, and elsewhere, and in other ways making ready for all eventualities.

In 1965, the General Assembly again deplored the military buildup in South Africa and the continued growth of foreign investment there, requested an arms embargo, called the continued existence of apartheid a threat to international peace and security, and called anew for at least economic action by the Security Council under Chapter VII.[101] An attempt to enlarge the Committee on Apartheid during 1966, no doubt in an attempt to involve those states which had not approved earlier calls for sanctions against South Africa, was frustrated by the refusal to serve of the United States, the United Kingdom, France, and twelve others. This precipitated further attacks on their "participation" in apartheid. Some, like France, which has not even agreed to the arms embargo with which the other major powers are officially co-operating, opposed generally the interventionary aims of the United Nations in this case; others, while supporting the ends, apparently objected to the somewhat precipitous ways in which the committee conducted its investigations and made its condemnations.[102]

While some sixty-one states have apparently applied an eco-

Africa, see William A. Hance, "Efforts to Alter the Future: Economic Action," in Leiss, *Apartheid*, 95 ff.; *Atlas*, January, 1965, pp. 22 ff. (the cases for and against sanctions); and Segal, *Sanctions Against South Africa*, esp. pp. 62–84 (legal aspects), 107–119 (strategic implications), 120–134 (trade), 135–152 (petroleum), 153–166 (gold), 167–185 (the impact on the United Kingdom), 186–196 (the impact on the United States), 204–233 (the impact on the High Commission Territories).

On military measures, see chap. 7 in Leiss, *Apartheid*.

For the author's general views on the lack of efficacy of economic measures alone against a determined, prepared state which considers that its vital interests are at stake, see Rita F. Taubenfeld and Howard J. Taubenfeld, "The Economic Weapon: The League and the United Nations," *Proc. Am. Soc. Int. Law* (Washington, D.C., 1964), pp. 183 ff.

101. See Res. 2054A and B (XX), December 15, 1965. On events in 1965 generally, see "Issues Before the 21st General Assembly," *Int. Conciliation*, No. 559 (September, 1966), pp. 114–119.

102. For replies of governments, see UN Doc. A/6356 (S/7387) (June 29, 1966). See also UN Docs. A/6226 (April 6, 1966), p. 3; A/AC. 115/SR. 72 (May 6, 1966), esp. p. 4; A/AC. 115/SR. 70 (June 29, 1966), para. 20. The Soviet Union accepted. See *UN Press Release*, WX/248, July 1, 1966.

nomic embargo, the major Western powers and the "old" Commonwealth have not limited trade, except in arms. Any obligatory enforcement action under Chapter VII has been resisted for economic reasons, the fear of disastrous loss of trade and investment (especially in view of the probable ineffectiveness of economic measures if used alone), and an unwillingness to go beyond economic measures to the use of force and the supplying of men, ships, and arms for a potentially bloody fight.[103] The Council's resolutions have been worded in terms of Chapter VI, which deals with the "peaceful settlement" of disputes and does not provide for mandatory action.[104]

Despite the United Nations' concern, foreign investment is heavy and continuing, with the United Kingdom's total commitments in the area alone estimated at perhaps $3 billion, and white immigration continues, presumably attracted by the economic opportunity in Afrikanerland, where a renewed boom has been in progress since 1961, and where foreign investment earns high returns and a white man has a good life and cheap native help.[105] Moreover, in response to Black African and international pressure to achieve a "non-racial" society, South Africa has unified under the Afrikaner banner.[106] The late Dr. Verwoerd's Nationalist party won a three-to-one majority in the general election held in early

103. On the United Kingdom, see UN Doc. A/SPC/SR. 472 (December 6, 1965), p. 10, and see sources on sanctions cited n. 80 above. See also, e.g., France (Doc. A/SPC/107 [December 3, 1965], p. 2), United Kingdom, and United States. For other responses to the embargo resolutions, see Secretariat summary in A/AC. 115/L. 143 (July 13, 1965).

104. See, e.g., Sec. Council Res. 191 (June, 1964).

105. For attacks on Western (i.e., United Kingdom, United States, and French) investment (in South Africa especially, but in other areas of southern Africa as well) and for documentation, see A/AC. 115/L. 133, June 6, 1965 (report on investments by the Committee on Apartheid); A/AC. 115/L. 36 Rev. 2, August 22, 1966 ("Foreign Investment in the Republic of South Africa," report by the Secretariat); and New York *Times*, October 26, 1966 (comments of Mr. Achkar), *Wall Street Journal*, July 13, 1966. United States investment is on the order of $650 million and annual United States–South African trade is at about $400 million. On the fury of Black African states at the continuing trade and investment, at loans from the West and even from the IBRD and the IMF to South Africa and South African firms, see New York *Times*, March 2 and May 12, 1966, and *UN Press Release*, WS/253, August 5, 1966, p. 6. On the boom, see *Economist*, August 7, 1965, esp. p. xxi.

106. On the unifying effect, see "Why South Africa is the West's Business," *Economist*, August 7, 1965, p. xii. See this article generally for a survey of South Africa.

1966, with white opposition parties all but disappearing.[107] The present solidarity of all major white groups, Afrikaner and English, behind the government is clear. While some changes may be in view, Verwoerd's successor, Vorster, has reaffirmed the sanctity of apartheid.[108] Thus far, at least, despite the views of the "new" Commonwealth members, the older members of the club have been unwilling to chastise this former member at the risk of damage to themselves.

Southern Rhodesia. Southern Rhodesia is, in the view of most of the world's nations, technically still a colony under British legal control, though in revolt against the motherland. Here, the issue is the postindependence constitutional bargain and consequently the political control of the country after independence. At present, some 217,000 whites rule Rhodesia's 150,000 square miles and 4 million natives with nearly absolute control.

Historically, Rhodesia was never subjected to very firm British control.[109] Conquered by Rhodes on his own behalf, it was long run as a private preserve. After World War I, the white population rejected union with South Africa and, instead, in 1923 adopted a constitution according the colony almost complete self-government. Under British pressure, a federation with Nyasaland and Northern Rhodesia was formalized in 1953, with complete independence as a functioning "multi-racial society" and "full membership in the Commonwealth" for the combined entity as the asserted goal. The federation had a brief life; the vast

107. See New York *Times*, April 3, 1966, p. E9. The main opposition party, the Union party, went so far as to try to outdo the Afrikaners by suggesting open aid to Rhodesia. See New York *Times*, March 14, 1966. On the opposition parties, see Joseph Lelyveld, "Minority of One" (re Mrs. Suzman), *New York Times Magazine*, March 20, 1966, p. 34; Nadine Gordimer, "Why Did Bram Fischer Choose Jail?" *ibid.*, August 14, 1966, p. 30.

108. See editorial, New York *Times*, September 14, 1966, pp. 15, 18.

109. On Rhodesia in history, see Douglas G. Anglin, "Unilateral Independence in Southern Rhodesia," *Int. Journal*, XIX (1963/64), 551 ff.; Herbert J. Spiro, "The Rhodesias and Nyasaland," in Gwendolyn M. Carter, ed., *Five African States* (Ithaca, N.Y., 1963). On the UN developments in 1965/66, see *Issues* (1966), pp. 67–77.

On the rule of law in Southern Rhodesia before UDI, see Gaius Ezejiofor, *Protection of Human Rights under the Law* (London, 1964), pp. 234–244.

In general, see James M. Boyd, "The Rhodesian Tangle," *Vista*, II, No. 1 (July–August, 1966), 33–39; *Time*, August 26, 1966, pp. 18–25; David Barton, "A Look at Rhodesia," *Vista*, I, No. 4 (January–February, 1966), 29–35.

native majorities, with voting rights, in the other areas were suspicious from the outset of Southern Rhodesia's white-controlled government, which denied similar voting rights to its non-white majority. When that federation began to break up, Southern Rhodesia adopted a new constitution (1961) removing the United Nations' reserved powers but retaining British sovereignty. Thus, by 1961, the "colonial" relationship was already largely formal. Nevertheless, legal independence was withheld over the issue of the lack of adequate constitutional provision for African voting rights and parliamentary representation.

In 1962, the United Nations first acted affirmatively with respect to Southern Rhodesia, despite Britain's assertion that this was her private affair when, in June, the General Assembly asserted that the area was a non-self-governing territory and called on the United Kingdom to suspend the 1961 constitution and protect the native population.[110]

In 1963, agreement with the United Kingdom was reached to dissolve the federation as of January 1, 1964, and the United Kingdom vetoed a Security Council proposal that the United Kingdom not transfer sovereignty or federation military forces to the government of Southern Rhodesia. The Assembly then adopted resolutions with the same terms, asking also that there be no independence without majority rule based on universal suffrage.[111] The "old" Commonwealth members abstained or refused to participate.

In Rhodesia, demands for independence grew, but the British, under Commonwealth and African pressure, refused approval since there was still no firm commitment to eventual majority rule. In 1964, the United Kingdom asserted that it would not accept a unilateral declaration of independence (UDI) and in late spring the Security Council urged all states to ignore any UDI. In October, 1965, the General Assembly condemned any

110. G.A. Res. 1747 (XVI), June 28, 1962. The General Assembly earlier asked its Special Committee to determine whether or not Southern Rhodesia had attained independence. See G.A. Res. 2745 (XVI), February 23, 1962. The "old" Commonwealth uniformly opposed this resolution; the newer members supported it.
111. For discussion, see S/7382, pp. 133 ff. The vetoed resolution is in S/5425/Rev. 1. See G.A. Res. 1883 (XVII).

attempt to seize independence and called on the United Kingdom to suppress any rebellion if one broke out. On November 11, 1965, Southern Rhodesia, despite urgent British warnings and threats, declared, unilaterally, its independence.

Immediately after the unilateral declaration of independence the General Assembly called on the United Kingdom to end the rebellion and asked the Security Council to consider the matter. On November 12, meeting at the United Kingdom's request, the Council condemned the UDI and called on all states to deny recognition to the Smith regime and to refrain from aiding the rebels.[112] No state to date has recognized Rhodesia's independence.

Although the United Kingdom had theretofore insisted that the United Nations had no competence to deal with the internal affairs of the territory, it now believed the matter of "minority rule" to be of world concern, though still Britain's responsibility.[113] On November 20, in response to the African states' demands, the Council condemned the "usurpation of power" and called on the United Kingdom to bring the regime to an immediate end and to take measures that would allow the people of Southern Rhodesia "to determine their own future." It called on all states not to recognize or establish diplomatic relations with the illegal authority; to refrain from providing the regime with any assistance or encouragement, particularly arms, equipment, and military material; and to sever economic relations and institute an embargo on oil and petroleum products. It also asked the OAU to assist in implementing this resolution.[114] This was thus a call for complete economic sanctions against the rebel government, including a petroleum embargo. Following the Lagos conference, a Commonwealth Sanctions Committee was set up. In early 1966, Prime Minister Wilson predicted that sanctions would end the rebellion "in a matter of weeks";[115] he was wrong.

112. See G.A. Res. 2024 (XX) and Sec. Council Res. 216 (1965).
113. UN Doc. S/PV. 1257 (November 12, 1965), p. 12.
114. Sec. Council Res. 217 (1965), UN Doc. S/PV. 1257 (November 12, 1965), p. 12. Some international organizations such as GATT, ILO, UNESCO, and WHO, have suspended official communications with Southern Rhodesia, and all experts serving under the auspices of the United Nations Development Programme have been withdrawn to Zambia.
115. See editorial, New York *Times*, February 1, 1966.

Since UDI, the United Kingdom, under great Commonwealth and international pressure from the new states, has reaffirmed its sovereignty over the area, has adopted a full range of economic sanctions, and has obtained overwhelming United Nations support for all nations to do the same. Pressured by the African members of the Commonwealth, it has now asked the United Nations for mandatory (compulsory) economic sanctions to replace voluntary measures, though the scope of the embargo is not all-inclusive. Britain has also made it clear however that no military force will be used to retake the colony, despite demands by the African states.[116] Britain has also made it clear that it would prevent a United Nations use of force, what Prime Minister Wilson has called a "Red Army in Blue Berets."[117]

In April, 1966, two tankers appeared near the port of Beira, Mozambique, apparently loaded with petroleum for Rhodesia. The Security Council, meeting at the United Kingdom's urgent request, declared that the "resulting situation constitutes a threat to the peace." It called on Portugal "not to receive at Beira oil

---

116. On demands for the use of force, see among many, Draft Sec. Council Res. S/7285/Add. 1 (May 11, 1966), which failed at the 1285th meeting (May 23, 1966) by 6-1-8; debates in the fourth committee in 1966, GA/T/1573–1580; *UN Press Releases*, WS/261 (September 30, 1966), p. 22 (Nigeria); WS/263 (October 14, 1966), p. 3 (India), p. 10 (Gabon), p. 12 (Iraq); WS/264, p. 3 (Zambia), p. 4 (Mali), p. 6 (Madagascar), p. 7 (Congo), p. 10 (Ceylon), p. 11 (Somali Rep.). On African feeling about Rhodesia generally, see John Hargreaves, "Pan-Africanism after Rhodesia," *World Today*, XXII (February, 1966), 57–63.

In answer to suggestions from Africa that the British will never use force against a "white" area, Boyd, "The Rhodesian Tangle," points to the American colonies and to Cyprus and Ireland in this century. There is undoubtedly little feeling in the United Kingdom for violence against Rhodesia however (*ibid.;* A. LeJeune, Dallas *Morning News*, September 20, 1966, p. D2. See also New York *Times*, September 15, 1966.

117. See Barton, "A Look at Rhodesia," p. 35, n. 10; Brit. Info. Serv., November 12, 1965, No. T.83, p. 15. The United Kingdom has nevertheless reaffirmed that independence will not be granted unless six principles are met, including: (*a*) Unimpeded progress to majority rule, already enshrined in the 1961 constitution, to be maintained and guaranteed; (*b*) Guarantees against retrogressive amendment of the constitution; (*c*) Immediate improvement in the political status of the African population; (*d*) Progress toward ending racial discrimination; (*e*) The British government would need to be satisfied that any basis proposed for independence was acceptable to the people of Rhodesia as a whole; (*f*) The "need to ensure that, regardless of race, there is no oppression of majority by minority or of minority by majority." See Southern Rhodesia, Documents Relating to the Negotiations between the United Kingdom and Southern Rhodesian Governments, November, 1963–November, 1965, Cmnd. 2807 (London, November, 1965), pp. 99–100, and Brit. Info. Serv. Docs. T.69, October 11, 1965, and T.2, January 25, 1966.

destined for Rhodesia" and "not to permit oil to be pumped" through the Beira-Umtali pipeline, and requested all states to divert any of their vessels "reasonably believed" to be carrying oil for Southern Rhodesia. In addition the Council called on the United Kingdom to prevent "by the use of force if necessary" the arrival at Beira of vessels "reasonably believed" to be transporting oil to Southern Rhodesia.[118] The Council thus, for the first time, authorized a state to carry out a Council decision taken under Chapter VII ("Action with Respect to Threats to the Peace, Breaches of the Peace and Acts of Aggression") of the Charter.

The United Kingdom succeeded in preventing the unloading of these tankers, but the Smith regime, bolstered by receipt of supplies (especially petroleum from and through South Africa and Mozambique), appears to have the internal economic situation well under control.[119] Sanctions have reportedly rallied the

118. Sec. Council Res. 221 (April 9, 1966). Rhodesia, in response, severed most of its remaining ties with the United Kingdom.

In discussing this move, France found no threat to the peace but did not interpose a veto (S/PV. 1277, p. 51) while the United States called it a "grave" step but supported it (S/PV. 1276, pp. 47–50). See generally John Carey, "The UN and Human Rights: Who Should Do What?" *Bull. of the Sect. of Int. & Comp. Law,* Am. Bar Assoc., July, 1966, pp. 9–20, at 11–14.

119. The country is only partially industrialized and relies primarily on coal, which is abundant, and not on oil for 75 per cent of its power. Its needs from the outside world are relatively limited and can apparently be supplied by South Africa which has adopted a most friendly "business as usual" policy.

On the irritant but not major effects of the sanctions, see report of a UN expert, *UN Press Release* WS/231 (March 4, 1966), pp. 3–4; and New York *Times,* May 27, 1966, August 9, 10, 1966 (Anthony Lewis), September 24, 1966 (P. M. Smith), September 25, 1966 (P. M. Smith), October 2, 3, 1966.

On British application of the sanctions and sanctions generally, see *Economist,* December 11, 1965, February 19, 1966, March 19, 1966, April 9, 1966. On South African aid to Rhodesia, see e.g., *Economist,* February 26, 1966. On Rhodesian countersanctions, see also New York *Times,* November 19, 1965. In 1964, half of Rhodesia's exports (about $210 million) were to the United Kingdom and the Commonwealth. See generally New York *Times,* December 19, 1965, p. E4.

On the effects of sanctions and Rhodesian countermeasures on Zambia, see e.g., New York *Times,* December 17, 1965, March 20, 1966, September 7, 1966. After an initial impact, the economy has straightened out but Rhodesia's place in trade has been gradually taken over by South Africa, which may in time cause similar difficulties. See *Int. Financial News Survey* (IMF), XVIII, No. 41 (October 14, 1966), 341.

On conditions in Rhodesia generally, see also New York *Times,* January 5, 1966, February 12, 1966, March 25, 1966 (Middleton), July 22, 1966.

For UN reports on conditions in Rhodesia, see A/6300/Add. 1, Parts I and II, October 7, 1966 (in general and on foreign economic and other interests). For attacks on foreign interests, see also A/AC. 109/SC.2/SR.24, June 2, 1966 (Committee of 24, meeting of May 9, 1966).

country behind the regime.[120] A few early internal strikes and disorders connected with UDI were quickly and easily crushed; potential native resistance is hampered by internal divisions in native leadership; and a few "invaders," allegedly armed with Chinese and Soviet weapons, have apparently been summarily dealt with by security forces (which include native troops).[121] Internally, the regime has resorted to wartime repressive policies including strict censorship, import and export controls, a ban on strikes and demonstrations protesting independence now, and an increase in restrictive arrests.[122] In response to the economic sanctions, it has elevated economic information on its current markets and sources of supply to the status of state secrets.

With the aid of South Africa and Portugal, Rhodesia has thus far stood fast against sanctions participated in not only by all the Commonwealth but by most other nations as well. The pressure from the African states to take aggressive action, to punish South Africa and Portugal for aiding the revolt, and even to punish the United Kingdom if the revolt is not soon ended has been constant and unremitting.[123] The United Kingdom's indication at a Commonwealth meeting in September that it would seek mandatory sanctions, but not military action, if an accord was not reached by late 1966 clearly left many Commonwealth members unhappy.[124]

120. See, e.g., Anthony Lewis, New York *Times*, August 12, 14, 1966, p. E3, April 10, 1966, p. E1; September 15, 1966.

121. On dealing with invaders, see New York *Times*, April 30, 1966. On the crushing of early dissension, see New York *Times*, November 21, 1966, p. E3, November 30, 1965. On internal divisions among native leaders, see Barton, "A Look at Rhodesia," pp. 29–35; Lawrence Fellows, "The Other—and First— Rhodesians," *New York Times Magazine*, November 21, 1965, p. 36. The local chiefs have been given broad independence and reportedly support the present regime. See New York *Times*, December 4, 1965, p. E2.

122. On censorship, see New York *Times*, February 9, 1966.

123. See, e.g., on the pressures by the "Anti-Colonial Committee" (the Committee of 24), A/AC.109/158 (April 21, 1966); A/AC.109/167 (June 7, 1966); A/AC.109/188 (June 29, 1966). On more drastic Security Council resolutions, see S/7285 (May 10, 1966), S/7285/Add. 1 (May 11, 1966), S/7285/Add. 2 (May 12, 1966). Nine African states—Algeria, Congo (Brazzaville), Ghana, Guinea, Mali, Mauritania, Sudan, Tanzania, and the United Arab Republic—broke diplomatic relations with the United Kingdom. Ghana and Sudan have re-established their relations with the United Kingdom.

124. For the Commonwealth communiqué, see New York *Times*, September 15, 1966. On a similar statement at the UN, see *UN Press Release*, WS/263 (October 14, 1966), p. 8, and *British Record*, No. 15 (September 26, 1966), pp. 2–3. On dissension at the meeting, and Zambia's departure when mandatory sanctions and force were ruled out for the present, see New York *Times*, September 14–16, 1966.

Indeed, we have reached the point where some of the newer members have threatened Britain with expulsion from the Commonwealth over the issue of Rhodesia![125]

South-West Africa. The question of South-West Africa, while of great current concern to those interested in the problem of the development of international institutions, can only receive brief attention here. It is the subject of a great number of recent studies. Potentially, it may prove to be a major test for the advocates of international sanctions. It is, however, a world rather than a Commonwealth problem.

South-West Africa, a German colony before World War I, was captured by South African forces in 1915. In 1917, the British Cabinet decided that South Africa should be allowed to annex the area, but in the peace settlement it was formally transferred for *administration* to the Union of South Africa by the Principal Allied and Associated Powers, acting on behalf of the League.[126] The League Council confirmed and defined the transfer as a Class C mandate, to be administered as an integral portion of the mandatory, with relatively few specific obligations on the mandatory. It was, however, to promote the well-being of the inhabitants and to make reports and submit certain disputes to the P.C.I.J. and was barred from modifying the status of the territory without the Council's consent.[127] The international concern with South-West Africa was thus formalized and has continued for almost fifty years.

Of the former mandates, South-West Africa was the only one which neither achieved independence directly nor was placed under the trusteeship system of the United Nations. In 1946, South Africa argued at the United Nations for full incorporation

---

125. On Britain and the new Commonwealth, see, e.g., New York *Times,* January 23, 1966, p. E5, and September 4, 1966, p. E2.

126. See, e.g., Alexander Stewart, *The Sacred Trust* (Johannesburg, 1963), p. 17 *et passim,* and statement by Smithers, U.K. Representative, March 22, 1961, reprinted in Whiteman, Digest (1963), I, 707–708.

127. See, e.g., *Jour. of Comp. Leg.,* 3d ser., IX (1927), 111.

For an account of South Africa's policies in the mandate, see Robert L. Bradford, "The Origin of the League of Nations' Class 'C' Mandate for South-West Africa and Fulfillment of the Sacred Trust, 1919–1939" (unpublished Ph.d. dissertation, Yale, 1965).

of the territory into the Union. The General Assembly refused to accede to the request and the Union government decided then not to proceed with incorporation but to maintain the status quo.[128]

It is today an area of over 317,000 square miles of difficult country inhabited by some half million people, 73,000 of whom are white, making the racial ratio about one white in seven.[129] It has been administered by South Africa largely in accordance with her own views of apartheid and other classifications based on race.

Ever since the United Nations refused, in 1946, to accept South African annexation of the mandate, questions concerning the status of the territory have been before the United Nations. Of great importance are the several decisions of the International Court of Justice (ICJ) concerning the mandate. On July 11, 1950, for example, the court held unanimously that the territory remained an "international Mandate" and that the Union, "acting alone, has not the competence to modify the international status of the Territory," for to do so required United Nations consent.[130] By twelve votes to two, the court decided that South Africa "continues to have the international obligations stated in Article 22 of the Covenant . . . and in the Mandate . . . as well as the obligation" to transmit petitions and make reports under United Nations supervision. By a much narrower vote of eight to six, however, it was also held that South Africa was not obliged to place the territory under the trusteeship system, though all the judges

128. For summary, see Int. Com. of Jurists, *South Africa and the Rule of Law* 83–90 (1960), and sources cited. See also *Brit. Year Book Int. Law, 1936*, XXIV (London, 1947), 386.

129. On conditions in South-West Africa, political, legal, economic, and social, see e.g., A/AC. 109/PET.535/Add.1 (September 27, 1966), esp. on labor; A/6000/Add.2 (September 28, 1965), Committee of 24; A/6300/Add.2 (September 20, 1966), Committee of 24. See also Dissenting Opinion of Judge Mbanefo in ICJ, South-West Africa Cases, Second Phase, Judgment of July 18, 1966.

For the South African view of conditions in South-West Africa, see statement of De Villiers at the General Assembly on September 26, 1966, in A/PV.1417 (September 26, 1966), and the Separate Opinion of Judge Van Wyk (South Africa) in ICJ, South-West Africa Cases, Second Phase, Judgment of July 18, 1966. See also Philip Mason, "Separate Development and South West Africa: Some Aspects of the Odendaal Report," *Race* (London), V, No. 4 (1964), 83–97.

130. International Status of South-West Africa, advisory opinion, July 11, 1950, *ICJ Reports* (1950), pp. 128 ff. The majority view was also that of the United States government on both issues (see Whiteman, *Digest*, I, 715–720).

agreed she could do so. The court was quite clear overall that the mandate had not lapsed. In additional advisory opinions in 1955 and 1956, the court dealt with questions of voting in the United Nations concerning South-West Africa and of the hearing of petitions from the territory,[131] but South Africa, while taking pains to preserve a separate status of sorts for the mandate, gave no evidence of acceptance of the import of the 1950 opinion, never reporting, for example, on conditions in the area.

To counter the lack of response to these advisory opinions, most of the United Nations members urged the African states which had been members of the League to bring a contentious case against South Africa over the territory. This, it was felt, would make further, more vigorous action easier to support and to explain at home for states traditionally imbued with a respect for courts and law and legal remedies, most particularly the United States and also, perhaps, the United Kingdom, states which might otherwise be reluctant to see the organized international community interpose itself forcefully between a sovereign and its "wards" in enforcement actions in which they might well be called upon to bear much of the contributions and sacrifices.

Thus, on November 4, 1960, the governments of Liberia and Ethiopia filed identical applications against South Africa asking the court to adjudge that South-West Africa is a territory under the mandate; that South Africa continues to have the international obligations stated in Article 22 of the Covenant of the League of Nations and in the mandate for South-West Africa as well as the obligation to transmit petitions from the inhabitants of the territory; and that the supervisory functions are to be exercised by the United Nations. All these were essentially matters

131. In the matter of Voting Procedure on Questions Relating to Reports and Petitions concerning the Territory of South-West Africa, Advisory Opinion, June 7, 1955, *ICJ Reports* (1955), the court stated, unanimously, that decisions of the General Assembly with respect to South-West Africa were "important questions" within the meaning of Article 18(2) of the Charter. This called for decision by a two-thirds vote, not a unanimous decision as might have been needed in the League Council, nor a simple majority as is the case for other questions in the General Assembly. In Admissibility of Hearings of Petitioners by the Committee on South-West Africa, Advisory Opinion, June 1, 1956, *ICJ Reports* (1956), pp. 23 ff., the court, by eight to six, stated that oral hearings by petitioners from the territory were permissible, although the League had no such procedures (in contrast to the Trusteeship Council of the United Nations, which did).

already covered by the earlier advisory opinions. In addition, perhaps the most important claim was that South Africa had failed to perform her prescribed duties in that she practiced apartheid in South-West Africa (discriminated on a racial basis), adopted arbitrary and unjust laws for the area, placed military bases there, and in other ways failed to fulfill her obligations adequately. Under Article 7 of the mandate agreement, it was asserted that South Africa was obliged to litigate these questions with interested League members. Significantly, South Africa made its appearance to contest the case.

At first, South Africa resisted on jurisdictional grounds, urging, *inter alia*, that these states lacked standing to sue, at least with respect to the general question of treatment of persons within the territory. In 1962, by vote of eight to seven, the court asserted that it did in fact have jurisdiction to hear the matter, that these states could bring this suit.[132]

Then, on July 18, 1966, the court, after six years of proceedings, dismissed the case on the ground that the applicants had no legal right or interest in the subject matter of the claim.[133] By vote of eight to seven, with the president, the Australian Spender, having cast a double vote to break a tie, the minority of 1962 on the issue of jurisdiction became the majority,[134] and the court's opinion did not reach the merits at all. Judge Fitzmaurice, the other regular

132. For comment, see Elizabeth S. Landis, "South West Africa in the International Court: Act II, Scene I," *Cornell Law Quar.*, XLIX (1964), 179; R. B. Ballinger, "The International Court of Justice and the South West Africa Cases: Judgment of 21st December, 1962," *So. Afr. Law Jour.*, LXXXI, Part I (1964), 35; David Barton, "Apartheid and the World Court," *Vista*, I, No. 6 (May–June, 1966), 42 ff.

133. The decision is now in print. For a brief account of the case, see Ernest A. Gross, "The South West Africa Case: What Happened?" *Foreign Affairs*, XLV (October, 1966), 36–48; "Issues Before the 21st General Assembly," *Int. Conciliation*, No. 559 (September, 1966), 60–67. For a recent South African statement on the decision, see A/6480 (October 20, 1966).

For background, see also Nordau, "The South West Africa Case," *World Today*, No. 3 (March, 1966), 122–130; "The World Court's Ticklish Case," *Nation*, No. 14 (April 4, 1966), 389–393.

134. Joining President Spender (Australia) in the procedural majority were Judges Fitzmaurice (United Kingdom), Gros (France), Morelli (Italy), Spiropoulos (Greece), van Wyk (ad hoc judge appointed by South Africa), and Winiarski (Poland). Dissenting were Judges Forster (Senegal), Jessup (United States), Koo (Republic of China, Vice President of the ICJ), Koretsky (USSR), Padilla Nervo (Mexico), Mbanefo (Nigeria, ad hoc judge appointed by applicants), and Tanaka (Japan). Not participating were judges Ammoun (Lebanon), Zafrulla Kahn (Pakistan), and Bustamante y Rivero (Peru).

member of the court with a Commonwealth background and legal training, joined with President Spender in a restrictive reading of the Covenant and the mandate agreement.

Clearly the most significant political result of the decision was the immediate return of the question of South-West Africa to the organized international political arena. The African states, which had been urged over the years by the West to wait patiently for the expected orderly, legal defeat of South Africa, were outraged. The court's action was called one "to confound its advocates and give joy to its opponents,"[135] an "abdication of responsibility," a "slap in the face."[136]

For some fifteen years, the United Nations had tried to gain supervision over the territory with no success.[137] Over many of these years, South Africa was able to count on at least an abstention if not a no vote from members of the "old" Commonwealth but by the mid-fifties this was changing a bit. The old members still opposed direct pressure on South Africa to negotiate in 1959—as in Resolutions 1360 (XV) and 1361 (XV)—and 1960 and the United Kingdom tended to continue at least to abstain even when the others voted yes.[138]

Moreover, in 1963, when the General Assembly, by vote of eighty-four for, six against and seventeen abstaining, adopted Resolution 1899 (XVIII) which contemplated the use of sanctions if South Africa moved too "aggressively" with respect to South-West Africa, the United Kingdom joined South Africa in voting no, while Australia, Canada, and New Zealand abstained in the face of the affirmative votes of the "new" Commonwealth members (the United States and France were also opposed).

---

135. *UN Press Release* WS/261, September 30, 1966, p. 22 (Nigeria).
136. See, e.g., *UN Press Release* WS/251, July 22, 1966, pp. 3–4. As evidence of African ire, an appropriation of $72,500 for salaries and clerical expenses of the court was blocked in the fall of 1966, even though the monies had already been spent. See New York *Times*, October 11, 1966. Kenya proposed that a way be sought to disqualify the majority judges. See *UN Press Release* WS/261, September 30, 1966, p. 18. See also statement of the representative of Cameroons, *UN Press Release* WS/260, September 23, 1966, p. 5. Several states have demanded the reorganization at least of the court on more "equitable" geographic lines. See, e.g., *UN Press Release* WS/261, September 30, 1966, pp. 18 (Kenya), 19 (Ethiopia), 22 (Burundi), and WS/263, October 14, 1966, p. 13 (Sudan).
137. See, e.g., Wainhouse, *Remnants of Empire* (1964), pp. 52–57.
138. E.g., on Res. 1565 (XV) and Res. 1702 (XVI).

More recently, in 1965, the General Assembly again condemned South Africa over its actions in the territory, condemned apartheid, warned that partition of South-West Africa would violate the mandate and that annexation would be aggression, and asked the Security Council to watch over this "serious threat to international peace and security."[139] The ICJ's rejection of the South-West Africa case came in the summer of 1966, and during the ensuing United Nations session, almost every nation demanded that the United Nations should assert control over South-West Africa. The African and some other states insisted on the immediate creation of a United Nations authority there. Even those states which usually counsel caution, such as the United States, were equally clear that the mandate persisted; that apartheid was reprehensible and intolerable; and that South Africa, having failed in her duties, should be ousted as mandatory.[140] As a result, on October 27, 1966, the General Assembly by 114 to 2 (Portugal, South Africa)—with France, the United Kingdom, and Malawi, which has special problems of dependency on South Africa, abstaining—resolved that the mandate was terminated; that South Africa had, "in fact, disavowed the Mandate," and that the territory is henceforth "a direct responsibility of the United Nations." Thus, the Commonwealth, including the dominions, took a forthright stand. South Africa has called the resolution illegal and has stated that it "will resist with all the power at its disposal any attempts which endanger the safety of our country or of the peoples committed to our care."[141]

The United Nations, faced with a division among its members over how rapidly it should attempt to proceed in forcing South Africa out, has moved cautiously in the early months of 1967. As with the effectiveness of pressures on South Africa over other issues, much depends on the willingness of the United Kingdom

139. Res. 2074 (XX), December 17, 1965. The resolution was adopted by a vote of 85-2-19. The Security Council also called for an arms embargo in Res. 181, August 7, 1963; it reaffirmed that call in Res. 191, June 18, 1964. For South Africa's protest of Res. 2074 see letter of December 21, 1965, A/6219.

140. See statements of Ambassador Goldberg, September 12 and October 12, 1966, New York *Times*, September 23 and October 13, 1966. The dissenting judges in 1966 were clear that the mandate persisted. See, e.g., Judge Jessup's opinion. The court's opinion does not reach this point.

141. See New York *Times*, October 13, 1966.

Conspectus

Robert R. Wilson[*]

The foregoing chapters of the symposium have dealt with selected elements of international and comparative law as they have arisen in various contexts in the relations of Commonwealth states. These relations involve much besides law, but for the present purpose emphasis has been limited, in so far as possible, to the latter. The broad scope of materials presented by the respective authors perhaps justifies a summary view of the essays in perspective.

I

It has seemed appropriate to have Professor Braibanti's chapter precede others in the volume, since his submission in regard to the role of law in general would seem to justify presentation of specific topics considered in the other chapters. The author emphasizes the crucial need for strengthening legal elements in the attainment of viable institutions. He stresses the importance of law as an agency of social change and as a source for diffusion of attitudes, ideas, and norms. While his thesis is one of general applicability, he illustrates it principally with references to Pakistan and on the basis of his extensive experience and research in that Commonwealth state. Acknowledging that the law has been imperfectly articulated and sometimes even viewed as a contaminant, he submits that a mature political system must be characterized by focused accountability, clarity of policy, courageous acceptance of decision-making by officials, and a high degree of rationality.

[*] James B. Duke Professor of Political Science, Duke University.

The kind of study of the political which Professor Braibanti envisages in fact transcends law, but he submits that the political must be rooted in legal analysis if it is to have significance. The argument is enriched by specific examples, particularly from phenomena in Asia. The analysis provides appropriate setting for other contributors to the volume to present selected subjects in the fields of international and comparative law of the Commonwealth.

II

Professor Jennings' essay on state succession proceeds from the basic proposition that a new state enjoys rights and accepts duties under international law not only because of its succeeding a particular state but also, and perhaps more importantly, because of its becoming a member of a family subject to that law. Noting the relative importance of treaty law in the totality of that which a newly independent state accepts, the author sees political considerations as ground for treaty continuity and the rule of law as needed only for the residuary and occasional case.

In Commonwealth practice, temporizing declarations on succession have emanated from some very new foreign offices. Professor Jennings does not feel that there has been serious modification of an old rule that treaties do not survive at succession; in novation he finds tendencies to carry over certain categories of obligations. A striking fact in Commonwealth history is that there has been a gradual process of evolution in which a *continuing* person has been involved, so that in a sense there are no *new* states in the Commonwealth and treaties have actually been made in contemplation of the change of personality which has occurred. Taking a teleological approach, the author submits that even before their complete independence the dominions may be regarded as having attained a true international personality, and the latter continues as the period of guardianship comes to a close. By the end of the nineteenth century the older dominions had the right, as a necessary ingredient of their independence, to withdraw from British-made treaties. There were claims of the right to withdraw from most-favored-nation commitments and, in the twentieth century, for example, claims of rights to withdraw from the Warsaw Convention.

Professor Jennings is in agreement with Professor D. P. O'Connell that in the matter of succession involving delict, it is perhaps unrealistic to attempt distinction between liquidated and unliquidated claims. The author concludes that since a treaty is in form an obligation rather than a general law, there is need for recognizing in the terms of succession that a new state may inherit treaties because they were made in contemplation of its eventual statehood.

III

In his chapter on "Colonial Participation in International Legal Processes" Professor Deener presents a historical survey and offers suggestions as to the possible effects of past practice and of current developments. Involved is the distinctive role which the older Commonwealth states have had, as contrasted with that of the very new Commonwealth members, in the process of assenting to and helping to shape customary and treaty rules. The author notes the manner in which, even before becoming fully independent, the dominions had come to have part in influencing practice in international legal relations and how, with this background, they have been little disposed to question customary law which had come to be existent at the time of their acquiring full statehood. In contrast, the attitude of the very new Commonwealth states toward international legal rules that have come to be established may well be affected, it is suggested, by the fact of their not having participated, as the former dominions have had opportunity to participate, in the custom-making process that has resulted in the present system of rules on such matters as state succession and jurisdiction over territory.

Professor Deener raises the question whether the newer members' participation, upon attaining independence and without having had the experience older members have had, will result in the socialization of these newly emerging communities into the traditional type of international legal system. Involved, the author suggests, is a question of means whereby the demands of the newer states can be met while at the same time other (well-established) participant members in the international legal system continue in their demands. While Professor Deener does not feel that any definite conclusions seem to be justified as yet, he suggests the possibility that the principles of international law might conceivably be defined, in the light of reason, to a greater and more universally acceptable perfection. He does not dismiss, however, the possibility that the present international legal structure may disappear and that it may be replaced by several cultural and regional systems through a kind of *modus vivendi* of uneasy coexistence.

IV

The mutual relations of English and Islamic law with the indigenous customary law of different communities have posed continuing problems in Commonwealth development. Assessing the effect in the Indian subcontinent, Professor Anderson discerns the development of an "Anglo-Mohammedan law." English law was superimposed to some extent upon Islamic law, as the latter had earlier come to prevail over indigenous customary law. The adjustment involved Clive's obtaining fiscal administration and civil jurisdiction from the Mogul emperor in Delhi, and the India Company's taking over criminal jurisdiction. In the provinces, as distinct from the Presidency towns, English law was introduced largely under the umbrella of "justice, equity and good conscience." Summarizing the position which came to exist with respect to Islamic law in the subcontinent, the author finds it to have been excluded by statute from such spheres as crime, evidence, and procedure; to have been applied, in questions of pre-emption, to Muslims and such Hindus as had accepted this principle into their customary law, under "justice, equity and good conscience" (except in Madras); and to have been applicable to Muslims as of right in family law, gifts, and *waqfs*.

As to Zanzibar, Professor Anderson (restricting his attention to the period prior to the recent revolution) points out that the same judges sat at times as the British court exercising Her Majesty's jurisdiction and at others as the Zanzibar court exercising the jurisdiction of the Sultan. In the latter the Islamic law was, in civil matters, accepted as the fundamental law, but had been ousted to a considerable extent by statute law; and in the law of crime and evidence it had been completely excluded.

The author contrasts this with Northern Nigeria, where there was virtually no mention of Islamic law in any statute before 1956, although Islamic law was in fact applied more extensively than anywhere else outside the Arabian peninsula. Native courts, highly developed at the time the British protectorate was instituted, continued to handle an extraordinarily high percentage of cases, civil and criminal; and many of the emirs' courts tried even capital cases under Islamic law. This posed a number of problems, and following the report of a panel of jurists (of which Professor Anderson was a member), it was decided to replace Islamic criminal law by new codes. The author notes, however, that Islamic law remains applicable as the personal and family law of Muslim litigants.

V

Considering "The Common Law and Native Systems of Law," Professor Green submits that the introduction of the British concept of the rule of law has been one of the least objectionable features of British imperialism. The existing law applied to territory acquired by cession or conquest until amended by the King. After the initial introduction of common law in the colonies there was a tendency to introduce legislation specifying the parts of English law which were to be applicable and the date of applicability. (The author points out that anomalies were not unknown.) The interplay between the common law and native law sometimes elicited, as the author explains, judicial utterances as to repugnancy between barbarism and civilization.

Professor Green offers the opinion that the position taken by the United States concerning American Indian custom has been more enlightened than that which tends to be usual with respect to the interplay of English law and local law in British overseas possessions. While the introduction of the common law into native societies has led to some modification of local native customs found to be unacceptable to Western Christian society and has expanded the rule of law as understood in Christendom, judges essaying a mixture of the two have tended, the author submits, to disregard local conditions and sensibilities. With respect to the common law, Professor Green suggests that English lawyers must be prepared to see adaptation of this law (and of themselves), lest there be in the new countries a rejection of the influence of the common law, rather than the recognition of its comprising but *one* of the various systems designed to serve the local people's needs.

VI

In her study of "International Rendition in United States–Commonwealth Relations" Professor Alona Evans points out that the 1931 extradition treaty which the United States has with the United Kingdom also applies as between each of seventeen other Commonwealth states and the United States, on the basis of "devolution" or "temporizing" arrangements. The author directs attention to the scheme drawn up by Commonwealth law ministers in 1966 relating to determination of what constitutes a political crime. There is suggestion that desirable results for Commonwealth states might be effected through subsuming Commonwealth members to "foreign" states under the 1870 British statute on extradition or the extradition statutes of other Commonwealth states. With respect to the problem of double criminality, the author points out that some anomalies might grow out of the statutory basis for extradition from Australia to the United States. The matter of extraditing nationals receives separate attention. As to the basis for action upon an extradition request, Dr. Evans notes that standards of evidence are not the same as those for *conviction*. Expulsion procedure is "less cumbrous" than extradition, and the author observes that the political offender is vulnerable to informal extradition.

In concluding, Professor Evans draws attention to similarity in the practice of common-law states, to some informal methods in use between the United States and certain Commonwealth states, and some movement toward establishment of a basis for legal extradition, such as that between Sierra Leone and Guinea. She refers to the awareness that a fugitive offender is not a mere pawn between the asylum state and the requesting state, and points to evidence of concern for the protection of the individual, as reflected in the recent scheme formulated by Commonwealth law ministers.

VII

The international law of jurisdiction, and national policies with respect to monopolistic and restrictive trade practices, constitute a background for Mr. Feltham's study of "Extraterritorial Application of Antitrust Legislation" as viewed from the standpoint of Commonwealth states. Considering the law and practice of four Commonwealth states—Canada, the United Kingdom, Australia, and India—the author proceeds from the principle that parliamentary power is unlimited but the actual intent must be found, and if this is unclear there is a presumption that Parliament generally intends legislation to apply to acts within the state. There has been some reactive legislation for the protection of local interests, and there is also some reactive jurisprudence in response to United States law.

As to the practice of particular Commonwealth states, the author refers to Canadian and Australian legislation making reference to the Statute of Westminster, 1931, as having been retroactive and as having removed limitations on the Canadian and Australian Parliaments insofar as extraterritorial effect is concerned; but acts will not be interpreted as having extraterritorial effect unless such intention is evidenced by the statutes. As to United Kingdom legislation, it is noted that the supremacy of

Parliament is not limited, as far as British courts are concerned, by rules of international law. However, the Restrictive Trade Practices Act, 1956, contains clear indications of Parliament's intention to limit possible extraterritorial application of the statute. Australia's Trade Practices Act, 1965, does not evidence such limited scope, but a recent decision of the High Court of Australia indicates that the courts will be loath to give extraterritorial extension to the Australian legislation. India has as yet no legislation on the subject, the author notes, but there is some indication in the tax laws that Parliament might give wide scope to any legislation which may be proposed in the future.

VIII

Questions of public law, both international and constitutional, have arisen in the Commonwealth over the matter of sanctions during the period of League of Nations and United Nations history. The chapter on "The Commonwealth and International Sanctions," by Rita F. Taubenfeld and Howard J. Taubenfeld, emphasizes that not merely Commonwealth problems but world problems are involved. Since the number of Commonwealth states has so greatly increased since creation of the United Nations, and policies of apartheid have come under continuing attack during this period, the role of Commonwealth states in this context has increasingly invited study. The role of international organization in connection with the employment of sanctions against Italy three decades ago has become largely a matter of historical interest, but careful re-examination of the facts involved may have continuing utility for policy-makers.

The authors point out that the question of apartheid has been before the United Nations since 1952, when thirteen member states, including India and Pakistan, placed the matter on the agenda as presenting a threat to world peace. Subsequently other Commonwealth states have become very much involved. Initially the United Kingdom, Australia, and New Zealand joined South Africa in urging that the United Nations lacked competence to discuss this "internal" matter and in the view that international peace was not endangered, but later a strong tide of feeling developed against considering apartheid a mere domestic jurisdiction matter. Despite the growing movement in this direction, as the authors note, mandatory economic sanctions recommended by a group of experts did not become a reality. While there was eventually in the Commonwealth a sanctions committee and Commonwealth states' opposition to apartheid in South Africa became a matter of policy, the older members have been hesitant to enforce sanctions at economic risk to themselves. The Rhodesian independence issue has, in the meantime, led even to threats by some new Commonwealth members of expelling the United Kingdom from the Commonwealth. The more dramatic developments in this whole general area have related principally to international organization law and policy rather than merely to international and comparative law in the practice of Commonwealth states.

Index

Abdulhusen Abhai decd., Re, 91
Abu Hanifa, 64
Abul Fata v. Russomoy, 72
Abyssinia, 197
Adegbenro v. Akintola, 98
Aden: and Regulation IV of 1827, 67; and waqfs, 73
Adeyinka Oyekan v. Musendiku Adele, 106n
Adv.-Gen. of Bengal v. Ranee Surnanoye Dossee, 83n
Afrikanerland, 209
Agreement between the Parties to the North Atlantic Treaty Regarding the Status of their Forces (1951), 109n
Albania, 185
Alcoa case, 159
Alcoa rule, 165
Algeria, and diplomatic relations with the United Kingdom, 215n
Alliance for Progress, 19
American Banana Co. v. United Fruit Co., 159, 160
American Bar Association, 140
American Indians, 83, 96–97, 98–99, 101–102, 106, 107, 227–228
Amoabeng v. Mills, 90
Amodu Tijani v. Secretary, Southern Nigeria, 97
Anglo-German Naval Treaty (June 15, 1935), 182–183
"Anglo-Mohammedan law," 64, 71, 226
Angola, 208
Anguillia v. Ong Boon Tat, 88n
Anonymous (1722), 82
Anthropology of law, 25
Antitrust legislation, extraterritorial application of, 130–173, 229–230
Apartheid, 203–210, 217, 219, 221–222, 230–231
Application of Chase Manhattan Bank, 139n
Arab law, 61n
Arens, Richard, 15
Arguelles case, 110n
Aristocracy of the robe, 4, 8
Aristotle, 3, 10

Armah v. Government of Ghana, 117
Arton, Re, 122
Asquith of Bishopstone, Lord, 88–89
Atkin, Lord, 101
Aurangzib, 65
Australia: antitrust legislation in, 148, 157–168, 229–230; and apartheid, 205, 230–231; constitution of, 98; and Convention relative to the Disposal of Real and Personal Property, 46n–47n; and double criminality, 120, 228; and extradition, 111n, 115n, 120, 122, 123, 228; Extradition Acts (1903–1950), 110n; and extraterritorial application of antitrust legislation, 131, 157–168; Full Court, 158; High Court, 157, 168, 230; Industries Preservation Act (1906–1950), 157, 159–162, 166, 167–168; and International Agreement for the Suppression of Obscene Publications, 47n; International Organizations (Privileges and Immunities) Act (1948), 50n; International Organizations (Privileges and Immunities) Regulations (1959), 50n; and League of Nations Covenant, 53; and most-favored-nation treaties, 37; Parliament, 160, 163, 168, 229; and postal conventions, 51n–52n; and Radio Telegraph Convention (1932), 52; and Republic of South Africa, 206, 220, 230–231; and sanctions, 202, 205, 206, 220; and South-West Africa, 220; and specialty, 122; and state succession to treaties, 44; and Statute of Westminster (1931), 163, 229; Trade Practices Act (1965), 164–167, 230; Trade Practices Act (1966), 167–168; Trade Practices Tribunal, 164, 166; treatment of Indians in South Africa, 204, 205; and United Nations, 202, 204, 206, 220, 230–231; and Versailles Conference (1919), 53; mentioned, 81
Australian and New Zealand—Eastern Shipping Conference, 158